高等院校"十三五"规划教材——经济管理系列

外贸英语函电

蔡惠伟　编　著

清华大学出版社
北京

内 容 简 介

本书是一本国际经济与贸易专业核心课程的实战教程，取材真实，内容覆盖面适当，包括外贸交易过程的所有环节，如：与外方建立业务关系、资信调查、询盘、发盘、还盘、促销、下订单、签约、包装、投保、装运、索赔理赔、安全收汇以及参加展会、灵活贸易、各种商务活动的文件处理等。反映了当今世界进出口业务的现实，例文能真切反映交易的实际过程，注重培养学生的实际应用能力，直面企业对学生的就业需求。编排特别讲究教学法，体例设计高度符合教学需要，方便任课教师组织课堂教学。

本书适合国际经济与贸易专业的学员、外贸工作者以及有需要同外商进行有效沟通的其他专业在职从业人员参考使用，可以作为大学教学用书、公司培训用书以及自学参考用书。

本书封面贴有清华大学出版社防伪标签，无标签者不得销售。
版权所有，侵权必究。侵权举报电话：010-62782989 13701121933

图书在版编目(CIP)数据

外贸英语函电/蔡惠伟编著. —北京：清华大学出版社，2019（2024.7重印）
（高等院校"十三五"规划教材——经济管理系列）
ISBN 978-7-302-53397-9

Ⅰ. ①外… Ⅱ. ①蔡… Ⅲ. ①对外贸易—英语—电报信函—写作—高等学校—教材 Ⅳ. ①F75

中国版本图书馆 CIP 数据核字(2019)第 178802 号

责任编辑：陈立静
装帧设计：刘孝琼
责任校对：周剑云
责任印制：宋　林

出版发行：清华大学出版社
网　　址：https://www.tup.com.cn, https://www.wqxuetang.com
地　　址：北京清华大学学研大厦 A 座　　邮　编：100084
社 总 机：010-83470000　　邮　购：010-62786544
投稿与读者服务：010-62776969, c-service@tup.tsinghua.edu.cn
质量反馈：010-62772015, zhiliang@tup.tsinghua.edu.cn
课件下载：https://www.tup.com.cn, 010-62791865

印 装 者：三河市科茂嘉荣印务有限公司
经　　销：全国新华书店
开　　本：185mm×260mm　　印　张：17.75　　字　数：425 千字
版　　次：2019 年 9 月第 1 版　　印　次：2024 年 7 月第 7 次印刷
定　　价：49.00 元

产品编号：077235-01

前　言

　　经过 30 多年的改革开放，到中国正式加入世界贸易组织第 15 年的时候，中国已经成为全球第二大经济体、世界第一大贸易国、世界第一大吸引外资国和世界第二大对外投资国。"十九大"报告中有关 2035 年和 2050 年的宏伟蓝图，让我们憧憬，催我们奋进！今后 30 年是我国由贸易大国向贸易强国演变的时期，这段时间也正是我们完成中华民族伟大复兴、实现"中国梦"的时期。

　　中国进入新时代，社会生活的各个方面都在发生迅速而深刻的变化，教育领域中人才培养的理念和模式也要跟上时代的步伐。以往那种重学历、重证书、重应试的做法必定要让位于重能力、重实践、重素养的理念和探索。社会需求、企业需求、家长需求、学生需求必然得到尊重。由此，人才对社会经济发展和创新转型的贡献度也必将大大提高。

　　在这样一个新时代，每个年轻人都会有出彩的机会。投身于外贸领域的 90 后和 00 后应该是幸运的，大环境大趋势很好，进出口经营权、电报电传传真等概念离我们越来越远和越来越陌生，电子邮件、微信、移动支付、人民币跨境支付系统、人民币国际化、跨境出口电商、中欧班列、全自动码头、中国进口博览会等新概念扑面而来并伴随左右。国际环境、政策环境、技术手段等都发生了巨大的变化。

　　与此同时，竞争也日益激烈。因此，对年轻人的要求也更高了，光会应试考证书死读书是注定适应不了竞争要求的。就外贸领域而言，年轻人要精通外贸专业知识、熟练运用外语、尽早吸收前辈经验，出口成章，落笔成文，同时善于做跨文化的沟通者，这种功夫始终是外贸人的看家本领。

　　"外贸英语函电"系高等院校国际经济与贸易专业学生的必修课程。它将专业知识和专业写作技能有机地融为一体，紧扣外经贸专业知识和外经贸工作的具体运作环节，既可提高英语文字的表达能力，又可培养具体业务的处理能力。

　　该课程集专业知识、工作经验和熟练应用英文于一体，切实提高学生的竞争力，满足企业与社会对大学生的需求。该课程向学生提供的知识与技能会让学生应聘时变得底气十足，上班后第一天就能用上，而且天天要用；不做外贸的同学毕业以后只要与外方沟通，不管从事何种工作，也能极大地受益于本课程所提供的知识与技能。

　　作者在高校从事本课程的教学工作已有二十余载，经常想到父母把孩子一手养大，孩子又经过 12 年的寒窗苦读，才来到一所大学学习，这是多么不容易的事！而学生坐在教室里听老师讲课，背后是家长望子成龙、望女成凤的期待，还有莘莘学子学有所成的渴望，所以每次上课都对课堂带着一份敬畏和责任，这么多年来，这份敬畏感和责任感丝毫没有减少，也因此而突发奇想，有一天原创了一句话自勉："一次不愉快满意的授课是对学生与职业的辜负。"既然选择了这个职业，就要把课上好！

　　其实，老师为学生的辛勤付出，学生是看得懂记得住的，并且会以不同的方式表现出来，譬如学生先后给作者两次测评满分以及 99.71 分、98.82 分和 97.5 分的高分。

　　以下摘录几段学生写的课程学习小结。

国贸 021 张丽达："一个学期的外经贸英语函电课程即将结束，我感到学得的知识、增长的见识、学到的经验都难以计数。尤其是老师风趣幽默的讲解，让我们感受到了什么叫作寓教于乐。老师在课堂上与我们分享他自己的经验，这对我们这些即将走向工作岗位的大三学生来说是非常宝贵的财富。此外老师还纠正了学习英语的错误方法……"

国贸 023 邹娱："我觉得这门课程对我们系学生以后工作的帮助非常大……我前一段时间去一家外贸公司面试实习生……由于学习过这门课程，所以我面试时信心很足。当面试官要求我翻译一封外贸函件时我觉得得心应手，这正是这门课给我的收获……"

国贸 021 陈维安："这门课程的学习对我来说可谓收获丰富，对于外贸函电的格式、内容有了深刻的认识……蔡老师充分结合自己从事外贸工作中的经历，为我们上了精彩的课程，我很佩服和欣赏蔡老师的学识渊博，同时很感谢老师的认真教导！"

国贸 021 周锡飞："外贸函电一堂课胜读英语三两月。缘何？重点课程精于课之内容，亦因师之人格。最钦佩恩师之处在于既精通外文又善出口成章之国文。岁月流逝掉的中文精粹重新出现在同学的视野里，这是我十几年英文学习的最大收获，也是许多外文授业者忽略的方面，所以我特别钦佩老师这一点……"

国贸 091 毕长江："……大学三年级课程很多，但这门课是我在这一学期，甚至我目前的学习生活中最精彩的一门课。别出心裁的授课方式，所有人的互动参与，独特的考核测评，相信在今后的很长时间里我都会对这一段学习经历记忆犹新，而《外经贸函电教程》这本教材也会成为我今后工作的必备参考书之一。"

国贸 091 王京玉："……蔡老师将课堂内容与工作经验相结合，深入浅出，丰富了课堂内容，为我们带来接连不断的精神盛宴。对于这门课的特点，我总结了以下几点：①课程内容紧密联系实际，重在应用。②老师上课风趣幽默，精彩国文与绝妙英文穿插交错，引人入胜。③老师上课极有耐心，给每一个同学锻炼的机会，不错过每个人……"

国贸 092 郑作昕："……我要感谢老师每堂课对信函的逐句翻译，加强了我的理解，还有老师以及学长学姐的生动鲜活的经历，都对我触动很大，启发很多，我会将所学所得运用到以后的学习和生活当中，不辜负老师的期望……"

保险 090 查娜："作为大四即将毕业的学生，很希望以后学弟学妹选择这门课。我本人在美企和香港的贸易企业实习过，经贸外语是从事贸易必备的基本素质……很多人不以为大学很重要，但是随着年龄和阅历增长，会深切体会到用时方恨少的感觉。因此，我大学的最后一堂课，很荣幸由蔡老师轻松诙谐的讲课方式收尾，希望我以后的人生能用到课程内容……"

英语 122 董燕："……不由地感叹，时间过得好快，在蔡老师的指导下，这门课即将接近尾声，正如每次听蔡老师的课一样，两个多小时的时间总在轻松愉悦的氛围中不知不觉地流逝。蔡老师讲课很有特点……使得外经贸课上得风趣而又有吸引力……作为英语专业大一的学生，我觉得这门课让我收获了不仅是专业上的知识，还有许多平时课堂上学不到的东西……总而言之，老师让我获益匪浅……"

制药 122 张维："选修《外经贸英文函电》是我大一下学期最有收获的事情……古人云'书中自有黄金屋'，我认为学习一定要实用，而从这门实用的选修课中，我受益的不仅仅是外贸专业的知识，更是发展的眼光和广阔的视野。这门课就像黄金，我相信，它一定会在我今后的学习和工作生活旅途中灿灿发光！"

学校教务处网站上的学生评教系统保存的学生评语也很有意思(直接拷贝系统原始记录)：

学生 1 的评语

很实用的一门课程，老师讲解得很详细。

学生 2 的评语

诙谐幽默，内容翔实，旁征博引，妙趣横生，引人入胜！谆谆教诲，如醍醐灌顶，余音绕梁，三日不绝于耳，三月不知肉味！啊~~~~~O(∩_∩)O 哈！

学生 3 的评语

讲课熟练，能用身边的例子激励我们学习！

学生 4 的评语

蔡老师是大学很少能给学生很多启发的老师！老师自身的水平和修养也很高。在这个课上学到了很多东西。

学生 5 的评语

这是我大学三年以来遇到的英语口语最好的老师，风度翩翩，满腹经纶，教书育人！

学生 6 的评语

好

学生 7 的评语

希望学校能更多地开展类似蔡老师这样的实务型课程。

学生 8 的评语

与实际工作联系很大，信息量充足，对我们很有裨益。

讲课风趣、收获很多。

蔡老师很幽默，和同学们能够和谐相处，讲课有方法！

老师讲课思路很好，学生确实很有收获。

非常非常非常好。

真是一位好老师!

老师具有很宽广的情怀，将教学与生活结合，给学生很多人生的启迪，对学生有很大的启发，学生受益匪浅，老师语言温和，为人师表温润如玉，学生十分喜欢。

这样的文字多得很，字里行间都透着对课程、老师和母校的一片深情，每当看到都能感到一股浓浓的暖意。甚至有一个班的校友毕业 20 周年返校，远道而来点名要见老师，这种喜悦真的让我很欣慰和满足。

本书首先是为学生而写！作者知道学生喜欢什么样的教材，能让他们学得既实又活又有趣，感觉能打通教室与办公室、专业与企业、校园与社会之间的围墙，学到方法，习得能力，毕业时离开校园大门的那一刹那内心是无比自信的！

其次也为有缘的同行而写！现在做老师不容易，各种考核很多，压力不小。作者也知道老师喜欢什么样的教材省事省力又好用，愿意用了一年又一年——其实其内容与练习的安排已经预埋了教育学、心理学、成人学习理论和教学法的原理——本书不光有真实、实战的内容，地道的语言，更有前辈经历与经验的有机融入——所谓"功夫在诗外"。

本门课程先后被称为本专业的"核心课程""主干课程""重点课程",作者本人被评为"主讲教师",获得过教学研究"优秀论文一等奖""优秀教学成果奖""优秀畅销书一等奖"等众多荣誉,在业界收获了同行的高度评价以及市场的广泛接受。本书的前身《外经贸函电教程》曾经创下一年两印、多年连印,在近百所高校使用的记录。相信此次积二十余年教学之功力重新编撰的教材也一定会受到广大师生的喜爱和业界的好评。

蔡惠伟
于上海梅陇

对教师的心里话

感谢您慧眼识珠选用本书作教材！

有一个有趣的问题，让我们一起来探讨一下。现在我们做老师不容易，那么最大的敌人是谁呢？可能就是手机和手提电脑！这两样东西接上互联网，另一头就是一个无边无际、无穷无尽又精彩无比的信息海洋，而90后又是信息时代的原住民。因此，如果老师讲课没有两把刷子，就会出现老师学生各自为战的课堂奇观。

有研究表明，人完全具有自控能力通常要在24岁之后。因此，23岁之前的年轻人自制力一般是不够的，而在校生的年龄段基本属于这个阶段。所以靠说教是无法让学生安心听课的。这里我们引入心理学的两个概念——"间接兴趣"和"直接兴趣"。前者指对于某事物本身并没有兴趣，而是对于这种事物未来的结果感到需要而产生的兴趣。本课程与社会实践高度一致，对应聘和职业生涯具有非常特别的重要价值，因此，学生一般都很重视，也就是说其"间接兴趣"的水平都很高。后者是指由于对事物本身感到需要而引起的兴趣。这种直接的探究事物的认识倾向对提高学习成绩的作用往往比"间接兴趣"的作用还大。本课程一个明显的特征是综合性。学生学了十多年的英文、若干年的专业基础课和专业课、学会了操作电脑，在这门课里全能用上，而且要求真正地把英文作为工作语言，把专业知识融会贯通，写出清楚简洁/礼貌得体/老练的信函、传真和电子邮件来。因此，要善于给学生创造情景、提出要求，让学生自己探索，等学生有所思、有所悟、有所求的时候再加以引导，让其表达、讨论和探索，所谓"不愤不启，不悱不发"，那么学生就会产生学习和配合课堂活动的积极性、主动性和创造性，加上不断地给予鼓励，用好皮克马利翁效应，整个课堂就会愉悦起来，师生关系就会和谐正向起来。

因此，在移动互联网时代，要上好"外贸英语函电"这样的课程，光有外贸专业知识、英文功底，外加更好的实践经验，尽管已经很优秀了，但还是不够的，还需要心理学知识、多种成人学习理论和教学法等知识，将众多领域的知识和灵活应用糅合在一起，才能使学生感觉两节课90分钟就像20分钟一样，一会儿就愉快地结束了！而且期待下周再听你的课！如果教师的讲解本身像磁石一样富有吸引力，再加上互动环节，学生哪有时间玩手机呢！在有温度的课堂里听课，学生也不想玩手机啦！

有了好的食材，还要有大厨的高超厨艺，才能炒出一桌好菜；有了好的教材，同样需要老师的高超教学艺术，才能有令人愉快、满意、难忘的课堂！

能够让学生抵挡得住手机诱惑的老师很可能是个有功夫的老师！

作者在20多年的教学生涯中，先后遇到全日制本科生、大专生、二学位学生、脱产和不脱产的成教院和网络教育学院的学生，还有来自世界各地不同母语的留学生，以及企业培训学员，他们的基础和特点是有区别的，所以养成了研究学生特点的习惯，从学生的"学情"出发，再对标课程要求和工作标准安排教学活动，就会有良好的教学效果。

本门课程要求教师通过课堂讲授、案例分析、模拟训练等方法，使学生掌握阅读、翻译和草拟英文函电的基本知识和技能，培养学生正确理解外商来函、来电并译成通顺中文的能力，使学生能用英文撰写一般的往来函电，能正确理解、翻译和拟写英文单证、合同和协议等。

您可以根据总课时数、学生原有的水平、接受能力等因素综合考虑，选择需要讲解的课文内容和练习方式、强度等。建议安排好学生课后的复习内容和要求，第一单元重在讲解三种文本的外在格式。其余单元重在讲深、讲透、讲活五个例信，有时间可以讨论和分析案例，有答案的练习让学生自己课后对照练习。事实上，本书为各位教师的自由发挥提供了广阔的空间。本书涉及的读者跨度极大，各个层次的读者都可以各取所需。您尽可以巧妙地利用本书提供的种种便利。

对同学的建议

我想对各位同学说的是：受过本课程的训练，再去外贸公司做业务，上手会很快！没有过四六级也没关系，因为本教材超级强大！至于有人要去做跨境出口电商，那语言更不是问题了。也就是说，如果能够对本书读深、悟透、会用，那么基本上能安身立命了。另外，本人觉得在现在这个有利的大环境下，各位志向要大点，要立志毕业三年领导同龄人，毕业五年领导比自己年龄大的人！不闹情绪不抱怨，树目标，找方法，有行动。

大方向有了，具体的事情还是要脚踏实地地去做。就学习本课程而言，要善于提高课堂学习效率，课后及时复习稳固。前者要求各位专心听老师讲课，因为老师讲课时为大家提供了大量的鲜活信息，能让同学把知识学活了，进而转化为一种思维方式和工作能力。请把注意力放在听内容上以及课间课后的提问上，要让听课效率尽量不受授课风格的左右。这是上上策。课堂上一有机会就要敢于发言、参与讨论，课间课后要多多向老师请教，弄懂自己在课上没有明白的问题。

复习的标准是要讲得清每封例信的"人、事、物、理"，即什么人(买卖双方)、什么事情、什么标的物、什么道理(交易)。做练习也要有纪律，譬如除第一单元外，每个单元都有一个中译英的练习，做之前不能直接看附录中的答案，应该是自己先做一遍，再马上与附录中的答案对照，可以做一句对照一句。遵循这样的训练顺序，就会有收获，每次可以少做几句，分几次完成。天道酬勤，有付出就能体会到成就感。当然答案是供大家参考的，并非总是唯一的，允许有不同的正确译法。但涉及专业术语时，请务必严格把关，不要让对方误解或无法理解。

需要特别提醒诸君：把它作为一门专业课来学，而不是当作一般的英语课来学！国人学习外语的通病是以背单词为原点，以做语法、阅读题目为半径，以通过证书为连续剧的欢喜大结局，工作了才发现自己不会说、不会写，遇到外方不知如何有效沟通，眼巴巴地看着各种机会从身边溜走。

为了便于学员学习，本书每个单元都采用了篇幅较长的邮件或案例。实际工作中，有大量篇幅短小的往来函电，且行文有随意化的倾向，有的甚至可以称为"简陋"，而不是"简洁"了。作者主张大家在写邮件时还是以相对严谨为好，这样既能体现语言水准和个人修养，又能避免误解；篇幅倒是宜长则长、宜短则短。

编排说明

  每个单元开头都用英语做了适当而简要的介绍，之后是五个实战英语文本，主要是电子邮件，还有少量的信函、传真、合同或协议等。为了有利于读者模仿和记忆，专门概括了某一类函电的内容构成要点。接着，列出了与该单元相关的重要术语，它们是需要正确理解并掌握如何使用的专业内容，然后是该单元的小结，最后是六种类型的题目，请根据需要灵活使用。

  第一单元详细介绍了信函、传真和邮件的格式，其他的格式以第一单元为样本。

  读者看到的其他单元的邮件、传真和信函显示的正文之前的内容都只是表明该例信取自公司电脑保存原件的原始状态，如发件人、收件人、邮箱地址及保存的具体时间点，以彰显往来函电的真实性，而不是说我们自己在写信函、传真和电子邮件时也要模仿它们。第一单元的三个样本就是比较常用而规范的模仿对象。至于之后每个函电中的公司名称、地址、电话、邮箱、价格、人物等信息，为了保护公司的隐私，都做了相应的修改，但其内容除了错误和不当已经修改之外基本保持原状。从这些反映了交易实际过程的往来英文函电中读者能将国际贸易实务的理论知识和外贸实践活动真正结合起来并融会贯通，同时可以得到大量有益的启示，尤其是那些连续的邮件，日期和时差也明确地显示着(精确到小时、分钟和秒)，就像身处外贸公司在工作一样，如临其境，这是很难得的复盘体验和学习过程。

  衷心祝愿有缘的读者能发现本书的价值！若有错误或不当，尚祈鉴宥并拨冗惠告！

目 录

Unit One　Job Requirements and the Forms of Business Letters 1
　　Part One　Job Requirements 2
　　Part Two　The Forms of Business Letters 4
　　　　I. Traditional Business Letter 4
　　　　II. Fax 7
　　　　III. Email 8
　　Summary 9
　　Exercise 9

Unit Two　Establish Business Relations 13
　　Introduction 14
　　Business Letters 14
　　Pattern A of Business Letters 18
　　Relevant Terms 18
　　Useful Phrases 19
　　Summary 19
　　Exercises 20

Unit Three　Credit Inquiry 25
　　Introduction 26
　　Business Letters 27
　　Pattern B of Business Letters 31
　　Relevant Terms 31
　　Useful Phrases 32
　　Summary 32
　　Exercises 32

Unit Four　Enquiries and Replies 37
　　Introduction 38
　　Business Letters 38
　　Pattern C of Business Letters 43
　　Relevant Terms 43
　　Useful Phrases 43
　　Summary 44
　　Exercises 44

Unit Five   Quotations and Proforma Invoices ... 49

    Introduction ... 50
    Business Letters ... 50
    Pattern D of Business Letters ... 55
    Relevant Terms ... 56
    Useful Phrases ... 56
    Summary ... 56
    Exercises ... 57

Unit Six   Offers, Counter-offers and Re-counter Offers ... 63

    Introduction ... 64
    Business Letters ... 64
    Pattern E of Business Letters ... 68
    Relevant Terms ... 68
    Useful Phrases ... 69
    Summary ... 69
    Exercises ... 69

Unit Seven   Orders and Their Fulfillment ... 77

    Introduction ... 78
    Business Letters ... 78
    Pattern F of Business Letters ... 82
    Relevant Terms ... 82
    Useful Phrases ... 83
    Summary ... 83
    Exercises ... 83

Unit Eight   Sales Confirmation ... 89

    Introduction ... 90
    Business Letters ... 90
    Pattern G of Business Letters ... 95
    Relevant Terms ... 95
    Useful Phrases ... 95
    Summary ... 96
    Exercises ... 96

Unit Nine   Terms of Payment ... 111

    Introduction ... 112
    Business Letters ... 113

Pattern H of Business Letters 117
Relevant Terms 117
Useful Phrases 118
Summary 119
Exercises 119

Unit Ten   Packing 125

Introduction 126
Business Letters 126
Pattern I of Business Letters 129
Relevant Terms 130
Useful Phrases 130
Summary 130
Exercises 131

Unit Eleven   Insurance 135

Introduction 136
Business Letters 136
Pattern J of Business Letters 139
Relevant Terms 140
Useful Phrases 140
Summary 140
Exercises 141

Unit Twelve   Shipping Instructions and Shipping Advice 145

Introduction 146
Business Letters 146
Pattern K of Business Letters 150
Relevant Terms 150
Useful Phrases 151
Summary 151
Exercises 152

Unit Thirteen   Trade Disputes and Settlement 157

Introduction 158
Business Letters 158
Pattern L of Business Letters 164
Relevant Terms 165
Useful Phrases 165

    Summary 166
    Exercises 166

Unit Fourteen   Sales Promotion 173

    Introduction 174
    Business Letters 174
    Pattern M of Business Letters 178
    Relevant Terms 179
    Useful Phrases 179
    Summary 179
    Exercises 180

Unit Fifteen   Expos 185

    Introduction 186
    Business Letters 186
    Pattern N of Business Letters 190
    Relevant Terms 191
    Useful Phrases 191
    Summary 191
    Exercises 191

Unit Sixteen   Flexible Trade (I) 199

    Introduction 200
    Business Letters 200
    Pattern O of Business Letters 208
    Relevant Terms 208
    Useful Phrases 208
    Summary 208
    Exercises 209

Unit Seventeen   Flexible Trade (II) 213

    Introduction 214
    Business Letters 214
    Pattern P of Business Letters 219
    Relevant Terms 220
    Useful Phrases 220
    Summary 220
    Exercises 220

Unit Eighteen Miscellaneous 225

    Introduction 226
    Business Documents 226
    Relevant Terms 235
    Useful Phrases 235
    Summary 235
    Exercises 236

Appendix I 241

Appendix II 243

Unit One

Job Requirements and the Forms of Business Letters

外贸英语函电

Part One Job Requirements

When you work for an import-export corporation, you are always required to be able to do a lot of things, such as understanding the exact meaning of the incoming letters, translating Chinese version letters into English and replying your customers in English directly. The following three cases tell you what you need to do in your corporation.

Case One

Ms. Jiang graduated from university in June. After graduation, she was lucky to be employed by an import-export corporation. One day she was required to translate a fax message into Chinese. Ms. Jiang could get the main idea of it, but she found it difficult to translate the message exactly into Chinese. Now, suppose you were Ms. Jiang, what would happen if you were asked to do so? Please try to write down in proper Chinese.

Date: 18 June, 201*
To: Mr. Henry Ford
From: Ms. Vivian Ma
C.c.: Mr. Tony Gates
Re: ISSUE OF CHINA CERTIFICATE OF ORIGIN TO TONGGUAN ARGENTINA

Thank you for your co-operation in our current documentation operation.

We are informed by Tongguan Argentina that a new government regulation for customs clearance has been implemented. All factories should issue a China Certificate of Origin for all the products made in China, starting for shipments which will arrive in MONTEVEDEO and BUENOS AIRES on/after 11 Aug. For details, please see as follows:

Document type: Certificate of Origin issued by China Authority of Import and Export MUST BE WITH A STAMP IN THE OVERLEAF BY ATGENTINIAN CONSULATE (BEIJING BRANCH).

Effective Date: FCL shipment—starting from vessel ETD HK/China on /after 22 June.

Application: Please apply for the C/O before ETD and should send the C/O to WEM within 20 days after ETD.

C/O charges: We are now discussing the C/O charges matter and will inform you later.

Remarks: It is very important to state the invoice No. and date on the C/O (please find the attached C/O sample for your reference).

Air shipment: If you have air shipment, please inform us first.

Please find the attached revised shipping information and C/O sample. Should you have any questions, please do not hesitate to contact Vivian at 6732****.

Thank you very much for your attention.

Best Regards,
Vivian
Encl.

Unit One Job Requirements and the Forms of Business Letters

Case Two

Mr. Cai once worked for a US-founded corporation in Shanghai. One day, he was asked to send a letter of invitation to their business partner in both Chinese and English. The Chinese version invitation was finished first. Now suppose you were Mr. Cai, please translate it into English.

邀请函

朱嘉音处长雅鉴：

　　为了更好地使贵方了解国外先进的筑养路机械设备和施工技术，促进中国公路的建设和养护，本公司拟邀请朱嘉音女士、马同闻先生、赵起安先生、刘许富先生和高为军先生参观于今年9月20日在美国迈阿密市举行的国际筑养路机械展览，同时还将请你们参观一些著名的筑路机械制造工厂。

　　预计在美逗留20天，往返国际机票和在美期间食宿和交通将由本公司统一安排，费用自理。

　　请贵方惠予考虑，并及时答复为盼！

　　顺致

商安！

凯利机械贸易有限公司
总经理　江业成
201*年7月22日

Case Three

Edward, Mr. Cai's boss, received a fax message from his Australian friend, Mr. Dawson. Edward asked Mr. Cai to send a reply to Mr. Dawson in English directly after Mr. Cai's reading the following fax. Now suppose you were Mr. Cai, please reply to Mr. Dawson by fax according to the following fax message.

Date: 16 May 201*
To: Lihua Imp. & Exp. Co., Ltd
Fax: 86-21-642486**
From: Johan Dawson
Fax: (613) 9876****
Re: Freight

Dear Edward,

　　Apologies for not contacting you earlier, but things have been pretty hectic here.

　　Christina and I send our warmest regards to you, Julia, Mitchell, Brian and your extended family.

　　We have visited most of our friends, Frank (the naughty boy) rang yesterday from Tasmania and was asking—when is Edward coming?

I will be contacting you more frequently soon as I will be installing a PC (talking to a supplier this morning). It will be good to keep in touch more often.

Edward, can you do me a small favor? I hope our shipment has arrived in Melbourne but the shipping Company is saying to me that the goods have been cost port to port only—not door to door? The Melbourne Company has contacted the Shanghai forwarding agent who confirms this.

The thing is if it has been paid in full in Shanghai, I don't want to pay the charges twice. (The port charges, handling & transport charges are considerable).

Please respond to me by email or fax numbers above-mentioned.

I appreciate your helping me again, and look forward to hearing from you ASAP.

Both Christina & I are missing you and look forward to seeing you once again very soon.

Best regards,
Johan Dawson

The above-mentioned three cases tell you that you will be required to be able to do three things in your company, as below:

☑ translate incoming English version letters into proper Chinese;

☑ translate Chinese version letters into proper English;

☑ reply to your foreign customers directly in English after reading English version letters, faxes or emails.

Part Two   The Forms of Business Letters

I. Traditional Business Letter

Normally, a traditional business letter consists of seven standard parts and some optional parts. Here is a sample.

NEW EXHIBITIONS CO., LTD

P. O. BOX 699**
DUBAI - UNITED ARAB EMIRATES
MOBILE: + 971-83-6883***
TEL: + 971-5-1816***

FAX: + 971-5-1816***
salesmanager@emirates.net.ae
88ait@alibaba.com
WEB: www.abb18.ae

Unit One Job Requirements and the Forms of Business Letters

Date: 21 Feb. 201*

Sandy Han Stationery Co., Ltd.
Address:113* Zhongshan Road, Shanghai
Tel : 0086-21-6234*** Mobile: 1366789****
Fax : 0086-21-6234*** Zip Code: 200013
E-MAIL: sandy66@alibaba.com

Dear Sirs,

  INVITATION TO 3rd AFRICA, ASIA & MIDDLE EAST EXPO IN NAIROBI
  It is indeed our great pleasure to invite your company to participate in the most important event of the year to be held in Nairobi. As you know, Kenya serves as the gateway to a vast East-African market of over 400 million consumers.
  17th Africa, Asia & Middle East Expo is divided into 6 specialized segments under one roof, such as:
  1 - CONSUMEX ' 17
  Computers, IT, Peripherals, Consumer Electronics, Home Appliances, Office Automation, Satellite & Broadcasting, Wireless & Telecommunications, Stationery, Toys, Gift Items, etc.
  2 - FOOD-PAK ' 17
  Food & Beverages, Agricultural & Dairy Products, Fast Foods, Hotel Products, Fresh Frozen & Canned Foods, Kitchen Appliances, Packaging & Labeling Machines, Flexible Packaging, Disposable & Paper Products, etc.
  3 - BUILTECH ' 17
  Building & Construction Materials, Tools & Hardware, Safety & Security, Sanitary Ware & Bathroom Fittings, Ceramics, Marble, Electrical & Lighting products, Cables, Generators, Paints, Plastic & Rubber Products, etc.
  4 - AUTO & PARTS '17
  Automotive, Auto Spare Parts & Accessories (New & Used), Car Care Products, Tyres, Bearings, Aviation &Transportation Equipment, Oils, Lubricants, Greases, Auto Paints, etc.
  5 - MEDI+ PHARMA '17
  Healthcare & Medical Supplies, Pharmaceuticals & Drugs, Dental & Surgical Instruments, Skin Care, Hospital Equipment, Soaps, Detergents, Hygienic & Disposable Products, etc.
  6 - INTERTEKSIL ' 17
  Textiles and Garments, Fabrics, Men & Women Wears, Garments, Leather & Leather Products, Fashion Accessories, Perfumery, Cosmetics, Bags, Watches, Imitation Jewelry, etc.
  PARTICIPATION OPTIONS:
  OPTION # 01 (EXHIBITING) :
  USD 225 per sq.m. SHELL stand with basic furniture (Minimum 9sq.m).

> OPTION # 02 (ADVERTISING IN THE BUISNESS CATALOGUE):
> 9000 copies will be distributed to all major trade visitors during the exhibition.
> QUARTER PAGE 4-COLOR   USD 400
> HALF PAGE   4-COLOR   USD 750
> FULL PAGE   4-COLOR   USD 1,100
> The first two Expos were very successful! Enclosed please find the brochure about these expos. If your esteemed corporation is interested in entering the biggest export market in East Africa, please do not hesitate to contact us. We are looking forward to your favorable reply.
>
> Henry Smith
> Project Director
> NEW EXHIBITIONS CO.,LTD

These different parts are explained as follows:

(1) the letter-head;

(2) the date;

(3) the inside name and address;

(4) the salutation;

(5) the subject heading;

(6) the body of the letter;

(7) the complimentary close;

(8) the writer's signature and designation;

(9) the enclosure.

Of which, No. 5 and No. 9 belong to optional parts of a business letter, which you can choose to use or not. A typical business letter shall consist of all the remaining parts.

The layout of the above-mentioned letter is called *blocked letter style*. The following style is called *semi-indented letter style*. You can choose any one of them in business communications.

Exhibition Group

6**- Matao - SP - BRAZIL

ZIP Code 15990-8**

Phone & Fax: +55 16 283-8**

E-mail: export@exh.com.br

sales@export.com.br

Website: www.export.com.br

Date: 22 Jan. 201*

Sandy Han Stationery Co., Ltd.

Address: 13* Zhongshan Road, Shanghai

Tel: 0086-21-6234*** Mobile: 1366789****

Fax: 0086-21-6234*** Zip Code: 200013
E-MAIL: sandy66@alibaba.com

> Dear Sir/ Madam,
>
> We from Exhibition Group are having the pleasure to invite you to visit us at the most important metal working branch trade show in Latin America:
>
> **MECANICA 201***
>
> This fair will be in Sao Paulo city, Brazil, between the days 18 and 22, May, 201*, at the Anhembi park.
>
> To receive further information and your invitation, please send us an e-mail with your complete address for the confirmation: sales@brexport.com.br.
>
> We hope to have your esteemed company at these days at this important event.
>
> Best regards,
> Henry Smith

II. Fax

A Fax machine enables you to send or receive any documents immediately, including signature, table, chart or other information. It can work for you 24 hours automatically every day. In this way, we can keep in touch with our customers closely.

Different companies prefer to use different patterns of fax message. Generally speaking, the following particulars should be mentioned when you fax to your customer: names of the parties concerned(including the names of the sender and receiver), their companies, telephone numbers, fax numbers, date, pages. For example:

上 海 利 华 进 出 口 有 限 公 司
Shanghai Lihua Imp. & Exp. Co., Ltd.

Rm.9012 Union Building,	Fax: 86-21-645378**
1202 Zhongshan Road (N),	Tel: 86-21-645378**
Shanghai, 20026* China	E-Mail: lihua88@yahoo.com

Date: Aug 29, 201*
To: Mr. Roland Klein
Klein Underwood Company
Fax: 49-40-6378****
From: Shanghai Lihua Imp & Exp Co., Ltd.
Fax: 86-21-645378**

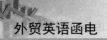

Re: Brochure sent for your reference

Dear Mr. Klein,

In compliance with your request in your Fax dated Aug. 28, we have sent you our latest brochure, by separate airmail, for your reference.

If you are interested in any item of our products, please let us know ASAP. We are looking forward to your specific enquiry.

Yours faithfully,
Henry Cai
Sales Representative

III. Email

Nowadays, email has become a most powerful tool in business correspondence, which is fast, cheap and convenient.

Normally, it is advisable for you to have only one subject for each email. Such letter also should be limited to cover less than one page because nobody likes reading overly long letters. Below is a sample.

To: roger@alibaba.com

Subject: Freight to West Coast USA

Dear Mr. Wang,

We are much honored to know your esteemed company at International Exhibition Centre. We send you a latest list of freight rate to west coast USA for your reference as follows:

WEST COAST USA

    PORT OF LOADING: SHENZHEN

    LOS ANGELES   LONG BEACH   CARRIER: NORASIA

    USD1,650/20GP   USD2,200/40GP   USD2,450/40 (YANTIAN/WED. ETA: 16DAY)

    OAKLAND SAN FRANCISCO   CARRIER:TMM

    USD1,700/20GP   USD2,250/40GP   USD2,520/40HQ(YANTIAN/MON. ETA: 16DAY)

    LOS ANGELES LONG BEACH OAKLAND SAN FRANCISCO CARRIER: SINOTRANS

    USD1,750/20GP   USD2,300/40GP   USD2,450/40HQ (CHIWAN/SAT. ETA: 15DAY)

    LOS ANGELES   LONG BEACH   CARRIER: MARUBA

    USD1,650/20GP   USD2,200/40GP   USD2,450/40HQ (YANTIAN/WED. ETA:18DAY)

    LOS ANGELES   LONG BEACH   OAKLAND SEATTLE   CARRIER:CSCL

    USD1,800/20GP   USD2,400/40GP   USD2,650/40HQ (YANTIAN/TUE. FRI. ETA: 14DAY)

    LOS ANGELES LONG BEACH OAKLAND TACOMA   CARRIER: LT/EVERGREEN

Unit One Job Requirements and the Forms of Business Letters

USD1,850/20GP	USD2,450/40GP	USD2,720/40HQ	(YANTIAN/THU. ETA: 14DAY)
LOS ANGELES	LONG BEACH	OAKLAND SAN FRANCISCO	CARRIER:WANHAI
USD1,900/20GP	USD2,450/40GP	USD2,750/40HQ	(YANTIAN/SAT. ETA: 14DAY)

If you have any questions, please do not hesitate to contact us directly. If you need more information covering other lines, please tell us, too. We are looking forward to cooperating with you in the near future.

Yours sincerely,
Henry Cai
Sales Representative
Shanghai Lihua Imp. & Exp. Co., Ltd.

Summary

Working in an import-export organization, you are required to do the following three things:

a) To be able to translate incoming business letters written in English into Chinese;

b) To be able to translate outgoing business letters written in Chinese into English;

c) To be able to reply to your customer in English after reading incoming business letters written in English.

There are different forms of business letters in business correspondence, including traditional business letters (handled by post office), faxes and emails. The last forms are now most commonly used in international trade.

Exercise

I. Choose the best answer

1. We are sending you by air our sample, together with a range of pamphlets ____ your reference.

  A. for   B. at   C. of   D. with

2. Quotations and samples will be sent upon receipt ____ your specific enquiries.

  A. for   B. at   C. of   D. to

3. We will make you a competitive offer ____ our products, September shipment.

  A. for   B. on   C. with   D. in

4. We assure you ____ our full cooperation.

  A. for   B. of   C. with   D. in

5. We will assist you ____ this respect.

  A. for   B. of   C. with   D. in

6. We have received the information you asked for in your letter ____ May 5.
    A. for   B. of   C. with   D. in

7. We must advise you to regard their request for credit ____ caution.
    A. for   B. of   C. with   D. in

8. We will be very glad to answer your inquiries ____ any time.
    A. for   B. at   C. of   D. with

9. We have extensive connections ____ food stores in cities and towns.
    A. for   B. with   C. of   D. to

10. We are pleased to have your enquiry ____ our products.
    A. for   B. of   C. with   D. in

11. ____ your information, we are also interested in other kinds of Chinese nuts in large quantities.
    A. Of   B. For   C. With   D. In

12. We quote this article ____ CNY158.00 per dozen.
    A. to   B. with   C. at   D. on

13. We are airmailing to you, ____ separate cover, a copy of our catalogue.
    A. with   B. on   C. under   D. for

14. We are looking forward with interest ____ hearing from you.
    A. with   B. on   C. by   D. to

15. We shall be glad to know whether they are ____ the wholesale trade.
    A. for   B. of   C. with   D. in

16. Any information you may give us will be treated in absolute ____.
    A. confident   B. confidential   C. confidentially   D. confidence

17. If you place your order with us ____ our products not later than the end of this month, we would ensure May shipment.
    A. for   B. of   C. with   D. in

18. Payment is to be made ____ an irrevocable L/C at sight.
    A. for   B. of   C. by   D. in

19. Other products are ____ the same high quality.
    A. at   B. of   C. with   D. in

20. If your answer is ____ the affirmative, please quote us your best price CIF New York.
    A. for   B. of   C. with   D. in

II. Supplementary Reading Material

Mr. Cai, author of this textbook, who has taught this course since 1991, is sure you will benefit a lot from this course. He trusts that it is quite worthwhile for you to spend a lot of time in studying this book in your spare time. You will find it very helpful, especially after you begin your business career. If you failed to do so, you would regret it. The following emails, which were written by two of Mr. Cai's former students in a casual way, were just the case in point. Please do

Unit One   Job Requirements and the Forms of Business Letters

not imitate the first email, it is only for your reference. The second one is better than the first one. They are as follows.

Email A

Dear Mr. Cai,

　　First I shall also wish u and ur family "Happy New year" ~~. I didn't see the e-card in ur mail though u promised to m~~~:(what a pity. And now I'm so glad to tell u that I'm working in an imp & exp company which is located in JIUJIANG Rd. The new life-style isn't suitable for me from the beginning, but I did remember once u said: self-image. So I hope I can get along with each colleague asap. I'm also appreciate to u that now I have to deal with some English business letters in my jobs. Till now, I'm feeling ur course is great important to m! xixi, I can feel u r smiling to m, at this moment:)

　　Can u tell m my score? It is not be good, is it? I think I'll trouble u with something in the future. Can I know ur fax no. and the call no.? Keep in touch with m, pls.

　　　　　　　　　　　　　　　　　　　　　　　　　　　　　　urs, faithfully,
　　　　　　　　　　　　　　　　　　　　　　　　　　　　　　J.T. Ma

Email B

Dear Mr. Cai,

　　Now your new semester begins, you must be busying in teaching, writing and studying. I beg you to pay attention to your health and remember that rest is always necessary.

　　Time is flying. Such feeling is stronger after graduation. I began my business career half a year ago. In the past six months, I learnt a lot and experienced a lot and made a great progress. During this period I really realized the importance of English, esp. your course, English for International Business Communication. I always keep this textbook in my office and consult it from time to time. However, I feel this edition is old, part of which has been not accustomed to the current social practice. Therefore, I am looking forward to your new book. When it is published, I will buy one and ask you to sign your name!

　　Next, I'd like to tell you something about my job. Now I am working for Zhejiang H.Y. Materials Co., Ltd. I spent one month in the workshop so as to be familiar with the products and then was assigned to the International Business Dept. and now I can do my job independently. As the raw materials are imported from Africa, a branch in Congo was established two months ago in order to assure the supply of raw materials. All the materials used for life and production for the Branch are supplied by ourselves, therefore, a new Imp & Exp company was established here so as to pave the way for the exportation of all the materials. Now I am also in charge of the export business. In fact, I am feeling my way to accumulate my experience, and I am very confident now and trust that I will do a much better job in the future!

Of course, that my work goes smoothly now is due to the good skills you built for me at university. I really have to say it again that your course really benefited me a lot! Thank you, Mr. Cai!

May you be happy on Teachers' Day.

Yours truly,
Chunyan Han

Unit Two

Establish Business Relations

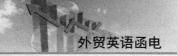

Introduction

In international trade, the first and most important step is to find your business partners in the international market. In order to find your potential customers in foreign countries, you have to write business letters or send fax messages or emails to them so as to establish business relations with them.

You can find your buyers or sellers through the following channels:
(1) The Internet;
(2) Trade fairs;
(3) Banks;
(4) Advertisements;
(5) Business directories;
(6) Friendly companies of the same trade;
(7) Chinese Commercial Counselor's Offices in foreign countries;
(8) Chambers of Commerce in foreign countries;
(9) Trade Points under UN organizations.

After you get the name and address of your aimed customer, you will write a letter to try to establish business relations with him, in which you should tell the receiver how his name is known, what you handle and what you want to do, that is what you want to sell or what you want to buy.

Business Letters

Email 1

From: damai-SALES(163) damai-sales@vip.163.com
To: lily <lily@ttll.com>
Cc: haomai-service <haomai-service@vip.163.com>
Subject: your email of Sept.3
Date: Friday, September 05, 201*   4:30 PM

Dear Sir or Madam:

Thanks for your e-mail dated Sept. 3. We are pleased to know your interest in our products. Please send us your specific inquiry for our products if you would like to establish a new relationship to cooperate with us. And do not hesitate to let us know your demand at your earliest convenience.

We are a producer and manufacturer specializing in brass ball valve, brass gate valve, flexible tubes, Teflon tape, sanitary fittings. Our products are of high quality and good design with very good reputation. In our many-year's export practice, we have furnished our customers with our high-quality goods and very competitive prices. We believe that we will have a brilliant future if we cooperate with each other.

Now we have many products entering your local market. We hope we could offer you our services and competitive prices to your entire satisfaction.

Finally, you could also view our web to get more information about us. We sincerely hope we could cooperate with you very soon.

Best regards,
Henry Cai (Mr.)
Export Manager

Shanghai Lihua Imp. & Exp. Co., Ltd.
Rm.9012 Union Building,
1202 Zhongshan Road (N),
Shanghai, China, 200235

Fax: 86-21-645378**
Tel: 86-21-645378**
E-Mail: sunmoon@vip.163.com

Email 2

From: billaffleck88@intnet.mu < billaffleck88@intnet.mu >
To: sullivan88@vip.163.com <sullivan88@vip.163.com>
Cc: xinqixiang@163.com <xinqixiang@163.com>
Subject: Export Director
Date: 201*/6/17 9:25:57

Dear Sirs,

We take this opportunity to introduce ourselves as a Commission Agent established in Mauritius 40 years ago and specializing in Building Materials and Hardware.

We have made a sound reputation in this market by catering for importers/wholesalers with whom we have developed good relationship throughout the years.

There is a regular demand in our market for all kinds of Sanitary Fittings and we invite you to send us by post your latest color catalogue together with your best FOB Lianyun Harbor prices so that we may contact our various customers to place their orders.

We earnestly hope to establish a long-term mutual benefit business relationship with your company in a near future and look forward to your prompt reply.

Best regards,
Bill Affleck
Big Ocean Trading Co., Ltd.

2** Poudriere street - P.O. Box 1988
Port Louis - MAURITIUS.
Tel: (230) 208-3815 / 321-2***
Fax: (230) 212-8643 / 208-6***
E-mail: billaffleck88@intnet.mu

Email 3

From: abdullah99@alibaba.com <abdullah99@alibaba.com>
To: sullivan88@vip.163.com <sullivan88@vip.163.com>
Cc: xinqixiang@163.com <xinqixiang@163.com>
Subject: request for price list
Date: 201*/6/17 9:25:57

Dear Mr. Sullivan,

We have received your price list through an email. While checking your price list, we noted that there are a few items not mentioned therein according to your products. We will be extremely grateful if you could send those prices according to our attachment. Your cooperation would be appreciated.

We, RTBO Franchise Development and Investment Division, a subsidiary of StarBOB Group based in Jeddah, Saudi Arabia, would like to introduce our company to your esteemed organization.

StarBOB Group has been operating in the Kingdom since 1947, presently it owns and operates a large network of manufacturing, distribution and service companies under the RTBO trademark. The RTBO Division is managed by a five-member board of directors and it has a work force of over 1,000 employees. This facility supplies 3,000 distribution centers and 40 showrooms located in all major cities of the Kingdom and the Middle East Region. With our existing network of regional offices & show rooms set in every city in Saudi Arabia, Lebanon, Egypt and emirates, we guarantee immediate and profitable result. This overwhelming presence in the Middle East is the core foundation of our Group's trade strength.

We are interested to market your product in Saudi Arabia. We would highly appreciate it if you could send us your price list and catalogues for our reference.

Looking forward to hearing from you soon.

Best regards,
Abdullah

Email 4

From: "mail.orientalresources.com" <sunmoon@orientalresources.com>
To: <STEVE@FOXMAIL.COM>

Unit Two Establish Business Relations

Subject: NICE TO MEET YOU AT THE CANTON FAIR IN GUANGZHOU AND CHINA SOURCING FAIR IN SHANGHAI
Date: Tue., 27 Apr., 201* 16:18:13 + 0800

Dear Sir/Madam,
Re: trade fair

We are so much delighted and honored to meet you at the CANTON FAIR in our booth: 20.1G37-48 (GREAT WALL), and at CHINA SOURCING FAIR in booth 3H06.

As one of the leading factory specializing in sanitary fittings, faucets, and valves, we are sincerely interested in establishing long business relationship and cooperation with your esteemed company.

Our products are mainly exported to the South America and Caribbean Market, some exported to Africa, South Asia and North America.

With reasonable prices, various and wide-ranged product lines, and flexible terms of payments, we enjoy a good fame and leading advantages out of hundreds of competitors in this line.

As you must have obtained our catalogues at the fair, you can list your choices and feel free to inquire us.

If you cannot find our catalogues, you may also find parts of the items at: www.asiaresourcing.com and do not hesitate to let us know, so that we can re-send catalogues for your reference.

We are looking forward to your reply at your earliest convenience.
Best Regards,

Sullivan Zhang
Export Manger

Email 5

From: alex808@alibaba.com <alex808@alibaba.com>
To: xinshidai-sales@vip.163.com <xinshidai@vip.163.com>
Cc: xinqixiang@163.com <xinqixiang@163.com>
Subject: new customer new cooperation
Date: 201*/3/13 9:25:57

Dear Sirs,

We have known your esteemed firm through our friend's company in Hong Kong.

Firstly, we'd like to introduce ourselves. We are a representative agent with more than 20 years of experience in Santo Domingo market. We have young and capable professionals. So, we think we are the ideal candidate to represent any types of line in our market.

For many years, we have been dealing in all kinds of plumbing fixtures through exporters in Taiwan and Hong Kong, who supply us with most of the products. However, owing to the constant advancement of raw material prices, currency appreciation and financial cost, the prices of these products have been increased so much that we cannot compete with many suppliers. Therefore, we are looking for new cooperator who can offer us good quality, competitive prices, prompt delivery and good service. We hope that we can establish business relation with you directly to manage your complete line of products.

We are an agent, so we request a stable commission of 3%~5% on different products. Actually, we have got some requirements from our customers. If you want to give us the opportunity to work with you directly, please sent us your best FOBC5 Shanghai or CIFC5 Caucedo Port covering the following items:

BM9112, BM9118, BM9128, BM9125, GQ41802, GQT61BL

We sincerely hope to cooperate with you for mutual benefits. Your early reply is appreciated.

Best regards,
Alex Garcia
East Asia Market Manager
Oso Panda International,
Calle Anacaona #1008, Bayona.
Santo Domingo, Republica Dominica.
Tel.: 809-50*-90** Fax: 809-50*-93**
E-mail: alex808@alibaba.com

Pattern A of Business Letters

When you want to establish business relations with your potential customers, you should tell the receiver:

a) how his name is known;
b) what you handle;
c) what you want to do, that is, what you want to sell or what you want to buy;
d) you are looking forward to his early reply.

Relevant Terms

catalogue 目录	pamphlet 小册子
brochure 小册子	price list 价目单
sample 样品	a trial order 试订单

续表

enquiry 询价	an enquiry note 询价单
a quotation sheet 报价单	customer 客户
manufacturer 制造商	wholesaler 批发商
retailer 零售商	Sale by Sample 凭样品买卖
Sale by Description 按规格说明售货	without any delay 毫不延误

Useful Phrases

deal in 经营	deal with 处理，与……做生意
specialize in 专营	furnish sb. with sth. 向某人提供某物
prior to 在……之前	seek for 寻找，追求
enter into business relations with sb. 与某方开展业务关系	upon receipt of 一俟收到
look forward to 期待	up to now 迄今为止
take the liberty of doing sth. 冒昧做某事	make sb. an offer for sth. 向某人发某物的盘
for one's information 告知某人	for one's reference 供某人参考
for one's inspection 供某人检验	for one's consideration 供某人考虑
as to 至于，关于	avail oneself of 利用
take pleasure in doing sth. 乐于做某事	be suitable to 适合于
through courtesy of sb. 承蒙谁的介绍	a wide range of 各式各样的
to acquaint sb. with sth. 使某人熟悉某物	in compliance with 按照，与……一致
by separate airmail 单独航空邮寄	with reference to 关于，有关
on the basis of 在……基础上	without delay 不延误
out of stock 无现货，已脱销	in short supply 供不应求
in large supply 大量供应	to our mutual benefit 对双方有利

Summary

In international trade, the first and most important step is to find your business partners in the international market. There are many channels through which you can find your buyers or sellers. In the first letter sent to your potential customer, you should tell him how his name is known, what you deal in, what you want to do, that is, what you want to sell or what you want to buy and you are looking forward to his early reply.

Exercises

I. Questions for review

1. Do you know what the main channels are through which you can establish business relations with your aimed customers?
2. What are the essential elements of the first enquiry?

II. Choose the best answer

1. We shall be glad to place an order with you ____ your products.
   A. with   B. at   C. on   D. for
2. We are interested in your plush products, details ____ our Enquiry Note attached.
   A. with   B. at   C. as per   D. in
3. Mineral products fall ____ the scope of our business activities.
   A. with   B. at   C. on   D. within
4. Upon receipt ____ your specific enquiry, we shall email you immediately our quotation sheet.
   A. for   B. of   C. with   D. to
5. We are looking forward ____ your prompt reply.
   A. for   B. with   C. to   D. of
6. If your price is competitive, we shall place a trial order ____ you for your new products.
   A. for   B. of   C. with   D. to
7. We are one of the largest exporters of animal products ____ this area.
   A. with   B. at   C. on   D. in
8. We enclose you our Enquiry Note No. 2311 and wish to receive your quotation sheet ____ your earliest convenience.
   A. with   B. at   C. on   D. within
9. The INVOICE and the PACKING LIST have been sent to you when we asked you ____ the forwarder details.
   A. for   B. of   C. with   D. to
10. There may be less communications ____ these two staffs, because before 15th we already booked the vessel from 18th to 25th. But one staff told us the vessel date is not sure now, it can be any day in next week.
    A. for   B. with   C. on   D. between
11. We learn from your letter ____ Dec. 23 that you are interested in establishing business relations with us for the purchase of our products.
    A. for   B. at   C. of   D. with
12. For your selection, we are sending you a list of the items which might be suitable ____

your market requirements.

    A. for   B. at   C. on   D. to

13. As we deal _____ sewing machines, we are glad to make you the following firm offer for your consideration.

    A. for   B. at   C. with   D. in

14. Most of the firm's suppliers either give only very short credit for limited sums or make deliveries _____ a cash basis.

    A. with   B. at   C. on   D. in

15. We should be glad to know whether they have the reputation _____ paying promptly.

    A. for   B. of   C. with   D. to

16. This information is given in confidence and without any responsibility _____ our part.

    A. for   B. with   C. on   D. in

17. We should find it most helpful if you could also supply samples of the various leather _____ which the gloves are made.

    A. for   B. with   C. of   D. in

18. Will you please send us a copy of your catalogue for gloves, _____ details of your terms of payment.

    A. for   B. with   C. on   D. in

19. The high standard of craftsmanship will appeal _____ the most selective buyers.

    A. for   B. with   C. to   D. in

20. It is quite probable that we may run short _____ supply.

    A. for   B. with   C. to   D. of

III. Translate the following sentences into Chinese

1. Please let us have your specific enquiry and our quotation will be emailed to you as soon as possible.

2. We thank you for your letter dated 18th November, in which you expressed your desire to establish direct business relations with us.

3. Please send us your latest catalogue showing your complete line of goods available for export.

4. We are seeking to establish a direct connection with your corporation, for we prefer your new makes.

5. If you can supply goods of the type and quality required, we may place regular orders for large quantities.

6. The following buyer is looking for products which are compatible with your business. Please kindly contact them for details.

7. Through the courtesy of Mr. McCurry, We learn that you are a big importer of light industrial products in your area, we take the liberty of writing to you to establish business relationship with you.

8. Our new product is especially designed for your market. We think this item will appeal to the most selective customers in your area.

9. We take pleasure in introducing ourselves as an exporter of this line in Shanghai to see if we can enter into business relations with you.

10. For any information as to our financial standing, we refer you to Bank of China, Shanghai Branch.

Optional Part

11. We are also interested in your other products in large quantities and shall send you specific enquiries later on.

12. Enclosed please find our latest illustrated catalogue and price list. The prices are on FOB Shanghai basis in US dollars.

13. We are pleased to know that you are a big buyer of air-conditioners in your area, we are a famous manufacturer in this line and hope to establish business relations with you.

14. From the Internet we find that you handle such product, we shall be much obliged if you send us your sample for our consideration.

15. We have noticed your advertisement in the magazine, we shall appreciate it if you send us your booklet for our reference.

IV. Translate the following sentences into English

1. 我们是一家专营陶瓷产品的出口商。
2. 我公司现在有各种地毯及其他纺织材料的铺地制品可供出口。
3. 我们接受客户来样、来图及按客户规格和包装要求供货的订单。
4. 请你方速报最新型号产品的 CIF 马尼拉最低价格。
5. 我们借此机会告诉你方我们希望把业务扩展到非洲市场。
6. 我们希望早日收到你方的具体询价单。
7. 一俟收到你方的具体询价，我们马上寄送样品并报最优惠的价格。
8. 随函寄上我公司新产品的价目单和商品小册子各一份。
9. 我们接受以客户的商标或品牌供货的订单。
10. 我们静候佳音。

V. Case Study

Send an email to your client, based on the information mentioned below.

上海利华人造毛皮有限公司于 1996 年成立，是一家中外合资企业，注册资金为 900 万美元。公司主要生产各类针织长毛绒及其制品。公司拥有先进的加工设备，生产用原料系优质进口材料，可年产 800 多万米的长毛绒面料。公司的主要产品有长毛绒玩具、服装、工艺鞋和包袋。注册商标为 KOALA，在欧美已经拥有众多的消费者。公司先后同十多个国家和地区的一百多家客户建立了良好的贸易关系，形成了较为完整的外贸渠道与销售网络，出口商品质量和服务质量在国际上均享有一定的声誉。

经过市场调研，发现在瑞典市场上中国的轻工业品拥有很好的声誉，于是决定拓展在该地区的业务。经了解，斯德哥尔摩的 ANITA CO., LTD. 是一家具有良好声誉的进口商。该公司的全称和详细地址为：

ANITA CO., LTD.

Vasagatan *

101 ** Stockholm

Tel/Fax:+46(0)8-506 53***

Email: anita88@sweden.com

请给客户发一封建立业务关系的邮件，要求格式完整、正确，主要内容包括公司介绍、可提供的产品介绍，说明随函寄上目录，并表达期待尽快与对方建立业务关系的热切愿望等。你公司的信息如下：

上 海 利 华 人 造 毛 皮 有 限 公 司

Shanghai Lihua Artificial Leather Co., Ltd.

Rm.8016 Jianguo Building,	Fax: 86-21-642578**
1208 Meilong Road, 200237	Tel: 86-21-642578**
Shanghai, China	E-mail: lihua66@alibaba.com.cn

VI. Discussion

1. Do you know any famous websites in international trade? Give your brief introduction about them to your classmates.

2. How can we benefit from the internet economy?

VII. According to the following appendix, please choose one of the target markets and then make an investigation to find out such facts: annual trade volume between this market and China, the structure of commodities, what the market needs most from China, what Chinese consumers' favorite imports are and the respective potential market demands.

Your Target Markets:

(A to Z) Afghanistan Albania Algeria Andorra Angola Anguilla Antarctica Antigua Barbuda Argentina Armenia Aruba Australia Austria Azerbaijan VIRGIN IS. Bahamas Bahrain Bangladesh Barbados Belarus Belgium Belize Benin Bermuda Bhutan Bolivia Bosnia-Herzegowina Botswana Bouvet Island Brazil Brunei Bulgaria Burkina Faso Burundi CANTON&E. IS Cambodia Cameroon Canada Canal Zone Cape Verde Cayman Central African Republic Chad Chile China Christmas Island Cocos Islands Colombia Comoros Congo Cook Islands Costa Rica Côte d'Ivoire Croatia Cuba Cyprus Czech Republic DRO.M.L Denmark Djibouti Dominican Rep. E.GUINEA East Timor Ecuador Egypt El Salvador Eritrea Estonia Ethiopia F.GUIANA F.POLYNESIA F.S.A.T Falkland Faroe Island Fiji Finland France Gabon Gambia Georgia Germany Ghana Gibraltar Greece Greenland Grenada Guadeloupe Guam Guatemala Guinea Guinea-Bissau Guyana H.M.ISL Haiti Honduras Hong Kong Hungary

Iceland India Indonesia Iran Iraq Ireland Israel Italy Jamaica Japan Johnston Island Jordan Kazakhstan Kenya Kiribati Korea DPRK Kuwait Kyrgyzstan Laos Latvia Lebanon Lesotho Liberia Libya Liechtenstein Lithuania Luxembourg MIDWAY IS(US) Macao Macedonia Madagascar Malawi Malaysia Maldives Mali Malta Marshall Island Martinique Mauritania Mauritius Mayotte Mexico Micronesia Moldova Monaco Mongolia Montserrat Morocco Mozambique Myanmar N. MARIANAS Namibia Nauru Nepal Netherlands Netherland Antilles Neutral Zone New Caledonia New Hebrides New Zealand Nicaragua Niger Nigeria Niue Norfolk Island Norway Oman P.I.T.T PLO Pakistan Palau Panama Papua New Guinea Paraguay Peru Philippines Pitcairn Poland Portugal Puerto Rico Qatar Reunion Romania Russia Rwanda S. YEMEN S.J.M.I S.T&P.IS SOUTH GEORGIA ST. KITTS-NEVIS ST. LUCIA ST.P&M ST.VINCENT Samoa San Marino Saudi Arabia Senegal Seychelles Sierra Leone Singapore Slovakia Slovenia Solomon Islands Somalia South Africa Spain Sri Lanka St. Helena Sudan Suriname Swaziland Sweden Switzerland Syria Tajikistan Tanzania Thailand Togo Tokelau Tonga Trinidad and Tobago Tunisia Turkey Turkmenistan Turks-Caicos Islands Tuvalu U.S.M.I UAE(United Arab Emirates) USA Uganda Ukraine United Kingdom Uruguay Uzbekistan VIRGIN IS.(US) Vanuatu Vatican City Venezuela Viet Nam W.A.F.I Wake Island Western Sahara Yemen Yugoslavia Zaire Zambia Zimbabwe

Unit Three

Credit Inquiry

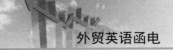

Introduction

A Credit Inquiry (Status Enquiry) is an examination of an importer's credit history. With the help of a Status Enquiry, an exporter can obtain such important information as the financial position, credit, reputation and business methods of other firms, that is, you can know your customer's conduct, capacity and capital. In this way, you will be able to decide whether or not to risk doing business with your customer, on the basis of how reliably he has kept his past promises.

In fact, any trader needs to make a credit inquiry if he intends to establish business relations with his prospective customers.

There are many methods of making a status enquiry. The most commonly used way is to write to a bank reference, but a bank is unwilling to give you information if you have no business relations with it. With the help of your own bank, you can get the required information.

Besides a bank reference, there are still many channels through which you can get the needed information, such as Chinese Commercial Counselor's Offices in foreign countries, foreign Commercial Counselor's Offices in China, Chambers of Commerce, business directories. If you consult business directories, you can get some basic information.

Nowadays business people prefer to make a status enquiry through other business houses of the same trade and enquiry agencies. The latter almost can obtain any customers' credit report in the world for you. Normally, the relative charges range from CNY600 to CNY6,600. A satisfactory Business Credit Report may contain detailed information and is indispensable for you to establish complete customer files and analyze operational and credit status of subject companies. Such report may cover more than 20 sections of content, including Important Events, Summary, Registration, Finance, Credit Record, Operations, Industrial Comparison, Risk Analysis, Credit Rating, etc. A Credit Report consists of only several paragraphs or as long as 20 pages.

In recent years, e-commerce develops rapidly. Some business websites also provide theirs members with customers' Credit Profile, in which they might tell you that the existence of this subject company and the correctness of the contact information were authenticated by a third-party credit agency in the same country of this company, such as follows:

Authenticated and Verified by ABC Research & Consulting Co. Ltd.

Company Name: A& B Trading Co. Ltd.

Contact Name: Jose Saramago

Country: Brazil

Address: 6**- Matao - SP - BRAZIL

ZIP Code: 15990-8**

Phone number: +55 16 283-8**

Fax number: +55 16 283-9**

E-mail: export@exh.com.br

Unit Three Credit Inquiry

    sales@export.com.br
    Website: www.export.com.br

Caution: Although companies with Credit Profiles have been independently verified, it does not mean that there is no risk in making transactions with those companies.

In providing a Credit Profile, they do not assume any part of the viewer's business risk and do not guarantee the accuracy, completeness, or timeliness of the information. They shall not be liable for any loss arising or resulting from reliance on this profile, nor from error or omission in preparing this profile.

As an importer, you can supply your foreign exporter with your reference, such as your own bank, golden customer, important supplier, agent, governmental institutes, so as to show your strong financial standing, high quality of your products, trustworthiness, excellent service and good reputation. Many exporters are also willing to make a status enquiry through enquiry agencies. For example, China Export & Credit Insurance Corporation is a famous one in China.

As an exporter, you'd better make credit inquiries through different channels to ensure you are dealing with trustworthy importers.

Business Letters

Letter 1

Shanghai   Lihua   Imp. & Exp.   Co.,   Ltd.

Rm. 606 Plaza Building,	Fax: 86-21-642578**
1302 Meilong Road, 200237	Tel: 86-21-642578**
Shanghai, People's Republic of China	E-mail: lihua88@alibaba.com

Harbor Imp & Exp Corp.
12 AB Road Sialkot,
Punjab, Pakistan
Zip Code: 51360
Phone: 92 432 26****
Fax: 92 432 26****
Dec.16, 201*

Dear Mr. Crabble,

    A purchase order from Joseph Smith & Son, Sialkot, Punjab, Pakistan for USD50,000 worth of merchandise listed you as a credit reference.

    We would appreciate any information you can provide on the credit history of Joseph Smith & Son, with your company. Key facts would include how long the owner, Joseph Smith, has had an account with you and whether or not he has any outstanding debts. We will keep any information you send us confidential.

I've enclosed a postage paid envelope for your convenience.

Sincerely,
Henry Cai,
General Manager

Letter 2

Harbor Imp & Exp Corp.

12 AB Road Sialkot,
Punjab, Pakistan
Zip Code: 51360
Phone: 92 432 26****
Fax: 92 432 26****
Email: harbor68@online.com.pk

Shanghai Lihua Imp. & Exp. Co., Ltd.
Rm. 606 Plaza Building,
1302 Meilong Road, 200237
Shanghai, People's Republic of China
Dec. 26, 201*

Dear Mr. Cai,

We are glad to tell you that we've got the information you asked for in your letter of Dec.16, 201*.

Joseph Smith & Son, Sialkot, Punjab, was established in 1991. Its registered capital was USD100,000. They are general importers and exporters, commission agents and manufacturers' representatives. Their main imports from China are textile, porcelain ware, house-hold electric appliance, hand tool. They are also wholesalers and retailers, trading principally with Afghanistan. We cooperated with this firm very well. It is always punctually meeting its commitments, but recently it seems to be getting into troubles because of overtrading.

Mr. Joseph Smith, the president, is understood to have experience in this line. We believe that business transactions with this firm will prove to be satisfactory. In the meantime, we consider them good for small business engagements. Larger transactions should be covered by L/C issued by Banks. However, this reply is without responsibility on our part.

We would be happy if we could be of some help to you in this matter.

Yours faithfully,
Earnest Crabble
Manager
Imp. Dept.
Harbor Imp. & Exp. Corp.

Unit Three Credit Inquiry

Letter 3

Shanghai   Lihua   Imp. & Exp.   Co.,   Ltd.

Rm. 606 Plaza Building,   Fax: 86-21-642578**
1302 Meilong Road, 200237   Tel: 86-21-642578**
Shanghai, People's Republic of China   E-mail: lihua88@alibaba.com

---

The Pacific Sydney Bank Ltd.
121* AB Road,
Sydney, Australia
Date: Dec.12, 201*

Dear Sirs,

　　Will you please be kind enough to obtain for us in confidence all the information possible respecting the financial position, credit history and methods of business of the following firm:

　　Kangaroo Trading Co., Ltd., 89 Warrawee Ave, Noble Park, Canberra

　　The only reference as given by Kangaroo Trading Co. Ltd. is their bank, Bank of Australia, Canberra. Any information you may provide for us will be treated in absolute confidence and without responsibility on your esteemed Bank.

　　We shall be much obliged if you can give us any information at an early date.

Yours sincerely,
Henry Cai,
General Manager
Shanghai Lihua Imp. & Exp. Co., Ltd.

Letter 4

The Pacific Sydney Bank Ltd.

Bank address: 3* Park Road, Milton, QLD 406*, Australia.
Shanghai Lihua Imp. & Exp. Co., Ltd.
Rm. 60* Plaza Building
1900* Meilong Road, 200237
Shanghai, People's Republic of China
Date: Dec.16, 201*

Dear Sir,

We are pleased to enclose a Credit Report regarding the below-mentioned firm, for which you asked in your letter dated Dec.12, 201*.

Kangaroo Trading Co. Ltd.,8* Warrawee Ave, Noble Park, Canberra

This is given to you in confidence and will, we trust, serve your purpose.

Truly yours,
Edgar Smith
Manager of Information Dept
The Pacific Sydney Bank Ltd.

Encl.

The information transmitted is intended only for the person or entity to which it is addressed and may contain confidential and/or privileged material. Any review, retransmission, dissemination or other use of, or taking of any action in reliance upon, this information by persons or entities other than the intended recipient is prohibited. If you receive this in error, please contact the sender and delete the material from any computer.

Letter 5

From: DAMAI-SALES(163) <damai-sales@vip.163.com>
To: Angela <angela@ttry.com>
Cc: XINSHIDAI-SERVICE <xinshidai-service@vip.163.com>
Subject: about Paul
Date: 201*/7/19 10:31:35

Dear Angela,

After contacting Paul again, we felt this person is not very reliable, although we still do not have enough time to go there examining the factory.

1) We have required him to send us printed catalogues many times. One time, he said "ok". Another time he said "it is finished". And the last time he said he only has catalogue in files.

2) We have asked him to let us know at least the Chinese name and address of this factory or send us his name card. He always either said it is not necessary, or said we have contacted many times with each other so both know each other.

3) We recalled memory that last time he told us he could not accept 70% payment after shipment just because there is one core part inside the MP3 is imported and subject to the fluctuation of the material greatly and easily. He told us he experienced that some clients may even waste ADVANCE T/T rather to be willing to execute the order when raw materials decreased a lot.

However, with second thought, we do not think there is any raw materials could cause over

30% fluctuation within short period, and if so there will lots of people doing investing on the material rather to produce MP3 for small profits! Because, even this core part fluctuates with over 10% increase, it also means it will have time to decrease over 10%.

4) They told us in this industry, no one will sell products by issuing Invoice in order to avoid taxes. And their purpose is to receive payment through company in Hong Kong so as to avoid further tax and duty. However, although to some extent, there are some reasons for people to do so, it is not an essential or always method to follow. To cooperate with such kind of people, you may feel very unreliable.

Anyway, we are still investigating this person and his factory. But till now, we do not believe this person.

Sometimes, you might face factory/boss is not trustful enough, and in some other cases, you may face some factory staffs doing bad things without letting the boss knows although the boss or factory is trustworthy. All these types will also cause you risks and loss. Please regard these situations with caution.

Best Regards

James

Manager of Export & Client Dept.

Shanghai Better Hardware Trade Co., Ltd.

ADD: No. 1991*, Meilong Road West, Humin Plaza Shanghai, #200237

TEL: 0086-21-642503**/642532**/642508** (ext.208)

FAX: 0086-21-642503**Website: www.betterhardware.com

Pattern B of Business Letters

Your Credit Inquiry should inform your receiver of the following particulars:
(1) The name of your customer and the address;
(2) What you need to know about your customer;
(3) Your assurance of keeping the reply as confidential.

Relevant Terms

Status Enquiry 资信调查	Credit Inquiry 资信调查
reference 资信证明人	bank reference 银行资信证明人
financial standing 财务状况	enquiry agency 咨询机构
Credit Report 信用报告	Credit History 信用记录

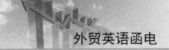

Useful Phrases

in some respect 在某些方面	in this respect 在这方面
assure sb. that… 向某人保证	assure sb. of sth. 向某人保证
for safety's sake 为安全起见	in strict confidence 严格保密
in absolute confidence 绝对保密	on an L/C basis 在信用证的基础上
be limited to 局限于	meet one's commitments 履行其义务
regard sth. with caution 谨慎对待某事	bring an action against sb. 控告某人
due to 由于	make delivery 交货
on a cash basis 现金方式	inform sb. of sth. 通知某人某事
inform sb. that… 通知某人某事	without security 无担保，无抵押
to the amount of 总计	in reply to 回复
to have confidence in sth. 对某事有信心	on one's behalf 代表某人
in view of 鉴于，考虑到	

Summary

  A Credit Inquiry (Status Enquiry) is an examination of an importer's credit history. With the help of a Status Enquiry, a foreign trader can know customer's conduct, capacity and capital so as to decide whether or not to risk doing business with the customer.

  Any trader needs to make a credit inquiry if he intends to establish business relations with its prospective customers. There are many methods of making a status enquiry.

  As an importer, you can supply your foreign exporter with your references to show your strong financial standing, high quality of your products, trustworthiness, excellent service and good reputation. As an exporter, you'd better make credit inquiries through different channels to ensure you are dealing with trustworthy importers.

Exercises

I. Questions for review

1. What is a Credit Inquiry?
2. What are the channels through which you can make a Credit Inquiry?
3. Why is it important to establish and maintain a good credit history?

II. Choose the best answer

1. Although Simpson Textile Imp & Exp Co., Ltd. has been a customer of ours, we do not

Unit Three Credit Inquiry

feel comfortable enough to vouch _____ them.

  A. for   B. with   C. to   D. of

 2. We have finished three transactions _____ this firm during the past two years. Each contract was less than USD20,000.

  A. for   B. with   C. on   D. from

 3. Their payments have been timely. It has a good reputation _____ the trade but we do not have any knowledge of their credit standing.

  A. for   B. of   C. to   D. within

 4. We suggest that you make additional enquiries _____ an agency.

  A. from   B. off   C. through   D. to

 5. Please make sure to ask your Bank to send Documents _____ International Courier so as to make it reach us next week.

  A. for   B. with   C. by   D. from

 6. We have followed all the legal requirements and gotten the Import License _____ the Ministry of Production and also the Authorization from the Central Bank.

  A. for   B. with   C. on   D. from

 7. We received the samples in good order and good quality, so we moved to the next phase _____ the business, which is actually placing an order.

  A. for   B. with   C. to   D. of

 8. I sent him a message which explained to him that my Company would never allow me to make payment _____ T/T to his Company.

  A. for   B. with   C. by   D. from

 9. We must check whether this company really exists even if we have to use Credit Company _____ check them out.

  A. for   B. with   C. to   D. of

 10. We will open L/C _____ the full amount and also we will require SGS CERTIFICATE OF INSPECTION to certify quality and quantity.

  A. for   B. with   C. to   D. of

 11. We suggest you may contact the manufacturer to confirm whether they have the same products _____ competitive prices, which is more trustful than Paul.

  A. for   B. with   C. to   D. of

 12. As you did not provide any information about how to issue the B/L yet, we will no longer amend the B/L anymore _____ this Friday, and such case will definitely cause a very big discrepancy against the L/C.

  A. for   B. with   C. to   D. after

 13. I have just called the Forwarder Agent in Caracas and complained to them why they did not call our company because our phone and Fax were listed _____ the B/L.

  A. for   B. with   C. on   D. from

14. Anyway, since the Container already arrived at the pier, we must solve this problem fast _____ any delay.
  A. for   B. without   C. by   D. from

15. We are facing very strong competition _____ AFGMETAL and please understand that they maintain very good price in our market.
  A. for   B. with   C. on   D. from

16. Kindly talk to Mr. McCurry to check out and update the prices according to the present market conditions so that we can maintain our share _____ our domestic market.
  A. for   B. with   C. in   D. of

17. We have adjusted all quotations to our clients about by 20% - 30% _____ a reasonable range.
  A. for   B. within   C. by   D. from

18. Of course, as a leading supplier, we will also buy some brass/zinc/alum raw materials _____ storage when the cost is in the lower lever, which will be mainly used for our old clients.
  A. for   B. with   C. to   D. as

19. New clients will get the prices _____ the latest raw material situation.
  A. for   B. with   C. to   D. as per

20. Considering our good friendship, we will not adjust prices greatly, but will increase only about _____ 5%~10%.
  A. for   B. without   C. by   D. from

III. Translate the following sentences into Chinese

1. This is a strictly confidential response to a request made by the firm.

2. Any statement on the part of this bank or any of its officers as to the standing of any person, firm or corporation, is given as a mere matter of opinion for which no responsibility, in any way, is to attach to this bank or any of its officers.

3. In answer to your inquiry of Dec. 16, we should not hesitate to trust Mr. Cai for any amount that he might order.

4. We feel free to say that you will find your dealings with him, not only entirely satisfactory, but also agreeable personally.

5. We have done business with both of these firms for 5 years and I am sure that they will be willing to furnish you with any information you ask for.

6. Judging from his purchases, he seems to be a man of considerable means.

7. The firm under inquiry enjoys a high reputation in the business circles for their punctuality in meeting obligations.

8. We have reason to believe they are highly respectable and trustworthy.

9. The above-mentioned information is given on the understanding that it is treated as strictly confidential.

10. This house has been remarkably successful, its connection is extensive, and with safe

firms, its reputation here is decidedly good.

Optional Part

11. Anita Co., Ltd. of your city intends to enter into business relations with us and has mentioned your esteemed company as reference as to their financial standing.

12. We shall be grateful if you tell us whether their financial standing is sound or not.

13. We regret that we have to send you an unfavorable reply because of the bankruptcy of their bank.

14. In reply to your enquiry of March.12, we take pleasure in informing you that they enjoy respect and unquestionable confidence in the business circle.

15. We are glad to enclose credit information regarding the above-mentioned company, which is given to you in confidence and shall be treated as strictly confidential.

IV. Translate the following sentences into English

1. 抱歉，由于10月1日到7日的国庆节七天长假而延误了回复。
2. 该公司是各种商品的进出口商，主要贸易对象是印度和巴基斯坦。
3. 我们将很感激你们在这一方面提供给我方的任何信息。
4. 他们总是能够因准时的交货、适中的价格和优异的质量而使客户完全满意。
5. 他们在国内外的业务联系很广，其财务状况相当稳健。
6. 你们在8月6日来信中提到的那样一笔数额的信用贷款似乎是安全的。
7. 该公司的困境在于管理不善，尤其是过额贸易。
8. 我们对这家公司的诚实充满信心。
9. 如果能让我们知道他们的财务状况是否相当好，那么我们会很高兴的。
10. 他们享有充分而及时履行义务的声誉。

V. Case Study

Debt Collection

Company QD is an exporter of timber in Northeast China. Company YK is an importer in Yokohama, Japan, who is an established customer of QD.

One day QD received an order from YK for timber. As YK was a regular buyer who enjoyed good reputation of paying promptly, QD made shipment in time on the basis of open account. However, QD failed to receive payment from YK in due time. So QD faxed a Debit Note to YK. But the importer refused to pay for the order owing to the bad quality of the timber.

QD made an investigation and found that there was no question about the quality of the timber, then made a phone call to YK, but the importer still refused to pay. So QD decided to bring an action against YK. But when they knew the high cost of lawsuit and the difficulty of enforcement, QD had to give up and regard this sum of money as a bad debt.

Fortunately, through the courtesy of a friend, QD came to know a credit consulting corporation (hereinafter called CR), who judged that full recovery was possible according to the evidence.

So, QD entrusted CR to collect this payment for goods. CR made a credit inquiry on YK so as to find the real reason of nonpayment. After investigation, CR found that YK premeditated this transaction. The boss of YK was an overseas student from China, and now settled down in Japan. Due to the high quality and low price of timber in Northeast China, he imported large quantity of timber from China every year. But recently, the consumers in Japan complained a lot about the quality of floor board made of timber from China, which resulted in the big drop of sales. So, the boss thought all the responsibility should wholly rest with QD. So he decided to refuse payment for this repeat order at the beginning of transaction.

CR phoned and faxed to YK time and again, discussing with the importer and analyzing the bad result of nonpayment. As a member of International Association of Commercial Collectors (IACC), CR would clamp down YK with seven local banks and thirty firms of the same line and disclose the fact it refused to meet its commitment to all its customers in Japan. Under such big pressure, the importer compromised and immediately made payment at full. YK stated that such thing would never occur again in the future.

Finally, QD achieved full recovery and decided to cooperate with debt collection agent on a long-term basis so as to reduce the risk of dishonor.

VI. Discussion

1. How do small/middle-sized trading companies recover overdue debts (receivables) in international trade?

2. Is it necessary for domestic imp. & exp. companies to make use of export credit insurance? Why?

Unit Four

Enquiries and Replies

Introduction

An enquiry is a request for a reply informing an importer of prices, catalogue, samples and/or a quotation sheet before placing an order with a prospective exporter. An enquiry is usually made by importers in international trade. Normally, a good enquiry shall include the following information:

- Minimum order quantity;
- Sample availability/cost;
- International standards met;
- Delivery time;
- Company brochure;
- Full product catalog;
- A response before a date.

An enquiry should be concise, specific and polite.

Suppose you were an exporter, how to maximize the value of every inquiry you receive? Here are some suggestions for your reference:

a) Reply to all enquires promptly, because buyer inquiries are valuable sales leads. Your response and the time it takes you to reply are critical to be successful. Reply today with complete information for best results. A reply should answer all the questions mentioned in the enquiry and samples should be sent to the prospective buyers as soon as possible. Of course, you may ask your receiver to share the cost by paying the postage, because sometimes sample cost is also a very heavy burden.

b) Update your sales inquiries database. The inquiries you receive form a valuable database of clients and prospects. Use this database to follow up or offer new products.

Business Letters

Email 1

To: huali88@alibaba.com
Subject: Enquiry for 4 Items

Dear Mr. Cai,

I was very pleased to meet you at Canton Fair and meet your colleague in Shanghai. We are greatly interested in your products.

We intend to place an order for one 20-foot container for the following items as a trial order. I'd like to say we are looking for the best and competitive price, FOB Shanghai, which enables us to start a long term business relations with you.

Unit Four   Enquiries and Replies

——Item No. 1508 Brass Ball Valve, with Brass Body, Iron Ball, Iron Stem, Aluminum Handle for the following size and weight:

1/2"	125g
3/4"	180g
1"	260g
1-1/2"	680g
2"	1150g
3"	2700g
4"	4800g

——Item No. 1582 Brass Ball Bibcock with Nozzle, with Brass Body, Iron Ball, Iron Stem, Aluminum Handle:

1/2"   180g

——Item No. 1236 Single Lever Bathtub Faucet with Hose, Shower and Holder.
——Item No. 1278 Single Basin Faucet with Brass Pop-up.
——Item No. 1898 Wall Mounted Kitchen Faucet with Spout.

So, please exert your best efforts to quote us your best price and let us know the quantity per carton for each item.

Best wishes
Jamie KALAJI
General Manager

GOG IMP & EXP CO., LTD
ALEPPO FREE ZONE
Syrian Arab Republic
P.O.BOX 78**
Tel: (00963) 21228****
Fax: (00963) 21228****
Email: jamie@scs-net.org

Email 2

To: huali88@alibaba.com
Subject: Enquiry for 8 Items

Dear Mr. Wang,

We are glad to know your esteemed company from Internet. We are anxious to place a trial order with you for the following 8 items:

—— Model #: 1508 — 10-inch Single-lever Kitchen Faucet in Elegant Design.
—— Model #: 1409 — 4-inch Lavatory Faucet with Brass Seat and Acrylic Handle.

—— Model #: 1318 —— 8-inch Kitchen Faucet with Lever Handle.

—— Model #: 1316 —— 4-inch Lavatory Faucet with Brass Seat and CP Zinc Handle.

—— Model #: 1312 —— 8-inch CP Plastic Kitchen Faucet with Brass Shank and Acrylic Handle.

—— Model #: 1315 —— 8-inch CP Plastic Kitchen Faucet with Brass Shank and CP ABS Handle.

—— Model #: 1526 —— 4-inch Plastic Faucet with Brass Shank and CP ABS Handle.

—— Model #: 1528 —— 4-inch Plastic Faucet with Brass Shank and Acrylic Handle.

We hope that you can send us the following information:

- FOB prices (for minimum order quantity)
- Minimum order quantity
- International standards met
- Delivery time
- Company brochure
- Full product catalog

As we find that there is a good demand here for these products, we will place the first order with you for the above mentioned articles within two months if your prices are competitive enough compared with those of other suppliers'.

Your early reply is awaited with much interest.

Best wishes,
Tom McEwan
Asst. Marketing Manager
TOM CONSUMPTION GROUP

P. O. BOX 57608,
DUBAI - UNITED ARAB EMIRATES
TEL: + 971 - 4 - 35136**
FAX: + 971 - 4 - 35136**
MOBILE: + 971 - 50 - 7686***
EMAIL: mcewan@emirates.net.ae

Email 3

From: HENRY-SALES(163) <henry-sales@vip.163.com>
To: steve88 <steve88@codetel.net.do >
Cc: hardwaresales <hardwaresales @vip.163.com>
Subject: price and quantity and production
Date: 201*/9/6 19:25:58

Dear Steve,

Thanks for your email dated Sept. 5.

As regards the price, after checking your PDF file, we found one price was wrong. The price for Item A93 should be USD2.95/SET, while in your file, it shows A93 is USD2.00. So please adjust the price of A93 from USD2.00 to USD2.95/SET.

The quantity you need for this time is very small, which will increase our production cost, because we could not take advantage of mass production, and it is hard to purchase necessary accessories with large quantities and chrome plating cost for each item has been increased 100%. So please consider whether you could increase the quantity for your order, otherwise we will have to adjust the prices according to your present small quantity.

Right now, we are entering the peak season, and our factory is extremely busy in production. The normal production period is 30 days, while now we need 40–50 days. Anyhow, we will exert our best efforts to insert your small order to finish it earlier after we finalize the price and quantity.

Best Regards,

Henry

Manager

Export & Client Dept.

Shanghai Better Hardware Trade Co., Ltd.

ADD: No.1991, Meilong Road West, Humin Plaza Shanghai, #200237

TEL: 0086-21-642503**/642532**/642508** (ext.208)

FAX: 0086-21-642503**

Website:www.betterhardware.com

Email 4

From: steve88 <donpope@online.com.mx>

To: HENRY-SALES(163) <henry-sales@vip.163.com>

Cc: hardwaresales <hardwaresales@vip.163.com>

Subject: price and quantity and production

Sent: Wednesday, September 08, 201* 6:18 PM

Dear Henry,

Thank you for your e-mail of Sept. 6.

Though quite small, I cannot increase quantities any more. Please believe me that I also wish to order bigger lots.

Anyway I will also check the possibility to increase quantity, but in order to do that I would like to ask you for the prices of the current quantities.

As for the production time, I will be really grateful to have your support on that. I realize I am placing my order late, but unfortunately I couldn't place it earlier.

I hope to receive the actual price for these quantities very soon and after that I will confirm either the current order or new one with increased quantities.

Your early reply is awaited.

Best regards,

Steve

Purchasing Manager

Water Heater & Gas Boiler Division

Don & Sons Co., Ltd.

Avenida Yucaton 9**8

Mexico City

Mexico

Email 5

From: HENRY-SALES(163) <henry-sales@vip.163.com>
To: steve88 <steve88@foreht.net.do>
Cc: hardwaresales <hardwaresales@vip.163.com>
Subject: closing dates
Date: 201*/12/6 15:21:58

Dear Steve,

Thanks for your email of Dec 4. We will have our New Year Holiday from Jan. 1st to Jan. 3rd.

As regards the traditional Lunar New Year Festival, we will have longer holidays. Every year almost all Chinese factories will be closed for the Traditional Spring Festival for a longer period. This time, the legal holiday is from Feb.13th to 19th, so our office will be closed during that period.

While, the factory, which is located in the rural areas, usually takes longer period —— maybe closed from Feb. 4th till Feb. 22th.

However the whole period will depend on the workers' returning situation, whose hometown are not in our factory area but in nearby provinces. This is to say, our production will be not guaranteed during the period of the forthcoming long holiday.

All our orders now are full until Feb. If you have new orders, please place them with us earlier, otherwise the shipment will be arranged very late.

Best Regards

Henry

Manager

Export & Client Dept.

Unit Four Enquiries and Replies

Shanghai Better Hardware Trade Co., Ltd.
ADD: No.1991, Meilong Road West, Humin Plaza Shanghai, #200237
TEL: 0086-21-642503**/642532**/642508**(ext.208)
FAX: 0086-21-642503**
Website:www.betterhardware.com

Pattern C of Business Letters

Normally, a good enquiry may include the following information:
a) Minimum order quantity;
b) Sample availability/cost;
c) International standards met;
d) Delivery time;
e) Company brochure;
f) Full product catalog;
g) A response before a date.

Relevant Terms

enquiry 询价	inquiry 询价
reply 答复	quotation 报价
quotation sheet 报价单	fax 传真
email 电子邮件，发邮件	sales representative 销售代表
chief representative 首席代表	

Useful Phrases

by separate post 另邮	excellent in quality 品质优良
novel in design 设计新颖	reasonable in price 价格合理
moderate in price 价格适中	competitive in price 价格有竞争力
excellent in craftsmanship 工艺优良	feel confident that 有信心
make payment 付款	draw one's attention to 提请某人注意某事
to be of the same high quality 相同的高质量	appeal to 吸引
sell fast 卖得快	in the market for 想买
on account of 由于，因为	without previous notice 不事先通知
at a more favorable price 以更优惠的价格	take advantage of 利用
be similar to 与……相似	at an early date 早日，尽快

Summary

An enquiry is a request for a reply informing an importer of prices, catalogue, samples and/or a quotation sheet. In international trade, an enquiry is usually made by importers, which should be concise, specific and polite.

It is advisable for you to reply to all enquiries promptly and update your sales inquiries database so as to maximize the value of every inquiry you receive.

Exercises

I. Questions for review

1. What is an Enquiry?
2. What particulars should be covered in a good enquiry?
3. How to maximize the value of every inquiry you receive?

II. Choose the best answer

1. We are glad to inform you that we have your name and address from the Internet. We shall be pleased to enter _____ trade relations with you.
   A. for   B. upon   C. with   D. into

2. We wonder whether you handle NACHI bearing. If you do, will you please send us a quotation _____ it (TAPE ROLLER BEARING 110 RUS 1).
   A. of   B. against   C. on   D. for

3. We specialize in importing machinery and equipment from all over the world _____ an equipment supplier of highway construction in China.
   A. with   B. in   C. as   D. at

4. We wonder whether you know who are selling NACHI bearing (TAPE ROLLER BEARING 110 RUS1). Could you tell us? We are ___ urgent need for it.
   A. with   B. in   C. as   D. at

5. We really appreciate your full cooperation during the past several years. We think we have developed a beneficial trade in your area ___ the basis of equality and mutual benefit.
   A. of   B. against   C. on   D. for

6. As to the new samples of our products, our statistics showed that we had a very heavy burden ___ sample cost.
   A. with   B. for   C. of   D. on

7. As you know, during the past years we always supplied small quantity of samples to our customers free ____ charge.
   A. of   B. against   C. on   D. for

Unit Four Enquiries and Replies

8. We not only had to pay the samples' cost, but also pay for the postage _____ express couriers, such as UPS, Fedex.

    A. for   B. to   C. with   D. into

9. However, our profit is getting smaller and smaller owing _____ the uprising prices of raw materials.

    A. for   B. upon   C. with   D. to

10. We could send samples by your account number, while we will supply the samples free of charge in normal small quantity _____ before.

    A. with   B. in   C. as   D. at

11. We feel sure that they will be glad to furnish you _____ any information you require.

    A. for   B. at   C. on   D. with

12. We need a regular supply of Bitter Apricot Kernels _____ cakes and candies.

    A. for   B. at   C. of   D. in

13. Quotations and samples will be sent _____ receipt of your specific enquires.

    A. for   B. upon   C. with   D. to

14. As this article falls _____ the scope of our business activities, we take this opportunity to express our wish to conclude some transactions with you in the near future.

    A. with   B. in   C. within   D. at

15. We assure you _____ our full cooperation.

    A. for   B. at   C. with   D. of

16. About a year ago an action was brought _____ the firm by one of its suppliers.

    A. of   B. against   C. on   D. for

17. We are large dealers in textiles and believe there is a promising market in our area _____ moderately priced goods of the kind mentioned.

    A. on   B. with   C. for   D. in

18. We would allow you a discount _____ 2%.

    A. with   B. for   C. on   D. of

19. The goods are excellent _____ quality.

    A. for   B. with   C. to   D. in

20. These leather handbags are fully illustrated in the catalogue and are _____ the same high quality as our gloves.

    A. for   B. of   C. to   D. in

III. Translate the following sentences into Chinese

1. What's your wholesale price on this item?

2. If Grade A is not available, Grade B will do.

3. Please tell us the Article Number of the Product.

4. Do you offer FOB or CIF?

5. Please quote us your best prices as soon as you receive our inquiry.

6. We have confidence in your bamboo wares.

7. I don't think price is a problem. The most important thing is that how many you can supply.

8. If your prices are more favorable than those of your competitors, we shall send you our order.

9. We hope this will be a good start for profitable business relations and assure you that your order will receive our careful attention.

10. Today we have sent you our illustrated catalogue through the "TNT" courier for your reference.

Optional Part

11. What lowest price can you quote for 50 bales of cotton for December shipment?

12. In reply to your enquiry of May 15, we send you several samples of wallpaper closely resembling to what you need.

13. The recent advance in the prices of raw cotton has compelled us to make a slight increase in the prices.

14. If you can meet our present requirements, please quote us your best CIF Hamburg, stating the earliest date of shipment and the discount you allow.

15. Thank you for your enquiry dated July 6, we send you a quotation sheet for your consideration. Of course, these quotations are all subject to our final confirmation.

IV. Translate the following sentences into English

1. 请报给我们你方 FOB 上海最具竞争力的价格，并将报价单发送至……

2. 我们正在核算出厂最低价，明天邮件发出供你们考虑。

3. 我们随函附上每件货物的照片和规格，相信你们能按照我方要求生产，并报出最优惠的价格。

4. 然而，最终做出决定之前，我们需要更多的信息。

5. 如果这一切都可能，能否请你们在 2 月 1 日之前给我们一个回复？

6. 为了给你们提供更多有关我公司的信息，随函附上我们最新的小册子供你们参考。

7. 我们渴望同贵公司建立起牢固的业务关系。

8. 看到你们在报纸上的广告，我们想请你方尽快寄送你方产品的最新价目单，并附以插图目录。

9. 回你方 10 月 12 日邮件的，现我方另外航空邮寄给你方我公司的小册子一份。

10. 如果你方报价可以接受，并且机器令人满意，我们会向你们定期下订单。

V. Case Study

Case A

----- Original Message 1 -----
From: Lorna
To: DAMAI-SALES(163) ; damai-service

Unit Four Enquiries and Replies

Sent: Tuesday, September 08, 201* 6:26 PM
Subject: new P/I urgent

Dear Jim,

It has been a long time since our last order. I hope this e-mail finds you well. Unfortunately I am placing my new order with emergency. Please see the attached file. I will stand by to receive your pro forma invoice. Are there any price changes? I hope that you will give me your earliest possible delivery date as soon as possible.

Thank you in advance for your cooperation and I hope to receive your prompt reply.

Best regards,

Lorna

Purchasing Specialist

Water Heater & Gas Boiler Division

TTRT LTD

----- Original Message 2 -----
===
From: DAMAI-SALES(163) <damai-sales@vip.163.com>
To: Lorna <Lorna88@ttrt.com>
Cc: damai-service <damai-service@vip.163.com>
Subject: new P/I urgent
Date: 201*/9/9 17:23:57
===

Dear Lorna,

Thanks for your email dated Sept. 8.

PRICE

I've checked your PDF file, and found there is one price was wrong. According to our last quotation DTD Jan.12th, 201*, the price for Item A85+E06 should be USD2.94/SET, while in your file, it shows A85 USD2.00, and E06 USD0.84, total just USD2.840. So please adjust the price of A85 from USD2.00 to USD2.100.

Besides, this time your quantity is still very small, which will increase our production cost because we could not make advantage of mass production, and it is hard to purchase necessary accessory with large quantities and the cost of chrome plating for each item has been doubled.

So please check whether you could increase the quantity, or we will have to adjust the prices according to your present small quantity. Thanks for your understanding.

PRODUCTION TIME

Right now, we are entering the peak season, and very very busy in production. The normal production period is 30 days, while now we need 40 – 50 days.

Anyway, we will check to see whether we could insert your small order to finish earlier or not after both sides finalize the price and quantity.

Best Regards,

Jim

Manager of Export & Client Dept.

Shanghai Better Hardware Trade Co., Ltd.

ADD: No.1991, Meilong Road West, Humin Plaza Shanghai,#200237

TEL: 0086-21-642503**/642532**/642508** (ext.208)

FAX: 0086-21-642503** Website: www.betterhardware.com

Case B

To: ellien88@alibaba.com

Subject: Inquiry for Bed Sheets for the Moscow Market

Dear Sir or Madam:

We are pleased to know from your website that you are a leading exporter in your area. We hope to establish direct business relations with you. We are an importer in Moscow for Bed Sheets, Sleeping Bags, Shower-bath, Curtains, Towels, Footwear, Headgear and Artificial Flowers. We are looking for Asian Suppliers.

We need Bed Sheets in Poly/Cotton 120 to 180 Thread Counts, Printed and Solid. Please send us your brochure for our reference.

Prefer to receive the following information by 31 March 200*:

FOB prices (for minimum order quantity)

Minimum order quantity

Delivery time

We are looking forward to your early reply.

Yours faithfully,

VI. Discussion

1. Many exporters complain that they often fail to receive any news after they reply to the foreign buyers' enquiries. What would you do if you were the exporter?

2. How do you distinguish a good one from many enquiries?

Unit Five

Quotations and Proforma Invoices

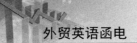

Introduction

A quotation (quotation sheet) is a statement of the prevailing prices of goods and services. The supplier is willing to supply goods or service at the prices on the terms and conditions mentioned in it. A quotation sheet will be sent to the prospective importer by the exporter after he receives an enquiry from the foreign buyer.

Proforma invoice is a kind of invoice which is made to inform importers of the cost of goods before shipment. It is usually used to apply for an import license, the establishment of an L/C or foreign exchange quota by the importer.

Contained in a proforma invoice are usually the descriptions of the goods, quantity, unit price, amount, port of loading, time of shipment, terms of payment and insurance coverage, etc. A proforma invoice serves as a quotation sheet when it indicates a prescribed period for which the price and conditions mentioned therein will remain valid.

Business Letters

Email 1

To: steven@aol.com
Subject: Quotation for Marble & Granite

Dear Mr. McCurry,

I am very pleased to receive your enquiry dated Oct. 4. We are confident that you will be satisfied with the high quality of our products. As you know all kinds of patterns are made of Granite or Marble, which are very beautiful and colorful. As this is your trial order, we quote you as follows:

Art. No: RTF-231:

Strip Slabstone Polished, no cut on edges (White Pearl Marble),

2000up x 650 x 18mm, Unit Price: USD 30.50/m^2, FOB Shanghai

Art. No: RTF-232:

Strip Slabstone Polished, no cut on edges (White Pearl Marble)

2000up x 580 x 18mm, Unit Price: USD28.90/m^2, FOB Shanghai

Art. No: RTF-321:

Polished Granite Table, Size: 800mm(Diameter) x 20mm (thick), Unit Price: USD 68.00, FOB Shanghai,

Art. No: RTF-322:

Polished Granite Table, Size: 1500mm(Diameter) x 30mm thick, Unit Price: USD 78.00, FOB Shanghai,

Unit Five Quotations and Proforma Invoices

Terms of Payment: confirmed, irrevocable L/C payable by draft at sight

Mode of Packing: in strong wooden crates

Time of Shipment: within two months upon receipt of L/C

Our quotation remains valid until the end of this year.

We also handle other ranges of products, such as Sculpture, Fireplace, Fortune Ball, Baluster and Rome Post. Please give us more specific enquiries if you are interested in our products.

We are looking forward to your favorable news.

Yours sincerely,

Henry Cai,

General Manager

Shanghai Lihua Imp. & Exp. Co., Ltd.

Rm. 606 Plaza Building,   Fax: 86-21-642578**

1302 Meilong Road, 200237   Tel: 86-21-642578**

Shanghai, People's Republic of China   E-mail: huali88@alibaba.com

Email 2

To: wick@aol.com

Subject: Quotation for Brass Ball Valve

Dear Wick,

Thanks for your e-mail of Oct 4. We are sorry for the delayed reply due to the 7 days' National Day Holiday in China. As requested, we quote you as follows on FOB SHANGHAI basis:

---Art. No.1316 Brass Ball Valve, with Brass Body, Iron Ball, Iron Stem, Aluminum Handle for the following size and weight:

1/2"	120g	USD0.82/PC
3/4"	170g	USD1.20/PC
1"	260g	USD2.18/PC
2"	1120g	USD8.60/PC
3"	2650g	USD21.80/PC
4"	4680g	USD40.105/PC

---Art. No.1426 Brass Ball Bibcock with Nozzle, with Brass Body, Iron Ball, Iron Stem, Aluminum Handle:

1/2   150g   USD0.95/PC

---Art. No.1532 Brass Angle Stop, with Brass Body, Metal Handle:

1/2x1/2   USD1.300/PC   135G

---Art. No.1546 Single Lever Bathtub Faucet with Hose, Shower and Holder:

USD14.85/PC for ϕ35 Catridge with Hose, Shower & Holder

USD15.50/PC for ϕ40 Catridge with Hose, Shower & Holder

---Art. No.1612 Single Basin Faucet with Brass Pop-up:

USD11.20/PC for ϕ35 Catridge with Pop-up

USD12.50/PC for ϕ40 Catridge with Pop-up

As the prices of raw materials are advancing, it is advantage to your interest to accept our quotation. Your early reply is awaited.

Yours sincerely,
Henry Cai,
General Manager

Shanghai Lihua Imp. & Exp. Co., Ltd.

Rm. 606 Plaza Building,　　　　Fax: 86-21-642578**

1302 Meilong Road, 200237　　Tel: 86-21-642578**

Shanghai, People's Republic of China　E-mail: huali88@alibaba.com

Email 3

From: XINSHIDAI-SALES(163) <xinshidai-sales@vip.163.com>

To: STEVE <steve88@fjfdfc.bg>

Cc: service of xinshidai <xinshidai-service@vip.163.com>

Subject: Quotation for Order #018 to Xinshidai

Date: 201*/2/2 17:00:17

Dear Steve,

Thanks for your email and call. We are glad to receive your new orders.

QUOTATION FOR NEW ORDER ON FOB Shanghai basis:

G-31 (CI 1583): USD0.435/PCS　　chrome plated 3-way diverter

E-03 (CI 1584): USD0.540/PCS　　1.3M PVC silver-wire Flexible

G-09 (CI1585): USD0.230/PCS　　white wall holder

H-19 (CI1586): USD4.050/PCS　　Brass Sliding bar chrome plated.

A-93 (CI1587): USD1.970/PCS　　Improved version (with every two holes close, open holes diameter 0.75MM)

Price increased due to the following reasons:

1) Raw Material Cu, Ni, ABS increased from your last order date(Nov. 20th, 201*) till today. (Feb. 2th, 201*)

Chrome-plating effected much by the Nickle material cost increase, and meanwhile due to the Ecological and Health reason chrome-plating factories are moving to remote rural areas which caused transportation cost higher. Besides, numbers of chrome-plating factory are decreasing due to the non-encouragement policy by the Government.

2) Chinese currency CNY got appreciation very quickly from Nov. to the present by about 4.2%.
3) Workers' salary (per hour) increased by about 50%-70% these years.

DELIVERY DATE

We are sorry to inform you that due to the Spring Festival, our factory will be closed from Feb.10th to Mar. 5th, 201*.

Our Shanghai office will be closed from Feb.18th to Feb. 25th, 201*.

This is the Chinese largest traditional festival all over the nation, during which rural areas will enjoy longer holiday and big cities will have a 7-day holiday.

And due to our already-full timetable on production for 4 containers to ship before the holiday, we could no longer insert any new order. All new orders will be arranged after receiving ADVANCE T/T and start production from Mar. 6th, 201*. It takes about 25-30days to be finished for each order.

Earlier confirmed and earlier ADVANCE T/T transferred orders will be arranged with priority after March.

We are sorry for not being about to finish your order in earlier March. And this is national wide problem, due to the traditional holiday.

We suggest that next time you'd better pay attention to our long holiday when you are going to place orders with us. For your information, except for the Spring Festival, we always have National Days from Oct.1th to 7th and Labor Holiday from May 1st to May 7th each year. These three holidays are relatively long holidays, which may cause manufacturers' delay on production.

price for BRASS less than 6000PCS:

Brass spout: USD1.230/PCS   more than 6000PCS.
Brass spout: USD1.355/PCS   less than 6000PCS.

Please confirm your quantity.

The above-mentioned quotations will be only valid till Feb.18th, 201*.

For your information, according the past records, raw materials will always increase greatly after Spring Festival because at that time all new orders come to China and cause the demand over supply.

At present, the decrease in the global market is also due to the coming Spring Festival. All Chinese factories are going to be closed and stop production, which cause no demand in the raw material market.

201* VISIT

For your information, from Feb. 21th to Mar. 22th, 201*, President William, Manager Catherine, and I will be out of office for business traveling to four countries visiting old clients, during which we may not being able to reply you on time.

Best Regards
Jim
Manager
Export & Client Dept.

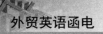

Email 4

To: sebestian@emirates.net.ae

Subject: Quotation

Dear Sebestian,

We are very glad to receive your inquiry dated Oct. 5, and thank you for your interest in our products.

We are pleased to inform you that all the items listed in your inquiry are in stock. These items are of high quality and have enjoyed a good reputation in the Middle-East area. We have got many repeat orders from our customers in Gulf countries. Of course, the prices quoted are also very competitive. You may rest assured that our products will be also marketable in your area.

Now we quote you our competitive prices as follows:

Art No. T1258:	USD69.50 Per Set CIFC3 Dubai
	USD57.70 Per Set FOBC3 Shanghai
Art No. T1356:	USD15.70 Per Set CIFC3 Dubai
	USD11.80 Per Set FOBC3 Shanghai
Art No. T1436:	USD30.10 Per Set CIFC3 Dubai
	USD25.40 Per Set FOBC3 Shanghai
Art No. T1789:	USD25.60 Per Piece CIFC3 Dubai
	USD21.20 Per Piece FOBC3 Shanghai

As the prevailing price in the international market is fluctuating, our quotations are subject to our final confirmation. Anyhow, if you accept them, please let us have your reply as soon as possible. By the way, please inform us when you will come to Shanghai, so that we can arrange the accommodation and timetable for your visit to our factory.

Your early reply is awaited.

Yours faithfully,
Henry
General Manager

Shanghai Lihua Imp. & Exp. Co., Ltd.
Rm. 606 Plaza Building,   Fax: 86-21-642578**
1302 Meilong Road, 200237   Tel: 86-21-642578**
Shanghai, People's Republic of China   E-mail: lihua88@alibaba.com

Sample of A Proforma Invoice

上海利华进出口有限公司
Shanghai Lihua Imp. & Exp. Co., Ltd.
形式发票
PROFORMA INVOICE

INVOICE NO:　　　　　　　　　　CONTRACT NO:
INVOICE DATE:　　　　　　　　　L/C NO:
SOLD TO MESSRS:　　　　　　　　TO:
　　　　　　　　　　　　　　　　FROM:

Marks & No.s	Description	Unit	Quantity	Unit	Price	Amount
		Total				USD

Shanghai Lihua Imp. & Exp. Co., Ltd.

ADD: Rm.608 Plaza Building, 1302 Meilong Road, 200237 Shanghai, People's Republic of China TEL: 86-21-642578** FAX: 86-21-642578** E-mail: lihua88@alibaba.com
TIME OF SHIPMENT: 30 DAYS AFTER WE RECEIVE 50% T/T
TERMS OF PAYMENT: 50% T/T+ 50% T/T
100% T/T TO COMPANY NAME: SHANGHAI LIHUA IMP. & EXP. CO., LTD.
BANK:
A/C.NO.　　　　　　　　　　　　　　　　SWIFT:

Pattern D of Business Letters

Generally speaking, a quotation sheet covers the following particulars:
a)　An expression of thanks for the buyer inquiry;
b)　Details of prices, quantity, amount, discount and terms of payment;
c)　An approximate date of delivery or date of shipment;
d)　The valid period;

e) Ending with a hope that the quotation will be accepted.

Relevant Terms

net price 净价	wholesale price 批发价
discount 折扣	allowance 补贴
retail price 零售价	current price 市价
prevailing price 现行价格	Gross for Net 以毛作净
More or Less Clause 溢短装条款	total value 总价值
valid period 有效期	commercial invoice 商业发票
proforma invoice 形式发票	

Useful Phrases

in duplicate 一式两份	in triplicate 一式三份
in quadruplicate 一式四份	in quintuplicate 一式五份
in sextuplicate 一式六份	in septuplicate 一式七份
in octuplicate 一式八份	in nonuplicate 一式九份
in decuplicate 一式十份	in twofold/threefold… 一式两份/三份
in two copies/three copies… 一式两份/三份	fall within 属于……的范围
apply for 申请	as requested 按要求
to be lower in price 价格更低	remain valid until 有效期到……
to be subject to 取决于，以……为准	amounting to 总计为
to the amount of 金额为	to one's satisfaction 使某人满意
lead to 导致	if possible 如果可能的话
if necessary 如果必要	with keen interest 怀有浓厚的兴趣

Summary

A quotation is a statement of the prevailing prices of goods and services. The supplier is willing to provide goods and service at the prices on the terms and conditions mentioned in it.

Proforma invoice is a kind of invoice which is made to inform importers of the cost of goods before shipment. It is usually used to apply for an import license, the establishment of an L/C or foreign exchange quota by the importer.

Contained in a proforma invoice are usually the descriptions of the goods, quantity, unit price, amount, port of loading, time of shipment, terms of payment and insurance coverage, etc.

Unit Five Quotations and Proforma Invoices

Exercises

I. Questions for review

1. What is a quotation sheet?
2. What is a proforma invoice?
3. What is contained in a proforma invoice?

II. Choose the best answer

1. Your samples are received with thanks. Based on the feedback _____ the customer, they gave us the following comments.
   A. for   B. with   C. at   D. from

2. All details _____ outer shell description, inner lining information, content description of the down jacket shall be supplied.
   A. as   B. of   C. with   D. for

3. Most serious problem is that the down feather is stitching out. You should use one more layer of cover _____ protect the down jacket.
   A. of   B. on   C. for   D. to

4. They want you to copy it exactly _____ weight, fabric construction, inner lining, main label and exact zipper details.
   A. within   B. for   C. in   D. at

5. Also the down content and appearance must be same _____ their samples because those are production samples and buyers are using those samples to confirm orders.
   A. as   B. of   C. with   D. for

6. Now the customer is very confident to place orders _____ us.
   A. for   B. with   C. to   D. in

7. Therefore, they want to ask you whether you can work on a few containers with them _____ receipt of approval samples.
   A. within   B. for   C. upon   D. at

8. They said you do not have to take all those orders _____ the factory is satisfied with their terms of payment as well.
   A. of   B. to   C. for   D. until

9. I will do my best to explain to the customer that we should have no problem to produce those goods _____ perfect conditions.
   A. within   B. for   C. at   D. in

10. The customer said once they feel the first few containers are acceptable then he will open letters of credit _____ the balance of whatever jackets you have available.
    A. as   B. of   C. with   D. for

11. We send you an offer _____ our new products.
    A. as   B. of   C. with   D. for
12. The goods of your specifications are _____ short supply.
    A. for   B. with   C. at   D. in
13. We anticipate your prompt response _____ this respect.
    A. for   B. with   C. at   D. in
14. We would, therefore suggest that you place your order with us _____ an early date.
    A. within   B. for   C. in   D. at
15. Damage _____ the goods was caused by heavy rain in transit.
    A. of   B. to   C. for   D. on
16. The goods _____ if your L/C had arrived by the end of December last.
    A. would be already shipped   B. must have already shipped
    C. had been already shipped   D. would have been already shipped
17. There is steady demand here _____ leather gloves of high quality.
    A. in   B. of   C. for   D. on
18. In _____ of quality, our make is superior.
    A. terms   B. term   C. connection   D. connections
19. You must be responsible for all the losses _____ from your delay in opening the covering L/C.
    A. arising   B. rising   C. arousing   D. have arisen
20. Unfortunately, we must _____ your offer for bicycles.
    A. reject   B. refuse   C. decline   D. turn down

III. Translate the following sentences into Chinese

1. You've already quoted a price of USD80.00 per box. Is there a discount for larger orders?

2. In accordance with your request in your Fax dated March 9, we are pleased to send you, under separate cover, a copy of our latest catalogue with the revised price-list.

3. Could you please send us a P/I of the following items for our customers in Nicaragua?

4. Owing to the recent advance in the prices of raw materials, we are forced to make a slight increase in the prices.

5. We feel that, in the following weeks, there will be further increase all round.

6. Our products have a more than 50% market share in your country, so we are very clear whether our prices are reasonable or not.

7. Due to the recent increase of the price of the raw materials, our quotation will be only valid for one week.

8. The prices of the raw materials may be higher in the near future and we'll have to recalculate our cost for your reference.

9. We assure you of our products with a high and stable quality as well as a superior

Unit Five Quotations and Proforma Invoices

service.

10. We wish to suggest, that you will take advantage of our offer, and immediately place an order with us, large or small.

Optional Part

11. We invite comparison of our prices with those of other manufacturers, and owing to the superior quality of our products, we believe that our quotations will be found the most advantageous.

12. Our quotation of Aug. 2 was made a very specially low figure, for the reason that we had this batch of goods in stock and we wanted to clear them before Aug. 31.

13. It is impossible for us to keep our quotation open for a week because of the frequent fluctuations in the international market.

14. The Proforma Invoice No. 131 covers goods against your Order No.116.

15. We take pleasure in making you the following offer, which is subject to your acceptance within seven days.

IV. Translate the following sentences into English

1. 我们随函附上购买你方产品的首份订单，相信你们可以给我们10%的折扣。
2. 目前我们的价格是特别低的。
3. 我们无与伦比的质量使我们得以收取比我们的竞争者更高的价格。
4. 尽管生产成本在上升，我们的价格一直保持稳定。
5. 除了产品质量一流，我方的价格也比其他供应商要低。
6. 只有在原材料当前价格不变时我们的报价才有效。
7. 我们能够向你方绝对保证质量。
8. 我们的产品在出厂之前都经过仔细测试，以便保证质量。
9. 我们保证这些货物在备妥装运时完好无损。
10. 在满足对这一商品的巨大需求方面，我们正面临极大的困难。

V. Case Study

Case A

To: phil@online.vien.net

Subject: Quotation for Washing Machine

Dear Phil,

Nice meeting you at Guangzhou Fair. I appreciate your great interest in our products. Now I have returned to my office in Shanghai.

We have checked the sea freight from Shanghai to Haiphong. As requested, we quote you our best price, CIF Haiphong as follows:

Model	Unit price	container (40')
LYC60-888 (5.5kg)	USD 165.00	152PCS
LYC55-666 (5.0kg)	USD 145.00	125PCS

As you know the price of raw material is advancing drastically, we have to remind you that our quotation remains valid only for two weeks. Please let us have your reply at your earliest convenience so that we can send you our P/I for your opening an L/C.

We await your early reply.

Best regards,
Creaty
General Manager

Case B

To: wick@qwev.net

Subject: Quotation for Forged Brass Ball Valve

Dear Wick,

Thank you for your e-mail dated Oct. 4, 201*.

In compliance with your request, we quote you the prices of these products as follows:

FOB Shanghai

LYC-11: Forged Brass Ball Valve, Forged Steel Handle and Brass Ball

Size	Price	Weight	Size	Price	Weight
1/2"	USD0.96	150G	3/4"	USD1.35	205G
1"	USD2.10	345G	1-1/4"	USD3.35	500G
1-1/2"	USD5.10	760G	2"	USD7.50	1220G
2-1/2"	USD16.10	2500G	3"	USD23.10	3510G

LYC-12: Brass Ball Valve, Steel Handle with Plastic Cover and Steel Ball

Size	Price	Weight
1/2"	USD0.88	155G
3/4"	USD1.30	225G
1"	USD1.80	340G
1-1/4"	USD3.20	580G
1-1/2"	USD5.50	930G
2"	USD7.10	1420G

Minimum Order Quantity: 10,000pcs

Delivery Time: 30 days upon receipt L/C

Sample availability/cost: Catalogue and Sample free of charge

International standards met: ISO9001

We are looking forward to your favorable news.

Yours sincerely,
Henry

Shanghai lihua Imp. & Exp. Co., Ltd.

Rm. 606 Plaza Building,   Fax: 86-21-642578**

1302 Meilong Road, 200237   Tel: 86-21-642578**

Shanghai, People's Republic of China   E-mail: huali88@alibaba.com

Unit Five Quotations and Proforma Invoices

VI. Discussion

1. What shall we pay attention to when we send a quotation to our foreign prospective importer?

2. What shall we pay attention to when we send a proforma invoice to our foreign prospective importer?

Unit Six

Offers, Counter-offers and Re-counter Offers

Introduction

An offer is an expression in which its offeror is willing to conclude a transaction with an offeree on the terms and conditions mentioned therein during its valid period. It can be classified into two categories: firm offer and non-firm offer. The former involves the exporter in contractual obligations, while the latter does not.

A quotation or a proforma invoice can also play the role of both a firm offer and a non-firm offer according to their contents.

After the importer receives an offer from its foreign supplier, he may ask to change one or some conditions and then give a reply to the seller. Such reply is called counter-offer. After the seller receives this counter-offer, he may think the reduction asked for is too much, or the date of delivery is too early, and whatever material alteration he makes, this amendment advice is called a re-counter offer. Of course, after the buyer receives this re-counter, he may send another re-counter offer to his seller. In this way, a business transaction is concluded after several rounds of such business negotiation. There could be many re-counter offers before a business transaction is concluded.

Business Letters

Email 1

To: sebestian@emirates.net.ae
Subject: Offer

Dear Sebestian,

We are very glad to receive your email dated Oct. 8, and thank you for your kindness.

As you know, our products have become popular in your area for their unique designs, attractive color and high quality. We trust that they will command a ready sale in your city. In compliance with your request, we quote you our competitive prices as follows:

Art No. T1258:   USD68.50 Per Set CIFC3 Dubai
Art No. T1356:   USD15.60 Per Set CIFC3 Dubai
Art No. T1436:   USD30.20 Per Set CIFC3 Dubai
Art No. T1789:   USD25.50 Per Piece CIFC3 Dubai

Minimum Order Quantity: One 20' FCL container for each Art No.

Packing: Art No. T1258, one set per carton, total 150 cartons to a 20'FCL.
           Art No. T1356, 12 sets per carton, total 200 cartons to a 20'FCL.
           Art No. T1436, 8 pieces per carton, total 250 cartons to a 20'FCL.
           Art No. T1789, 10 sets per carton, total 235 cartons to a 20'FCL.

Shipment: To be made within one month upon receipt of relevant L/C.

Payment: By confirmed, irrevocable L/C payable by draft at sight.

Insurance: To be covered by the seller for 110% of the invoice value against All Risks and War Risk.

As the prevailing price in the international market is fluctuating drastically, our offer remains valid for only one week. If you accept them, please let us have your reply as soon as possible.

We are looking forward to your favorable reply.

Yours faithfully,
Henry
General Manager

Shanghai Lihua Imp. & Exp. Co., Ltd.
Rm. 606 Plaza Building   Fax: 86-21-642578**
1302 Meilong Road, 200237   Tel: 86-21-642578**
Shanghai, People's Republic of China   E-mail: huali88@alibaba.com

Email 2

To: lihua88@alibaba.com
Subject: Counter-offer

Dear Henry,

Thank you very much for your offer dated Oct. 9.

To be candid with you, we like your products for their attractive designs and high quality, but we found that your prices appear to be on the high side. I am afraid that we have to point out that other suppliers in your area quoted us more attractive prices.

As our retailers in our city are unable to sell your products at your quoted prices and the orders we have in hand would be worth around USD200,000.00, we suggest you give us a discount of 8%. Besides, we have to remind you that the commission you granted for this transaction is 5%, instead of 3% indicated in your offer of Oct. 9. Furthermore, we accept terms of payment by D/P at 30 day's sight, which is our usual practice.

If you agree with us, we will immediately place our first order with you.

Your favorable reply is awaited.

Yours sincerely,
Sebestian
General Manager

NGS GROUP CO., LTD.

```
P. O. BOX 576**
DUBAI - UNITED ARAB EMIRATES
TEL: + 971 - 4    - 3525***
FAX: + 971 - 4    - 3525***
MOBILE: + 971 - 50 - 669****
EMAIL: sebestian@emirates.net.ae
```

Email 3

To: sebestian@emirates.net.ae
Subject: Re-counter Offer

Dear Sebestian,

We are terribly sorry that a mistake was really made due to typing. Yes, we did grant you a commission of 5%. It was negligence on our part. Please forgive us.

However, we have to point out that we quoted you competitive prices compared with other suppliers' and I am afraid that you shall take our excellent quality and attractive designs into your consideration. Above all, customers can make out different qualities.

In view of the good quality and the rising prices of raw materials, we really think it is very difficult for us to make any further reduction. However, as we are anxious to develop your market recently, we are prepared to give you an allowance and quote again as follows:

Art No. T1258:	USD67.50 Per Set CIFC5 Dubai
Art No. T1356:	USD14.80 Per Set CIFC5 Dubai
Art No. T1436:	USD28.90 Per Set CIFC5 Dubai
Art No. T1789:	USD23.50 Per Piece CIFC5 Dubai

As to terms of payment, we only accept L/C because this is the first transaction between us. We will be very pleased to consider other modes of payment after several smooth and satisfactory transactions with you. This offer is valid only for 5 days.

We sincerely hope that you will agree with us and let us have your acceptance so that we can start mutually beneficial trade relations as early as possible.

Yours faithfully,
Henry
General Manager

Shanghai Lihua Imp. & Exp. Co., Ltd.
Rm. 606 Plaza Building,   Fax: 86-21-642578**
1302 Meilong Road, 200237   Tel: 86-21-642578**
Shanghai, People's Republic of China   E-Mail: lihua88@alibaba.com

Unit Six Offers, Counter-offers and Re-counter Offers

Email 4

To: ravis@aol.com

Subject: Re-counter Offer

Dear Ravis,

It's very nice meeting you. The Canton Fair is over now, but there are some unpredictable cases:

We do not know why the prices of all the raw materials in our country are advancing rapidly, especially, BRASS and ZINC, which rose USD 500.00 per M/T and USD 200.00 per M/T respectively above the original prices we stocked. Plastic has increased USD250 per M/T, STEEL, USD300 per M/T. Unfortunately, the prices keep rising now. Such advancement started one month ago.

Under such circumstance, our normal production schedule has been greatly affected. We have to stop until the prices keep stable because it is extremely difficult for us to calculate the production cost.

Due to the recent 10% rise of the raw materials, we have to adjust our quotation, otherwise we have to bear a great loss. As you know, our margin of profit is only 5%. The market of raw materials here is out of order now, which you could know from media and other suppliers.

We are sorry that such change will bring you inconvenience. We sincerely hope that you will understand it. Once we can make you an offer, we will contact you immediately.

Yours faithfully,
Henry
General Manager

Shanghai Lihua Imp. & Exp. Co., Ltd.
Rm. 606 Plaza Building,   Fax: 86-21-642578**
1302 Meilong Road, 200237   Tel: 86-21-642578**
Shanghai, People's Republic of China   E-Mail: lihua88@alibaba.com

Email 5

To: lilycao@yahoo.com

Subject: Proposal

Dear Ms. Cao,

Thank you for your E-mail dated Oct. 5, 201*.

We are aware that the rate of Export Drawback has been decreased by 4% and the prices of raw materials have increased by 18%~30% not only in China but everywhere else.

The prices are higher than before but not for everything, the prices for brass, Iron & Zinc are increased but the plastic kept its price. Fortunately, we still keep a good and stable personal relation although great changes often happen in the market.

Art. No. CR1131: we would like to have this item exactly as the picture we sent to you, but we hope to know your best price for big quantity. You are right we are a big seller in the Caribbean Market.

We studied the market in our country and we found the prices you offered are not competitive. These prices should be our sales prices, so we would have no profit at all if we accepted your offer.

I propose that I can sell your items to our customers, you arrange production and take care of shipment from China to our city to the customers we appoint and we will open you the relative L/C.

We are well aware of the continual rise of the prices of raw materials and the decrease of Export Drawback Rate and the many fees on our side, we shall reach an agreement on a reasonable quotation as early as possible, which can make us start our cooperation.

If you agree to my proposal or you have another suggestion, please tell me.

Best regards,
Don Pope
General Manager

Don & Sons Co., Ltd.
Avenida Yucaton 6**
Mexico City
Mexico
Email: donpope@online.com.mx

Pattern E of Business Letters

In your counter-offer or re-counter offer, you shall mention the following particulars:
a) thank your partner for his offer or counter-offer;
b) tell him what shall be amended;
c) state your reasons directly why adjustment is necessary;
d) hope to receive favorable reply.

Relevant Terms

offer 发盘	firm offer 实盘
non-firm offer 虚盘	counter-offer 还盘
re-counter offer 再还盘	offering 提供的货，出售物
offeror 发盘人	offeree 受盘人

Unit Six Offers, Counter-offers and Re-counter Offers

Useful Phrases

place a first order with sb.for sth. 向某人下第一份订单购买某物	place a trial order with sb.for sth. 向某人下一份试订单购买某物
place repeat orders with sb.for sth. 向某人重复订货购买某物	place duplicate orders with sb.for sth. 向某人下与先前订单完全相同的订单购买某物
in no case 在任何情况下	place regular orders with sb.for sth. 向某人定期下订单购买某物
at popular prices 大众化的价格	to be light in weight 重量轻
to be candid with sb. 坦率地说	within the validity of… 在有效期内
without exception 没有例外	to be on the high side 偏高
compared with 与……相比	at a much lower price 价格更低
available from stock 仓库有现货，现货供应	in one's favor 对某人有利，以某人为受益人
in accordance with 按照，与……一致	meet a person halfway 与某人妥协，让步
convince sb. of sth/that 说服某人，使人相信某事	

Summary

A firm offer is an expression to sell goods at a stated price within a period of time. A non-firm offer cannot be accepted by an importer.

A quotation or a proforma invoice can be used as a firm offer or a non-firm offer.

Exercises

I. Questions for review

1. What is an offer?
2. What is a firm offer?
3. What is a non-firm offer?
4. What is counter-offer?
5. What is a re-counter offer?
6. When can a quotation or a proforma invoice be used as a firm offer?

II. Choose the best answer

1. We regret to inform you that our quotation has increased _____ 20% due to the advance of price of the raw materials and the production cost.

    A. in   B. on   C. by   D. at

2. In order to execute your order smoothly, we calculated the total volume and weight _____ your orders.

    A. with   B. on   C. of   D. to

3. We confirm that we can use 1x40' HQ to ship all the goods _____ your two orders.

    A. in   B. on   C. by   D. for

4. Please note that we must arrange shipment _____ the end of this year, because the export drawback rate will be reduced by 4% from Jan. 1st, 201*, which means next year's quotation will still rise.

    A. within   B. before   C. in   D. of

5. If you can accept our properly adjusted price, we'll use 1x40'HQ _____ ship these two orders in December.

    A. in   B. on   C. by   D. to

6. If you separate these two orders to use 2x20' containers, then one order will exceed the largest VOLUME _____ 1x20' container.

    A. within   B. before   C. in   D. of

7. So we are waiting for your final confirmation. Thank you _____ advance for your cooperation.

    A. within   B. before   C. in   D. of

8. Mr. Joseph Smith, the president, is understood to have experience _____ this line.

    A. within   B. before   C. in   D. of

9. We believe that business transactions _____ this firm will prove to be satisfactory. In the meantime, we consider them good for small business engagements.

    A. with   B. on   C. of   D. to

10. Larger transactions should be covered _____ L/C issued by Banks. However, this reply is without obligation on our part.

    A. in   B. on   C. by   D. to

11. We are of course _____ that the time for completion of your project has already been exceeded.

    A. know   B. to know   C. aware   D. sure

12. If you are interested, we will send you a sample lot, _____ charge.

    A. within   B. for   C. in   D. free of

13. You must be responsible for all the losses _____ from your delay in opening the covering L/C.

    A. arising   B. rising   C. arousing   D. have arisen

14. We are making you our quotation for shoes _____.

    A. as follows   B. as following   C. as follow   D. following

15. We thank you for your letter of May 5th, _____ your purchase from us of 5,000 tons Green Beans.

A. confirm   B. to confirm   C. confirming   D. confirmed

16. If we had been informed in time, we _____ them for you.

  A. reserve   B. will reserve

  C. would have reserved   D. will have reserved

17. Please make serious efforts to get the goods _____ immediately.

  A. dispatching   B. dispatched   C. to dispatch   D. being dispatched

18. We have been _____ with that firm for many years.

  A. making business   B. contacting

  C. dealing   D. supplying

19. As we are _____ the market for Table Cloth, we should be glad if you would send us your best quotation.

  A. in   B. on   C. entering   D. at

20. _____ our S/C No.6539 dated August 8, we wish to say that the goods will be shipped by the end of next month.

  A. With reference to   B. Refer to

  C. Referring   D. With refer to

III. Translate the following sentences into Chinese

1. Your unit price seems fair enough, but we're hoping for a higher discount rate.

2. We regret that we receive your email declining to purchase our new product because it is too expensive compared with that of other suppliers'.

3. We feel that a fair comparison in quality between our goods and those of other suppliers' will convince you of the competitiveness of our re-counter offer.

4. We do not deny that the quality of their products is slightly better but difference in price should, in no case, be as large as 12%.

5. After checking with our distribution center in your country about your question on bulk orders, we can still offer you the season discount of 20% off each large business shipment.

6. To facilitate the transaction, we counter offer as follows, subject to your reply reaching us before the end of this month.

7. Toward this end we would like to make you a special offer.

8. With thanks we acknowledge acceptance of your order dated July 6. The goods ordered will be shipped to you in the following lots upon the following schedule.

9. We regret to inform you that we have to decline your counter-offer, because recently we met a big dealer and our entire production is sold out in the next three months.

10. We regret that it is impossible to accept your re-counter offer, even to meet you halfway, because your competitors are offering considerably lower prices.

Optional Part

11. If we receive your order within the next week, we are prepared to give you a discount of 3%.

12. Now we look forward to your replying to our offer in the form of counter-offer.

13. When we place such a large order with other suppliers, we usually get a 2% to 3% discount.

14. We can reduce our price by 2% if you order exceeds more than 3000 sets.

15. We think an appropriate price should be around EUR220 per piece, FOB Hamburg.

IV. Translate the following sentences into English

1. 201*年1月1日以后我们国家的出口退税率要降低4%，我们的价格也会相应提高。所以我们希望你方尽早接受我们的再还盘。

2. 由于市场价格正在下跌，我们建议你们立即接受。

3. 坦率地说，我们遗憾地发现你方的价格偏高，所以我们建议你们给我方一个折扣，譬如6%。

4. 感谢你们5月15日的发盘，但我们必须指出你们地区的其他供应商给了我们更加有吸引力的报价，价格比你方低10%~15%。

5. 我们已经从你们的竞争者那里得到了一个更优惠的发盘，所以请给我们一个折扣，譬如在原价基础上减10%，以便开始我们的合作。

6. 另外，我们想再一次强调我们通常的支付方式是付款交单30天远期，这是我们与外国供应商交往的惯例。

7. 如果不是因为我们良好的关系，我们不会以这样的价格给你们发实盘。

8. 敬请告诉我们你方需要的数量以便我们可以相应调整我们的价格。

9. 如果你已经将所有因素考虑进去，你可能发现我们的报价比你们从其他地方得到的价格要低。

10. 我认为我们双方都坚持各自的价格是不明智的，让我们双方各让一半。

V. Case Study

The following five emails show you how the importer and the exporter bargained:

----- Original Message ----- (A)

From: "Steve McCurry" < Steve McCurry@fetty.bg<mailto: Steve McCurry@fetty.bg> >

To: "vip.163.com" <damai-sales@vip.163.com<mailto:damai-sales@vip.163.com> >

Cc: <damai@globalsourcing.com <mailto:damai@globalsourcing.com> >

Sent: Tuesday, January 10, 201* 12:40 AM

Subject: Mistaken quantity

Dear Jim,

I found out that I have mistaken the order qty of Item G26. Can you please do me a favor and reduce the number with 1000 pieces? It should therefore be 1800 instead of 2800.

Best regards,

Steve McCurry

-----Original Message-----(B)

Unit Six Offers, Counter-offers and Re-counter Offers

From: vip.163.com [mailto:damai-sales@vip.163.com]
Sent: Tuesday, January 10, 201* 3:19 AM
To: Steve McCurry
Cc: damai@globalsourcing.com <mailto:damai@globalsourcing.com>
Subject: Re: Mistaken quantity
Importance: High

Dear Steve,

Thanks for your email of Jan.10.

For your information, because the 2800PCS sliding bar is not the normal size, it is 38MM according to your requirement. So we have already bought the BRASS raw materials for 2800PCS after your confirmation on our P/I. We are sorry for not being able to change the quantities.

Also we would like to inform you that due to the GREAT increase on the domestic METAL raw material prices, all future quotations of metal product will be increased at least by 10% for brass items, and 14% for ZINC items (this is the price difference between last December and Present). Please be noted. If the increase or decrease occurs in future, we will adjust our quotation accordingly.

In addition, since most of the China factories and offices will be closed for the long Spring Festival, we estimate that after Feb.10th, the raw materials will be still on the increase tendency.

Best Regards,
Jim
Manager
Export & Client Dept.

Shanghai Better Hardware Trade Co., Ltd
ADD: No.1991, Meilong Road West, Humin Plaza Shanghai, #200237
TEL: 0086-21-642503**/642532**/642508** (ext.208)
FAX: 0086-21-642503**
Website: www.betterhardware.com
-----Original Message-----(C)
From: "Steve McCurry" < Steve McCurry@fetty.bg<mailto: Steve McCurry@fetty.bg> >
To: "vip.163.com" <damai-sales@vip.163.com<mailto:damai-sales@vip.163.com> >
Cc: <damai@globalsourcing.com <mailto:damai@globalsourcing.com> >
Sent: Tuesday, January 10, 201* 3:59 PM
Subject: RE: Mistaken quantity

Dear Jim,

We will highly appreciate it if you agree to do us a favor and withhold 1000 pcs of the Item

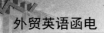

G26. They will be purchased at a later point by us, so you will not have any loss.

As regards the Prices:

According to LME.COM, the ZINC price increase since Dec is 8.7%. What sources do you use to check the raw materials prices? I find the quoted price increases too huge to be acceptable provided that your latest price quotations are only 1 month old.

Best regards,
Steve McCurry

-----Original Message-----(D)
From: vip.163.com [mailto:damai-sales@vip.163.com]
Sent: Tuesday, January 10, 201* 11:02 AM
To: Steve McCurry
Cc: damai@globalsourcing.com
Subject: Re: Mistaken quantity
Importance: High

Dear Friend Steve,

Thanks for your email.

MISTAKEN QTY

It is not guaranteed and workable for us to keep 1000PCS G26 as storage, because we do not know whether you will really buy them after our first order, and since we already paid these raw materials to the material supplier, but who pay for the storage?

As one of the leading manufacturer, we always respect all the orders from clients, no matter they are old or new clients. Once both sides signed the P/I, it will be fully effected with Law forces. And we never delay to arrange the production. That's also why our company enjoys fairly good reputation among the clients.

We also hope as our new client, your esteemed company is a promise-keeper who acts as what you said.

If you have any other problems, we will always try to help you to solve with joint efforts on basis of mutual understanding.

RAW MATERIALS

You may trace our email DTD Nov. 30th about the quotation for Item G26...

According to LONDON METAL EXCHANGE, the price for BRASS is USD4375 and ZINC USD1659 on Nov. 27th 201*, which is our last basis for the metal items. And today you can find the prices for BRASS is USD4689 and ZINC USD1980 on Jan. 9th, 201*, which means BRASS increased by 7.2% and ZINC by 19.5%. Anyway, we just want you get informed about this global situation. As for the next order price, we will discuss on basis of the actual future situation.

Best Regards,
Jim

Unit Six Offers, Counter-offers and Re-counter Offers

Manager
Export & Client Dept.

Shanghai Better Hardware Trade Co., Ltd
ADD: No.1991, Meilong Road West, Humin Plaza Shanghai, #200237
TEL: 0086-21-642503**/642532**/642508** (ext.208)
FAX: 0086-21-642503**
Website: www. betterhardware.com

-----Original Message-----(E)
===
From: " Steve McCurry" < Steve McCurry@fetty.bg<mailto: Steve McCurry@fetty.bg> >
To: "vip.163.com" <damai-sales@vip.163.com<mailto:damai-sales@vip.163.com> >
Cc: <damai@globalsourcing.com <mailto:damai@globalsourcing.com> >
Subject: RE: Mistaken qty
Date: 201*/1/10 21:03:20
===

Dear Jim,

MISTAKEN QTY

It was my personal mistake the 1000 pcs over-order, not a miskept promise. Anyway I take it you are not willing to do us this favor.

RAW MATERIALS

Thank you for your detailed explanation. Now I can trace your info and it makes sense. Anyway, let us leave the negotiations for a later point when we get ready for our next order and hopefully the materials prices will be better.

Best regards,
Steve McCurry

VI. Discussion

1. In recent years, the prices of raw materials change dramatically in the international market, how do a small manufacturer and exporter deal with such fluctuations? Give your example.

2. In making a counter-offer or a re-counter offer, asking your partner to reduce the quotation is sensitive and difficult. Try to find a case and explain to your classmates.

Unit Seven

Orders and Their Fulfillment

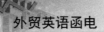

Introduction

If an importer is satisfied with the products offered by a foreign supplier, he will place an order with him for these articles. An order is an offer to buy, which is not legally binding until it is accepted by the seller.

An order shall cover the following particulars:

a) the buyer's name and address;
b) the order number and its date;
c) the descriptions of the goods, quantity, unit prices, article numbers, total amount;
d) the port of destination, the mode of packing, the time of shipment and the terms of payment, etc.

If you are lucky enough to receive a first order from a new importer, you'd better acknowledge it by telling him that:

a) you are much honored;
b) the quality of your products and your service are assured;
c) you also handle other similar products with the same high quality as the goods ordered;
d) you hope to establish a long-term business relations with him on the basis of equality and mutual benefit.

Normally, receiving an order is a good news for an exporter, but sometimes he may decline it because:

a) he is unable to supply the goods right now;
b) he is unsatisfied with the terms and conditions set forth in the order.

If an exporter accepts an order from a foreign buyer, the transaction will continue until its completion. If not, the exporter had better send a reply for the sake of courtesy. Such reply may consist of the following aspects:

a) thank the buyer for his order;
b) express regret at inability to accept it;
c) explain concisely the main reasons;
d) make a counter-offer, if necessary; or contact him if there is an opportunity in the future.

Business Letters

Email 1

TO: lihua88@alibaba.com
Subject: Acceptance

Unit Seven Orders and Their Fulfillment

Dear Moonshape,

Thank you very much for your offer dated Oct. 9. Having discussed with our chairman of the board, we decide to accept your terms and conditions and place a trial order for 100 washers, Model LLY55-868 at OEM type. We will place regular orders with you as long as the quality is up to our expectation.

Please send us your Sales Confirmation and tell us your warranty policy. We often give our customers one year's warranty.

We look forward to your early reply.

Best wishes,

Wick Coacher

General Manager

Tom Consumption Group

5**, Sayem Aldaher Street

Golail Industrial Zone

P. O. Box 9**

Jeddah, 21421

Saudi Arabia

Tel: 0096626823*** Ext: 3**

Fax: 0096626826***

Email: wick@ ttry.net

Web sites: www.ttry.net

Email 2

TO: lihua88@alibaba.com

Subject: Acceptance

Dear Ms. Xie,

I am very pleased to tell you that your products are well received by our customers here. This morning I discussed with my retailers and decided to place an order with you for the five items mentioned in our attached Order Form. They said they would sell them out by next February.

This order is subject to non-delay shipment before Chinese New Year- Spring Festival. Enclosed please find our Order Form.

We are looking forward to your prompt reply.

Lily

General Manager

NGS GROUP CO., LTD.

P. O. BOX 576**

DUBAI - UNITED ARAB EMIRATES
TEL: + 971 - 4 - 35256**
FAX: + 971 - 4 - 35256**
MOBILE: + 971 - 50 - 6696***
EMAIL: lily@emirates.net.ae
Encl.

NGS GROUP CO., LTD.

P. O. BOX 576**
DUBAI - UNITED ARAB EMIRATES
TEL: + 971 - 4 - 35256**

FAX: + 971 - 4 - 35256**
MOBILE: + 971 - 50 - 6696***
EMAIL:lily@emirates.net.ae
Order No. 158

Order Form

Oct. 9, 201*

Shanghai Lihua Imp. & Exp. Co., Ltd.
Rm. 606 Plaza Building,
1302 Meilong Road, 200237
Shanghai, People's Republic of China

Quantity	Descriptions	Art. No	FOB Shanghai
300	10-inch Single-lever Kitchen Faucet in Elegant Design	1508	USD18.60 each
400	4-inch Lavatory Faucet with Brass Seat and Acrylic Handle	1409	USD12.80 each
600	8-inch Kitchen Faucet with Lever Handle	1318	USD16.80 each
500	4-inch Lavatory Faucet with Brass Seat and CP Zinc Handle	1316	USD15.60 each
200	8-inch CP Plastic Kitchen Faucet with Brass Shank and Acrylic Handle	1312	USD16.90 each

Mode of Packing: in cartons.

Date of Shipment: within one month upon receipt of L/C.
Terms of Payment: by confirmed, irrevocable L/C payable by draft at sight.

                              Authorized and on behalf of NGS GROUP CO., LTD.
                                              Lily
                                         General Manager

Email 3

To: lily@emirates.net.ae
Subject: Your Order No. 158

Dear Lily,

We have accepted your Order No. 158 for our Faucets. Enclosed please find our Sales Confirmation No.MS-16 in duplicate. Please sign and return one copy to us for our file.

Now you are requested to establish a confirmed, irrevocable L/C in our favor covering the five items as soon as possible. We'd like to remind you that the stipulations in the relative L/C should be in exact accordance with our Sales Confirmation so as to avoid unnecessary amendments. You may rest assured that we shall not fail to make shipment in due time upon receipt of your L/C.

Your close co-operation is appreciated.

Yours faithfully,
Qiaoqiao
General Manager

Shanghai Lihua Imp. & Exp. Co., Ltd.
Rm. 606 Plaza Building,   Fax: 86-21-642578**
1302 Meilong Road, 200237   Tel: 86-21-642578**
Shanghai, People's Republic of China   E-mail: huali88@alibaba.com

Email 4

-----Original Message-----(A)
From: Qiaoqiao
[mailto: donpope@ttry.net]
Sent: Tuesday, October 10, 201* 21:07 PM
Subject: Re: your additional order

Dear Friend Don,
We are glad to receive your email dated Oct.10.
As requested, we will add 1,000 PCS of Item AQ-40 to fill in the 40' container. You may rest assured that shipment can be made before our Spring Festival.

However, we find the remaining space of the container can also be added another 1,000 PCS of Item AQ-40. So, if you can place an order for 2000 PCS, you will not have to waste freight. Please give us your final decision so that we can arrange production and email you the refined P/I. Please let us have your reply at your earliest convenience.

Best wishes,
Qiaoqiao
General Manager

Shanghai Lihua Imp. & Exp. Co., Ltd.
Rm. 606 Plaza Building,　　　Fax: 86-21-642578**
1302 Meilong Road, 200237　　Tel: 86-21-642578**
Shanghai, People's Republic of China　E-mail: lihua88@alibaba.com

Pattern F of Business Letters

In reply to a first order, your acknowledgement should tell the buyer:

a) welcome the buyer as one of your customers;

b) the quality of your products and your service are assured;

c) you also handle other similar products with the same high quality as the goods ordered;

d) you hope to establish a long-term business relations with him on the basis of equality and mutual benefit.

A reply rejecting an order may consist of the following aspects:

a) thank the buyer for his order;

b) express regret at inability to accept it;

c) explain concisely the main reasons;

d) make a counter-offer, if necessary; or contact him if there is an opportunity in the future.

Relevant Terms

first order 第一份订单	trial order 试订单
order form 订货单	order quantity 订货量
orderer 订货人	order as per sample 按样订货
order at best 以最好价格订购	repeat order 重复订货，指价格与先前相同数量不同的订单
duplicate order 指价格、数量与先前完全相同的订单	bulk buying 大批购买

Unit Seven Orders and Their Fulfillment

Useful Phrases

by the first available liner 由订得到的第一艘班轮装运	be aware of 意识到
for one's file 供某人存档	in stock 有现货
out of stock 无现货	point out 指出
finalize the transaction 达成交易	familiarize oneself with 使自己熟悉某事物
fluctuation of price 价格的波动	for the sake of convenience 为方便起见
to place one's order elsewhere 别处订货	owing to 由于
to confirm one's order 确认订单	execute an order 履行订货
cancel an order 取消订单	within the stipulated time limit 在规定的时限内

Summary

An order is an offer to buy goods, which is not legally binding until it is accepted by the seller. An order shall contain the particulars covering the buyer, the goods and the relative terms and conditions.

A first order from a new importer should be acknowledged promptly. It is also advisable for an exporter to send a reply to a foreign importer when declining an order because there may be business opportunities in the future.

Exercises

I. Questions for review

1. What is contained in an order?
2. How do you reply to a first order?
3. How do you decline an order?

II. Choose the best answer

1. In order to assist you in shipping our orders _____ the least difficulty we felt that we need to get more detailed information on the status of the fabric and also the factories where you propose to do the orders.

  A. with   B. of   C. for   D. in

2. You have requested for extensions _____ almost all the orders.

  A. with   B. of   C. for   D. in

3. We would like to inform that in most of the orders we have given you extensions and in a few orders we had given you more than one extension _____ requested by you.
    A. at   B. of   C. for   D. as

4. We have all the time accommodated you _____ giving extensions based on your request.
    A. by   B. of   C. for   D. on

5. We may not be _____ a position to go back to New York again for extensions, so we need to work on the ship dates more realistically.
    A. with   B. of   C. for   D. in

6. In order to do this, we need to get from your end a detailed Fabric arrival date into the factory for each order and _____ each color.
    A. by   B. of   C. for   D. on

7. On reviewing the details furnished to us this morning we find that you will again get _____ a situation where you will not be in position to ship our orders on time.
    A. with   B. of   C. for   D. into

8. We have finished three transactions _____ this firm during the past two years. Each contract was less than USD20,000.
    A. with   B. of   C. for   D. in

9. If you change the fabric order to a new mill _____ this crucial period it will be difficult for them to achieve the hand feel and the look which was approved by the buyer.
    A. at   B. of   C. for   D. as

10. Our suggestion will be to continue to work with the same mill where you have got the fabric developed earlier. Please ensure that the fabric quality is not compromised _____ any cost.
    A. as   B. of   C. for   D. at

11. We find your terms _____ and now send you our order for 3 sets of generators.
    A. satisfied   B. satisfaction   C. satisfactory   D. of satisfaction

12. The additional charge will be _____ your account.
    A. with   B. of   C. for   D. in

13. We regret to say that the prices you have bid are too low to _____.
    A. not accept   B. be acceptable   C. be accepting   D. be unacceptable

14. We cannot _____ our offer open for more than three days, so would you please email your acceptance.
    A. have   B. place   C. remain   D. leave

15. _____ any change in the date of delivery, please let us know in advance.
    A. There should be   B. Should there be
    C. There would be   D. Would there be

16. We shall be glad if you will _____ the matter at once and let us know the reason for the delay.

        A. look on   B. look for   C. look after   D. look into

17. _____ your prices are right, you will find a ready market for the products.

        A. Should   B. To provide   C. Provided   D. Provide

18. Quality of the present shipment is equal to _____ of last consignment.

        A. this   B. these   C. that   D. those

19. We hope that you will entrust us with more orders when you are again _____.

        A. in the market   B. on the market

        C. out of the market   D. at the market

20. As you are not familiar with the quality of the product, we recommend _____ a small quantity for trial.

        A. to buy   B. buy   C. buying   D. bought

III. Translate the following sentences into Chinese

1. At this time we are looking for a manufacturer who can do full production and final packaging of our patented devices.

2. We have large orders on hand, and will only work with producers who can guarantee timely production and delivery.

3. This letter confirms the recent change in your order…If this is acceptable, please sign and return the enclosed revised order form.

4. A satisfied customer is the best advertisement we can have, and our proudest boast is that we get a larger portion of trade just in that way.

5. We contacted our customers without wasting time, but very unfortunately we were late, as they particularly wanted the goods to arrive here in time for the Christmas sales.

6. If we had these samples at least one month earlier, we would have of course placed a very substantial order.

7. We acknowledge receipt of your Order No.116 for our ceramic products dated Nov. 12, 200*.

8. It is very difficult for us to get the goods in large quantity as well as make prompt shipment.

9. You may rest assured that we shall effect shipment in time upon receipt of your L/C.

10. It is regrettable to see an order dropped owing to no agreement on price; however, we wish to recommend you another specification at a lower price for your consideration.

Optional Part

11. We are quite satisfied with your products and there is a possibility of placing a repeat order in large quantities.

12. We thank you for your order of Sept. 12, which, we assure you, shall be executed in due course.

13. We hope that this trial order will lead to an enduring connection with you.

14. We have already emailed to you twice urging dispatch, and as you have failed to deliver

these goods on the date named, we have to cancel this order very regretfully.

15. We confirm having received your order dated July 6 for our new products. We assure you of our best attention to your order.

IV. Translate the following sentences into English

1. 由于国内市场的变化，我们想取消购买你方养殖珍珠的订单。
2. 恐怕我们没有能力供应你们所需要的数量。
3. 我们产品的优势是设计有吸引力，质量高，价格合理。
4. 由于出口成本的持续上升和我方产品优异的质量，我们几乎不可能再降价了。
5. 所有这些商品都是我们客户急需的，因此，我们希望你们尽早交货以便他们能够在圣诞节前售完。
6. 一俟收到你方的即期信用证，我们就安排由最早订到舱位的集装箱轮运出。
7. 也许你们还没有注意到我们经营的其他产品，我们另外航空邮寄给你方我们最新的目录供你们考虑。
8. 有关你方要买我们乐器的7月6日的订单，我们想通知你方这些货物正在生产中，10月底之前备妥待运。
9. 我们希望你们会对这批货物满意，并且期待着不久的将来能收到更多的订单。
10. 我们很高兴收到你方的重复订单，我们保证，它将被及时履行。

V. Case Study

-----Original Message-----(A)
From: Qiaoqiao
[mailto: donpope@ttry.net]
Sent: Tuesday, October 10, 201* 21:07 PM
Subject: Re: your additional order

The body of this email as per Email 4 mentioned above.

----- Original Message ----- (B)
From: Don Pope
To: lihua88@alibaba.com
Sent: Wednesday, October 11, 201* 8:12 AM
Subject: 1000pcs only!

Dear Qiaoqiao,

Thank you for your email of Oct. 9 and 10. We have amended the description details of Item AQ-40 as per your previous emails.

With reference to the quantity of this item, we have to say 1000 pcs is the maximum. As I explained to you before, my retailers still have substantial stock right now, this additional order is only to replenish my own inventory. Besides, I still have 3000pcs of Item XQQ-6588, which I had imported from my former supplier in Yancheng in September. Frankly speaking, I do not have to buy this item now because it will be over-stocked. However, I want to promote your products to my customers so that they can prefer your products in the future. That's why I have to say 1000pcs is maximum I can buy now. So, please understand my situation and accept 1000pcs for this additional order. So, please send me your refined P/I by return.

By the way, if you have received my samples of XQQ-6896 and 6898, tell me at once whether you can produce or not, please.

Best wishes,
Don
General Manager
Tom Consumption Group

5**, Sayem Aldaher Street
Golail Industrial Zone
P. O. Box 9**
Jeddah, 21421
Saudi Arabia
Tel: 0096626823*** Ext: 3**
Fax: 0096626826***
Email: donpope@ttry.net
Web sites: www.ttry.net

VI. Discussion

1. "The more orders you receive, the better." Is it right? Why?

2. How can you make your declining the buyer's order becomes a good beginning for you to retain a customer?

Unit Eight

Sales Confirmation

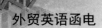
外贸英语函电

Introduction

The contract which is most commonly used in import and export is the formal written contract, i.e., a sales contract or a purchase contract; sometimes it is in the form of purchase order when countersigned by the exporter, or a sales confirmation when countersigned by the importer.

When there is a high degree of trust between the exporter and importer, with relative small amount, a short form of contract is adopted, e.g. a Sales Confirmation. When the transacted goods is very complicated, such as a kind of complete plant, and with a large total amount, long form of contract is used, e.g. a sales contract or a purchase contract.

Business Letters

Email 1

To: abbudula@emirates.net.ae
Subject: Your Order No. YR-86

Dear Shell,

We are very glad to receive your Order No.YR-86 for our pharmaceutical products. We are sending you, by separate airmail, our signed Sales Confirmation No. XW-66 in duplicate. Please counter-sign and return one copy for our file.

You may rest assured that your order will receive our best attention and the quality of our products will prove to be to your entire satisfaction.

As the date of shipment is approaching, please instruct your bank to issue the relative L/C in our favor as soon as possible, which shall reach us before Oct. 30 so as to avoid delay in shipment.

We trust you will let us have your L/C on time as usual. Our close co-operation will surely develop good relations between us.

Yours sincerely,
Snowen
General Manager

Shanghai Lihua Imp. & Exp. Co., Ltd.
Rm. 606 Plaza Building,   Fax: 86-21-642578**
1302 Meilong Road, 200237   Tel: 86-21-642578**
Shanghai, People's Republic of China   E-mail: lihua88@alibaba.com

Unit Eight Sales Confirmation

Email 2

To: garros@online.com.br
Subject: Your Order No. YL-68

Dear Garros,

We are much honored to receive your repeat Order No. YL-68 for our Titanium Ores. The high quality of our products and the smooth execution of your first order lead to further cooperation between us. We assure you of our full cooperation and trust that you will be satisfied with the high quality of our products.

We are sending you our signed Sales Confirmation No. YR-36 in duplicate via courier. Please sign and return one copy for our file. If there is any problem, please do not hesitate to contact us without delay.

As you need this batch of goods urgently, please instruct your banker to open the relevant L/C as soon as possible so that we can arrange shipment in due time.

We are looking forward to your early response.

Yours faithfully,
Henry
General Manager

Shanghai Lihua Imp. & Exp. Co., Ltd.
Rm. 606 Plaza Building,   Fax: 86-21-642578**
1302 Meilong Road, 200237   Tel: 86-21-642578**
Shanghai, People's Republic of China   E-mail: lihua88@alibaba.com

Email 3

S/C No.: MS-LY168
Date: Oct.12, 201*

The Seller: SHANGHAI LIHUA IMP. & EXP. CO., LTD.   The Buyer: NGS GROUP CO., LTD.
Address: Rm. 606 Plaza Building   Address: 5**, ** Street
1302 Meilong Road, 200237   P. O. BOX 576**
SHANGHAI CHINA   DUBAI UNITED ARAB EMIRATES
TEL: 86-21-642578**   TEL: + 971 - 4 - 35256**
FAX: 86-21-642578**   FAX:+971-4-35256**
E-MAIL: lihua88@alibaba.com   E-MAIL: sebastian@emirates.net.ae

Art. No. Commodity & Specifications	Unit	Quantity	Unit Price CIF DUBAI (USD)	Amount (USD)
1508 10-inch Single-lever Kitchen Faucet in Elegant Design	set	1200	USD18.60 each	22320.00
1409 4-inch Lavatory Faucet with Brass Seat and Acrylic Handle	set	2400	USD12.80 each	30720.00
1318 8-inch Kitchen Faucet with Lever Handle	set	2000	USD16.80 each	33600.00
1316 4-inch Lavatory Faucet with Brass Seat and CP Zinc Handle	set	2350	USD15.60 each	36660.00

TOTAL: USD123300.00

TOTAL CONTRACT VALUE:

SAY US DOLLARS ONE HUNDRED AND TWENTY THREE THOUSAND THREE HUNDRED ONLY.

PACKING: ART NO.T1508, 8 SETS PER CARTON, 150 CARTONS TO ONE 20'FCL.
ART NO. T1409, 12 SETS PER CARTON, 200 CARTONS TO ONE 20'FCL.
ART NO. T1318, 8 SETS PER CARTON, 250 CARTONS TO ONE 20'FCL.
ART NO. T1316, 10 SETS PER CARTON, 235 CARTONS TO ONE 20'FCL.

SHIPMENT: TO BE EFFECTED BY THE SELLER FROM SHANGHAI TO DUBAI UNITED ARAB EMIRATES WITHIN 30 DAYS UPON RECEIPT OF THE RELEVANT L/C WITH PARTIAL SHIPMENTS & TRANSHIPMENT NOT ALLOWED.

PAYMENT: THE BUYER SHALL OPEN THROUGH A BANK ACCEPTABLE TO THE SELLER AN IRREVOCABLE SIGHT LETTER OF CREDIT TO REACH THE SELLER BEFORE OCTOBER 20TH AND REMAIN VALID FOR NEGOTIATION IN CHINA UNTIL THE 15TH DAY AFTER THE TIME OF SHIPMENT.

INSURANCE: THE SELLER SHALL COVER THE GOODS FOR 110% OF TOTAL INVOICE VALUE AGAINST ALL RISKS AND WAR RISK AS PER AND SUBJECT TO RELEVANT OCEAN MARINE CARGO CLAUSES OF THE PEOPLE'S INSURANCE COMPANY OF CHINA DATED 1/1/1981.

REMARKS:

1. The buyer shall have the covering letter of credit reached the Seller 30 days before

shipment, failing which the Seller reserves the right to rescind this S/C without further notice, or to regard as still valid whole or any part of this contract not fulfilled by the Buyer, or to lodge a claim for losses thus sustained, if any.

2. In case of any discrepancy in Quality, claim should be filed by the Buyer within 130 days after the arrival of the goods at port of destination; while for quantity discrepancy, claim should be filed by the Buyer within 150 days after the arrival of the goods at port of destination.

3. For transactions concluded on C.I.F. basis, it is understood that the insurance amount will be for 110% of the invoice value against the risks specified in the Sales Confirmation. If additional insurance amount or coverage required, the Buyer must have the consent of the Seller before Shipment, and the additional premium is to be borne by the Buyer.

4. The Seller shall not hold liable for non-delivery or delay in delivery of the entire lot or a portion of the goods hereunder by reason of natural disasters, war or other causes of Force Majeure. However, the Seller shall notify the Buyer as soon as possible and furnish the Buyer within 15 days by registered airmail with a certificate issued by the China Council for the Promotion of International Trade attesting such event(s).

5. All disputes arising out of the performance of, or relating to this contract, shall be settled through negotiation.

In case no settlement can be reached through negotiation, the case shall then be submitted to the China International Economic and Trade Arbitration Commission for arbitration in accordance with its arbitral rules.

The arbitration shall take place in Shanghai. The arbitral award is final and binding upon both parties.

6. The Buyer is requested to sign and return one copy of this contract immediately after receipt of the same.

Objection, if any, should be raised by the Buyer within 15 days otherwise it is understood that the Buyer has accepted the terms and conditions of this contract.

7. Special conditions: (These shall prevail over all printed terms in case of any conflict.)

Confirmed by:

    THE SELLER   THE BUYER

SHANGHAI HUALI IMP. & EXP. CO., LTD.   NGS GROUP CO., LTD.

    XXX   XXX

GENERAL MANAGER   GENERAL MANAGER

Email 4

Purchase Contract

Ref: 6250

The Buyer (Party A):   The Seller (Party B):

Shanghai Lihua Imp. & Exp. Co., Ltd.   Juli Electronic Products Co., Ltd.

I. Party A places an order with Party B for the following articles, Party B shall duly supply it with the right quantity and quality.

Name & Specification	Quantity	Unit Price(tax included)	Total value(tax included)	Delivery Date
Mosquito Bat	63384	CNY6.18	CNY391,713.12	June.30, 201*

II. Standard of Quality

A: The quality of the export goods supplied by Party B must be up to the State Commodity Inspection Standard. The standard of quality is subject to the sample confirmed by the foreign importer.

B: Packing: Outer Packing: Carton; Dimension: 48×32.5×47cm; 76 pcs/carton; 834 cartons in total;

Inner Packing: Plastic bag.

Only the mark is printed on the carton, without telephone, fax.

C: Delivery Point: the warehouse designated by Party A.

D: Payment: Party A pays CNY50,000.00 as the down payment to Party B, the rest is paid immediately after Party A receives all the remittance from the foreign buyer and the value-added invoice from Party B (within 3-5 days after the foreign buyer remits the rest sum).

III. Miscellaneous

A: All the relative documents are the enclosures of this Contract.

B: All the samples and marks etc. offered by Party A so as to execute this Contract cannot be used by Party B or a third party without permission from Party A. Party B shall treat these in confidence on behalf of Party A.

C: Other stipulations:

a) As the delivery date is pressing, Party B must inform Party A of the quantity, weight, packages etc. in advance.

b) The quality of products must be in compliance with the sample confirmed by the foreign buyer.

c) The shipping mark is made by Party B. Party B shifts the goods immediately to the designed warehouse after Party B receives the Shipping Advice from Party A.

IV. Violation of Contract and Settlement of Disputes

The formation of this Contract, its validity, interpretation, execution and settlement of disputes shall be governed by the relevant laws and regulations of the People's Republic of China. Any disputes should be settled through friendly negotiation first. If not, both parties agree that any party could bring an action against another party in the buyer's law court.

V. This Contract comes into force after the two parties sign and seal. The validity commences on June 10, 201*, and terminates on Dec. 30, 201*.

VI. This Contract is made in duplicate, both parties hold one.

The Buyer (Party A): The Seller(Party B):

Unit Eight Sales Confirmation

…
Sealed by
Legal Representative/ entrusted representative
Signature
…

…
Sealed by
Legal Representative/ entrusted representative
Signature
…

Pattern G of Business Letters

When you send your signed S/C to your foreign buyer, your Fax or email should cover the following particulars:

a) you are sending your signed S/C or Contract by separate airmail;
b) the buyer is requested to counter-sign and return one copy for your file;
c) assure the buyer of the high quality of your products and your full cooperation;
d) urge the buyer to open the covering L/C in your favor.

Relevant Terms

business negotiation 商务磋商	acceptance 接受
Sales Contract 销售合同	Purchase Contract 采购合同
Sales Confirmation 销售确认书	Purchase Confirmation 采购确认书
express contract 明示合同	implied contract 默认合同
fixed-price contract 固定价格合同	long-term contract 长期合同
standard contract 标准合同	letter of intent 意向书
countersign 副署，会签	original 原件
copy 复印件	breach of contract 违约
violation of contract 违反合同	renewal of contract 续约
interpretation of contract 合同的解释	distribution channels 分销渠道
unfair competition 不公平竞争	

Useful Phrases

after protracted exchange of correspondence 经过旷日持久的函电往来	allow leeway 允许有回旋的余地
all parties concerned 有关各方	as below 如下
become effective 生效	come/go into effect 生效
come to an agreement 达成协议	beyond/without controversy 没有争议

续表

bring to a close 结束	by means of 凭借，依靠
consult with 咨询，请教	deviate from 偏离，背离
go contrary to 违背，与……背道而驰	

Summary

When an importer and an exporter finish business negotiation and are willing to conclude a business transaction, a formal written contract is always necessary to be signed by two parties. Such a contract may be called sales contract, purchase contract, purchase order or sales confirmation. They are adopted under different circumstances.

Exercises

I. Questions for review

1. What is a sales confirmation?
2. What is a sales contract?
3. What is a purchase contract?
4. When is a sales confirmation used?

II. Choose the best answer

1. On June 15, I booked a room for Chairman of Board at a five-star hotel _____ he flied to Shanghai.
   A. from   B. before   C. by   D. with
2. After he arrived, we discussed many things _____ our cooperation.
   A. as   B. to   C. at   D. covering
3. I accompanied the supplier and Mr. Shen all the afternoon. I witnessed their _____ the Purchase Contract smoothly.
   A. sign   B. to sign   C. be signed   D. signing
4. Yesterday morning I paid a special visit to Chairman of Board _____ he flied to Guangdong.
   A. before   B. while   C. where   D. under
5. As a matter _____ caution, Andy wants you to have a look at the Contract.
   A. from   B. in   C. of   D. according to
6. _____ there is nobody who can translate the contract, I feel it's my duty to do it.
   A. Before   B. So   C. As   D. That
7. Now I've just finished it, please check it. If there is no problem, please sign the Sales Confirmation and fax it to Mr. Shen immediately and pay the earnest money _____ T/T.

Unit Eight Sales Confirmation

A. in　　　　　B. for　　　　　C. to　　　　　D. by

8. We have over 25 years of experience in the international market, introducing new products _____ means of exclusive distributors that cover the Dominican market.

A. in　　　　　B. to　　　　　C. by　　　　　D. under

9. Please recheck the prices in your P/I, as you informed, you would increase 5% _____ normal price due to this small quantity.

A. in　　　　　B. to　　　　　C. as　　　　　D. on

10. We just make a new mold _____ our plastic faucet. Please check the Picture attached.

A. in　　　　　B. to　　　　　C. for　　　　　D. under

11. We look forward to your _____ reply.

A. favor　　　　B. favorably　　　C. favorite　　　D. favorable

12. This is to confirm our Order No.115 _____ the attached Excel Sheet.

A. for　　　　　B. as per　　　　C. about　　　　D. to

13. This chemical is made _____ a special formula.

A. from　　　　B. in　　　　　C. of　　　　　D. according to

14. _____ you have entered your new office building, you probably would like to refurnish it.

A. Now that　　B. So that　　　C. For　　　　　D. Because

15. Our display is _____ Stand 34, where you will find our new range of furniture.

A. in　　　　　B. to　　　　　C. at　　　　　D. under

16. Although _____ not particularly high, good prices are obtained.

A. sales is　　　B. sale are　　　C. sale is　　　D. sales are

17. If the first shipment proves _____, we shall place a repeat order.

A. to be satisfactory　　　　B. satisfaction
C. satisfied　　　　　　　　D. satisfy

18. It would be _____ your interest to accept our offer because you can hardly obtain similar supplies at our prices elsewhere.

A. in　　　　　B. of　　　　　C. to　　　　　D. on

19. We await _____ keen interest your trial order.

A. on　　　　　B. of　　　　　C. at　　　　　D. with

20. Thank you for your Fax dated Feb.12, we also confirm _____ your sample.

A. to receive　　B. receiving　　C. received　　D. having received

III. Translate the following sentences into Chinese

1. Do you have any comment on this clause?

2. Please check all the terms listed in the contract and see if there is anything not in conformity with the terms we agreed on.

3. We hope to be able to sign the contract by next Monday.

4. Let's congratulate ourselves that this transaction has been brought to a successful

conclusion.

5. This agreement shall evidence our mutual agreement to release, waive, cancel and terminate the contract between us dated June 1, 201*, without further recourse by either party.

6. The parties to that contract and to this agreement of mutual rescission desire to rescind that contract.

7. For the reasons set forth above, and in consideration of the mutual covenants of the parties hereto, the parties agree as follows:

8. The above-mentioned contract is hereby rescinded as of this day above written, and neither party shall have any further rights or duties thereafter.

9. Unless we immediately hear from you to the contrary, we shall confirm that the said changes and modifications are mutually agreeable.

10. If these terms are acceptable to you, please sign where indicated below and return together with your idea or proposal.

Optional Part

11. I agree to the terms concerning the mode of packing and the shipping marks.

12. The required L/C will be established in your favor upon receipt of your Sales Confirmation.

13. This contract contains basically all we have agreed upon during our negotiation.

14. If one side fails to honor the contract, the other side is entitled to rescind it.

15. Let's congratulate ourselves that this transaction has been brought to a successful conclusion.

IV. Translate the following sentences into English

1. 我已经准备好签署这份协议了。
2. 我们对条款没有问题了。
3. 如果一方不履行合同，另一方就有权取消它。
4. 随函附上我方第 NO. HW-116 号售货确认书一式三份，请签退一份供我们存档。
5. 一张保兑的不可撤销的凭即期汇票可兑付的信用证应立即开出。
6. 相关信用证中的规定必须与售货确认书中的条款完全一致，以避免随后的修改。
7. 要强调的一点是以我方为受益人的相关信用证必须由花旗银行开立。
8. 我们已经及时签署了售货确认书并按要求退回一份供你们备案，同时我们已经开出了相关信用证，它很快会到达你方。
9. 如果这个购买合同的执行令人满意，那么将来经常会有订单。
10. 请给我们你方签好的一式二份的售货确认书供我们会签，感谢你方的合作。

V. Case Study

Try to understand the following agreement:

CORPORATE SUPPLY AGREEMENT

This Corporate Supply Agreement ("Agreement") is effective as of this 1st Jan. 2006

("Effective Date"), between Koala-Kangaroo Electronics, limited, an Australian corporation, with offices at … Australia ("Koala-Kangaroo"), and _____, ("Supplier"). Koala-Kangaroo and Supplier agree to the terms set forth herein.

1. Definitions. The definitions set forth in Section 1 of Attachment 1 shall apply to this Agreement.

2. Scope and Integration. The Koala-Kangaroo Standard Terms and Conditions attached as Attachment 1 of this Agreement will apply to each sale by Supplier and purchase by Koala-Kangaroo of Products and Services. The Koala-Kangaroo Terms and Conditions are incorporated in all Purchase Orders issued by Koala-Kangaroo to Supplier whether or not the Purchase Orders include a reference to this Agreement. This Agreement is the entire agreement between Koala-Kangaroo and Supplier and supersedes prior or contemporaneous, oral or written agreements, representations and communications that are related to this Agreement's subject matter.

IN WITNESS WHEREOF, the Parties have caused this Agreement to be executed by their duly authorized representatives, as of the Effective Date in duplicate original copies.

Koala-Kangaroo Electronics, limited	SUPPLIER:
By:	By:
Name:	Name:
Title:	Title:
Date:	Date:

KOALA-KANGAROO STANDARD TERMS AND CONDITIONS FOR PRODUCTS AND SERVICES

1. Definitions

A. "Affiliate" means any entity that controls, is controlled by, or is under common control with a Party. "Control" means an entity owns or controls more than fifty percent of the voting stock or other ownership interest of another entity. References to "Koala-Kangaroo" include its Affiliates. Koala-Kangaroo and Supplier may each be referred to individually as a "Party" or collectively as "Parties" to this Agreement.

B. "Agreement" means these terms, the Koala-Kangaroo Purchase Order cover page, and any documents incorporated by reference.

C. "Confidential Information" means confidential or proprietary information disclosed by one Party to the other related to this Agreement (i) in any visually perceptible form, which is clearly marked as "confidential" or "proprietary", and (ii) in oral form, if it is identified as confidential at the time of disclosure and confirmed in writing within thirty days after disclosure. Whether or not marked or any notice having been provided, the unit price, quantity, schedule and build plans, Koala-Kangaroo product plans, technology roadmaps, and contracts always are

Confidential Information.

D. "Customer" means any entity or person that purchases directly or indirectly from Koala-Kangaroo.

E. "Deliver" or "Delivery" means delivery to the delivery point as specified on the Purchase Order and according to Section 6.

F. "Epidemic Failure" means Product defects exceeding two percent (2%) of quantity of Products shipped during any thirty day period within the warranty period that results in the Product failing in substantially the same manner, and such cause is technically confirmed by both parties, and which create a Customer impact, including (i) poor workmanship, (ii) noncompliance with specifications or industry standards, and (iii) use of incorrect or known defective parts or software, or a missing test sequence.

G. "Fixed Quantity Purchase Order" or "Discrete Purchase Order" means a purchase order for which the total quantity and delivery schedule are established when Koala-Kangaroo issues the order.

H. "Product" or "Products" means those products identified in a Purchase Order, including Software as defined in Section 7. For purposes of the warranty, intellectual property infringement indemnity and product liability provisions, "Product" shall not include any Koala-Kangaroo custom requirements, including without limitation, connectors, industrial design elements or any other Koala-Kangaroo-supplied or Koala-Kangaroo AVL-designated components.

I. "Purchase Order" means either a Blanket Purchase Order or Fixed Quantity Purchase Order when a distinction is irrelevant.

J. "Service" or "Services" means those services identified in a Purchase Order.

K. "Supplier" means the seller or licensor of Products or Services to Koala-Kangaroo.

2. Acceptance and Integration of Agreement

A. Supplier accepts this Agreement by acknowledging a Purchase order, delivering Products, or commencing Services, whichever occurs first. Offers and acceptances by the parties are expressly limited to the terms of this Agreement. Terms that are additional to or different from this Agreement are rejected by the parties. If this Agreement is construed to be an acceptance of an offer by Supplier, Koala-Kangaroo's acceptance is expressly limited to and is conditional on Supplier's assent to the terms of this Agreement, and each party rejects all additional or different terms.

B. This Agreement is the entire agreement between Koala-Kangaroo and Supplier and supersedes prior or contemporaneous, oral or written agreements, representations, and communications that are related to this Agreement's subject matter.

3. Lead Times

Material should be shipped not later then 21 days after PO is placed by Koala-Kangaroo.

A. Supplier will maintain adequate capacity to supply Koala-Kangaroo with a twenty percent increased quantity over Koala-Kangaroo's initial fifty two week forecast or the Fixed Quantity Purchase Order quantity, as applicable.

B. The minimum order size for parts sold in bulk is one part, and the minimum order size for parts sold in reels is one reel. Supplier will not charge Koala-Kangaroo extra on minimum size orders.

4. Product Changes and Discontinuances

A. Supplier will give Koala-Kangaroo six months written notice of any change to the form, fit, content, design, function, or part numbers of any Product. Supplier will not implement these changes in the Products Delivered to Koala-Kangaroo without Koala-Kangaroo's written approval. Supplier to send 4M Format with required information to Koala-Kangaroo for any change in product or Major process. Koala-Kangaroo QA &R&D will review change & after written approval from Koala-Kangaroo, Supplier can implement changes. Products/components observed with any changes without prior approval from Koala-Kangaroo will be treated as breaching the agreement & all such products will be Rejected & vendor have to decide for treatment of defective products.

B. Subject to Section 3.C, Koala-Kangaroo may change a Purchase Order by giving notice in writing to Supplier. Supplier will proceed with the change and will be entitled to an equitable adjustment in the performance schedule and purchase price for reasonable and unavoidable costs directly resulting from the change. Supplier will submit any claim for adjustment in writing to Koala-Kangaroo within thirty calendar days of Koala-Kangaroo's written notice.

C. Supplier will give Koala-Kangaroo six months written notice before discontinuing the manufacture or distribution of Products. During this period, Koala-Kangaroo has the option to purchase any quantity in a final buy of the discontinued Products and take Delivery within six months of the final buy date.

5. Price and Payment

A. Prices are listed on the Purchase Order.

B. Supplier may invoice upon either Delivery or on completion of Services. Payment of undisputed charges is due net 45 day payment terms (from date of invoice).

C. Supplier represents and warrants that the prices are the lowest prices for which Supplier has sold or is selling Products and Services, accounting for differences in quantity, schedule and other material terms. Supplier will reduce the price paid by (or refund an amount to) Koala-Kangaroo to the extent necessary to match the price provided by Supplier to its other customers for substantially similar Products or Services of substantially similar quantity.

6. Delivery, Inspection and Acceptance

A. Delivery by Supplier will be FOB (Incoterms 2000), shipping point. Supplier can invoice Koala-Kangaroo, once material is shipped to Koala-Kangaroo Limited.

B. The supplier shall provide all serial no. of the sets supplied under the invoice along with the packing list in every consignment, along with test reports to have better understanding for warranty replacement of parts.

C. It is agreed that Supplier will make every commercially reasonable effort to acknowledge Koala-Kangaroo's written notifications of receipt of non-conforming Product within 24 hours of such written notification. Samples of the non-conforming Products will be sent to Supplier if requested to do so within a reasonable time, also expected to be within 24 hours of such request. Supplier will work with the relevant Koala-Kangaroo team(s) to identify the root cause of the issue and develop an action plan of correction within 10 working days of sample receipt or sooner whenever possible. At that time, Supplier will issue an RMA for repair & replacement. Time is of the essence in these matters and both parties are expected to work together towards prompt resolution and to mitigate their damages, where applicable.

Products returned for 1 to 1 replacement (after authorization from Supplier) should be completed in 10 days.

D. Time is of the essence in the performance of this Agreement.

E. Field failures target <1% & Assembly line rejections/Predespatch inspection target 0%(as skd kit should not have any fault & for any SKD kit/CBU fault supplier to replace defective parts/Product on 1:1 basis along with duty & freight costs. Koala-Kangaroo & supplier to agree on product assurance test standards with mutual agreements.

7. License Grants

For the purposes of this Section 7, the term "Software" will mean: (i) software or firmware embedded in the Product; (ii) free-standing software that works with, or runs on the Product provided to Koala-Kangaroo, in either object code or source code, either at the time of Delivery or at any other time; and (iii) documentation relating to the software or firmware provided to Koala-Kangaroo. Unless otherwise provided in a separate license agreement between the Parties entered into by handwritten signature, Supplier grants Koala-Kangaroo a perpetual, irrevocable, worldwide, nonexclusive, fully paid-up license to use, modify, copy, reproduce, display, and create derivative works of Software; to assemble, edit, merge, translate, or compile additional copies of Software, including derivative works; and to support and maintain Software. Supplier also grants Koala-Kangaroo a perpetual, irrevocable, worldwide, nonexclusive, royalty free license to: (i) use, make or have made, demonstrate or have demonstrated, market or have marketed, offer or have offered for sale, sell or have sold, license, or have licensed, and otherwise distribute, or have distributed, Koala-Kangaroo products into which the Software has been incorporated; and (ii) provide end-users of these products a limited right to use the Software, which right will survive any termination or expiration of this Agreement. Koala-Kangaroo may, at its sole discretion, reproduce in whole or in part, any copyright notices or other proprietary legends belonging to Supplier on any copies that Koala-Kangaroo makes of the Software, including modified copies of the Software. Supplier's title to the Software will remain in and be the sole and exclusive property of Supplier. Koala-Kangaroo may allow third parties to exercise the rights and licenses granted in this Section 7 for the benefit of Koala-Kangaroo or Customers.

8. Representations and Warranties

A. For eighteen months from the date of shipment from supplier's site, Supplier warrants that Products are free from defects in materials and workmanship and conform to specifications, excluding damage caused by Customer's misuse, and do not contain viruses or other hidden mechanisms that would damage or interfere with the operation of the Products. Supplier warrants that at the time of Delivery, Products are owned or licensed by Supplier, free and clear of any liens or encumbrances. Supplier warrants that Products are new and contains new parts throughout. Supplier will, at its expense, promptly repair or replace defective Products and will pay for the costs of inbound and outbound transportation costs that are related to a breach of these warranties. The warranty includes replacement of panel & main PCBs within the above mentioned warranty period of 18 months. Supplier to supply 1% spares of total L/C Value in addition to 1:1 replacement for any failures occurring within warranty period.

B. In addition to the remedies in Section 8.A, if an Epidemic Failure occurs, Supplier will, at its own expense, immediately take remedial action for impacted and potentially impacted Products, whether in the field or in Koala-Kangaroo's inventory, under a corrective action plan approved by Koala-Kangaroo. Supplier will reimburse Koala-Kangaroo for all costs related to rectifying the Epidemic Failure, including, engineering changes and or Product repair or replacement costs. Supplier will also provide the following:

- Detailed defect analysis, quality improvement plans.
- Process standards and parameter detailed.
- Lot inspection report /Reliability Reports wherever requested

C. Supplier represents and warrants that it is in compliance with the insurance requirements in Section 15.

D. EXCEPT WHERE SUCH DISCLAIMERS ARE SPECIFICALLY PROHIBITED BY APPLICABLE LAW, SUPPLIER EXPRESSLY DISCLAIMS AND EXCLUDES ALL OTHER WARRANTIES, OBLIGATIONS, OR LIABILITIES, EXPRESS OR IMPLIED, ORAL OR WRITTEN, ARISING BY LAW OR OTHERWISE, INCLUDING THE WARRANTIES OF MERCHANTABILITY, FITNESS FOR A PARTICULAR PURPOSE, NONINFRINGEMENT OR THOSE ARISING FROM COURSE OF PERFORMANCE, COURSE OF DEALING OR USAGE OF TRADE.

E. Supply of RMA parts as against RMA approval 1:1 basis.

F. Supply of additional spares to Koala-Kangaroo at supplier's cost price. Spare parts(or compatible parts) availability for about 5 years after discontinuation of any product.

G. Replacement spares should be shipped no later than 7 days after approval is received by Supplier.

H. If Vendor wants to verify the defect, he may visit ONIDA factory and can verify the defect or can also ask for defective samples for their analysis. Cost of such samples dispatch and visit shall be born by supplier.

I. Supplier to settle down the lot replacement or compensation within 15 working days.

J. Corrective & Preventive actions report (CAR Report) from vendor along with free replacement for any components failures with in 18 months.

K. Site Quality engineer.

Vendor to cooperate with Koala-Kangaroo Quality engineer for any sort of predespatch inspection. Koala-Kangaroo may or may not depute quality engineer at supplier manufacturing location to perform predespatch inspection. Koala-Kangaroo Engineer can use supplier reliability lab for certain.

L. Koala-Kangaroo to put Cost poor quality to supplier for any cause like delay in delivery, Productivity loss, line Quality failures as per COPQ Format (PQF).

9. Service Practices

A. Supply of Service Manuals, Circuit Diagrams for all the models supplied to KOALA-KANGAROO before any new model dispatching.

B. Detailed Circuit Diagram (schematic) to carry out the component level repairs.

C. Regular Technical updates through Technical Notes/Service bulletins.

D. Modification Notes/Training to SVC engineers.

E. Change of product specification, change of parts notes, Common failures.

Inform in advance before launch of any new model with specification, Spare Parts compatibility with current model and technical support on the same.

Supplier shall authorize KOALA-KANGAROO to return the UNUSED/OBSOLTE MODEL PARTS and supplier shall reimburse the cost of UNUSED/OBSOLETE MODEL PARTS and issue CREDIT NOTE for the Spare Part value.

10. Indemnities and Limitations of Liability

A. Each Party will indemnify, defend, and hold harmless the other Party, its officers, directors, employees, contractors, and agents ("Indemnified Parties") from claims, damages, and expenses, including court costs and attorney's fees ("Damages"), for any death, injury, or property damage caused by the negligent acts or omissions, gross negligence, or willful misconduct, arising from or connected with the performance of this Agreement, caused by the indemnifying Party, its officers, directors, employees, contractors, or agents.

B. Supplier will indemnify, defend and hold harmless Koala-Kangaroo Indemnified Parties and Customers from Damages arising from claims by third parties resulting from an act or omission of the Supplier, including claims that Products or Services (i) are defective, (ii) are negligently designed, marked, marketed, or manufactured by Supplier, or (iii) fail to comply with any applicable law or industry standard. Upon receipt of written notification, Supplier will promptly assume full responsibility for the defense of any claims provided Supplier has full control of thereof.

C. Supplier will indemnify, defend, and hold harmless Koala-Kangaroo Indemnified Parties and Customers from Damages arising from any actual or claimed infringement or violation of any patents, trademarks, mask works, copyrights, trade secrets or other intellectual property rights, and defend any suits based on the use, license, distribution or sale of Product by Koala-Kangaroo or Customers. If the use or distribution of any portion of the Product is enjoined, then Supplier will, at its expense and at Supplier's option, (i) procure the right for Koala-Kangaroo and Customers to continue using or distributing the Product, (ii) modify the Product so that it becomes non-infringing while maintaining equivalent or superior functionality, or (iii) replace the Product with non-infringing product of equivalent or superior functionality. If none of the three alternatives is acceptable to Koala-Kangaroo, then Koala-Kangaroo may return all or part of the Products at Koala-Kangaroo's option, and Supplier will refund the price in full, less a reasonable amount for accumulated depreciation, based upon the industry-recognized life cycle of such Products.

D. Supplier will not agree to any settlement agreement that affects any Koala-Kangaroo Indemnified Party or Customer without Koala-Kangaroo's prior written consent. Koala-Kangaroo may, at its own expense, actively participate through its own counsel provided Koala-Kangaroo does not interfere or hinder Supplier in its defense or negotiations and provided further that at all times Supplier maintains control of such defense or negotiations.

E. EXCEPT FOR BREACHES BY EACH PARTY OF THEIR RESPECTIVE CONFIDENTIALITY OBLIGATIONS AND EACH PARTY'S STATUTORY LIABILITIES WITH RESPECT TO PERSONAL INJURY, DEATH AND TANGIBLE PROPERTY DAMAGE, IN NO EVENT WILL EITHER Koala-Kangaroo OR SUPPLIER, WHETHER AS A RESULT OF BREACH OF CONTRACT, TORT (INCLUDING NEGLIGENCE), OR OTHERWISE, HAVE ANY LIABILITY TO EACH OTHER OR TO ANY THIRD PARTY FOR ANY INDIRECT, PUNITIVE, SPECIAL, INCIDENTAL, OR CONSEQUENTIAL DAMAGES.

11. Confidentiality

A. During the performance of this Agreement and for five years from its termination, the Parties will (i) restrict disclosure of Confidential Information to employees and contractors who have a "need to know" for performance of this Agreement and (ii) handle Confidential Information with the same degree of care, but at least reasonable care, the receiving Party applies to its own confidential information. Except as provided in Section 7, this Agreement does not grant any proprietary rights, including any license, implied or otherwise, in Confidential Information.

B. Confidential Information does not include information that is (i) previously known to, or received rightfully by the receiving Party without any obligation of confidentiality, (ii) distributed by the disclosing Party without restriction, (iii) publicly available other than by unauthorized disclosure by the receiving Party, or (iv) independently developed by the receiving Party.

Confidential Information may be disclosed to a governmental authority law fully demanding Confidential Information, if the receiving Party provides timely written notice to the disclosing Party so the disclosing Party has a reasonable opportunity to object to the scope of the governmental demand, and confidentiality is otherwise maintained by the Parties after the disclosure. Koala-Kangaroo may be developing products similar in functionality to the Product; the receipt of Confidential Information by Koala-Kangaroo from Supplier will not prohibit Koala-Kangaroo from developing products.

12. Compliance with Laws and Ethical Standards

Supplier, on behalf of itself and its suppliers and subcontractors as related to this Agreement ("Supply Chain"), represents and warrants that Product is produced, manufactured, and supplied, and Services are rendered in compliance with applicable jurisdictions' laws, regulations, and standards, including those concerning environmental protection, freedom of association, wages, and humane treatment of workers, and those laws and other standards specified in Exhibit A.

13. Termination

A. If one Party is in material breach and fails to cure the breach within thirty days of notice of the breach, the other Party may terminate this Agreement by giving written notice to the breaching Party. Koala-Kangaroo may terminate this Agreement for convenience forty-five days after giving written notice to the Supplier. In the event of a termination for convenience by Koala-Kangaroo, Koala-Kangaroo shall be liable to pay Supplier for (i) the full value of the total quantity of finished goods not yet delivered as required by the maximum weekly Requirements Report within the Manufacturing Cycle Time calculated at the current price of finished Product not yet Delivered as of the date of termination, plus (ii) actual cost of all work in process, plus (iii) actual cost of raw materials unique to the Product, in each instance limited to the maximum inventory level in the Requirements Report for each week of the Manufacturing Cycle Time. Either Party may terminate this Agreement immediately by giving written notice to the other Party if: (i) the other Party files or has filed against it a bankruptcy petition of any type, makes an assignment for the benefit of creditors, or goes into liquidation or receivership, (ii) the other Party ceases to conduct business in the normal course, becomes insolvent, enters into suspension of payments or moratorium, admits in writing its inability to pay debts as they mature, or avails itself of or becomes subject to any other judicial or administrative proceeding relating to insolvency or protection of creditors' rights, or (iii) the direct or indirect ownership or control of the other Party existing on the Purchase Order date changes materially and may adversely affect the rights of the terminating Party, including the acquisition of ownership or control by a competitor of the terminating Party.

B. The terms of this Agreement that are intended to survive termination will survive, including Sections 2, 4, 7, 8, 9, 10, 11 14 and 15.

14. Force Majeure

Neither Party will be liable for delays in Delivery or performance caused by the following: acts of God, including natural disasters; acts of terrorism; acts of civil or military authority, including war or embargoes; epidemics; and riots; if the delay alleged to result from the event is (a) beyond the actual control and without fault or negligence of the delayed Party or its respective Supply Chain, and (b) not resulting from failure to comply with applicable law or this Agreement. Within ten days of the occurrence of the force majeure, the Party claiming a force majeure will provide the other Party with written notice, including the estimated delay and actions being taken or planned to avoid or minimize the impact of any delay. The Party claiming a force majeure will have the burden of establishing that a force majeure has occurred and has delayed Delivery or performance. If a force majeure event results in a delay of more than fifteen days and Delivery or performance cannot be completed within an additional fifteen days, the other Party may cancel any further Delivery or performance, including pending Deliveries, with no liability. Supplier will use commercially reasonable efforts to minimize the delay.

15. Governing Law and Dispute Resolution

A. The laws of Australia, disregarding its conflict of law provisions, govern this Agreement. The Parties disclaim application of the United Nations Convention on Contracts for the International Sale of Goods.

B. Koala-Kangaroo and Supplier will attempt to settle any claim arising out of this Agreement through good-faith negotiation. The following process will be used to resolve disputes. The Parties will submit the dispute in writing to a senior executive from each Party. If the dispute is not resolved within thirty days, either Party may demand non-binding mediation, the cost of which will be shared equally by the Parties, except that each Party will pay its own attorney's fees. Within forty-five days after written notice demanding mediation, the Parties will in good faith choose a mutually acceptable mediator. Mediation will be conducted in Sydney. If the dispute cannot be resolved through mediation within ninety days, either Party may submit the dispute to a court of competent jurisdiction. Use of any dispute resolution procedure will not be construed under the doctrines of laches, waiver, or estoppel to adversely affect the rights of either Party. Either Party may resort to judicial proceedings for intellectual property disputes or if interim relief is necessary to prevent serious and irreparable injury.

C. The state and courts in Sydney, Australia will have the exclusive jurisdiction and venue for any action under this Agreement and Supplier irrevocably agrees and submits to the exclusive venue and jurisdiction of these courts.

D. Even if a dispute arises Supplier will not interrupt or delay Delivery of Products or performance of Services or terminate any licenses granted under this Agreement, unless (i) a court of competent jurisdiction or Koala-Kangaroo has granted authority to do so, or (ii) Koala-Kangaroo has terminated this Agreement pursuant to Section 12.A.

E. IN THE EVENT OF ANY DISPUTE BETWEEN THE PARTIES, WHETHER IT RESULTS

IN PROCEEDINGS IN ANY COURT IN ANY JURISDICTION OR IN ARBITRATION, THE PARTIES HEREBY KNOWINGLY, VOLUNTARILY, INTENTIONALLY AND HAVING HAD AN OPPORTUNITY TO CONSULT WITH COUNSEL, WAIVE ALL RIGHTS TO TRIAL BY JURY, AND AGREE THAT ANY AND ALL MATTERS SHALL BE DECIDED BY A JUDGE OR ARBITRATOR WITHOUT A JURY TO THE FULLEST EXTENT PERMISSIBLE UNDER APPLICABLE LAW.

16. Other Terms and Conditions

A. Authority. Each Party represents and warrants that (i) it has obtained necessary authorizations to enter into this Agreement and to perform its obligations, and (ii) the execution and performance of this Agreement does not violate any bylaw or other governing authority of the Party and (iii) this Agreement is a binding obligation.

B. Business Interruption and Recovery Plan. Supplier will provide, and annually update, a written business interruption and recovery plan, including business impact and risk assessment, crisis management, information technology, disaster recovery, and business continuity. Supplier will notify Koala-Kangaroo in writing within twenty-four hours of activation of the plan.

C. Insurance. Supplier will (i) maintain statutory Workers' Compensation, Employer's Liability, Broad Form Commercial General Liability, and Business Automobile Liability Insurance on behalf of Supplier and its subcontractors, and Contractual Liability Insurance for liability under this Agreement, in each instance of at least $1,000,000 (U.S.) combined single limit; (ii) maintain insurance covering its assets and operations in an amount sufficient to fund the costs of compliance with the Business Interruption and Recovery Plan required by Section 15.C of this Agreement; (iii) name Koala-Kangaroo as an additional insured and, under the Commercial General Liability policy, include a cross-liability endorsement; (iv) provide a waiver of subrogation in favor of Koala-Kangaroo under the Workers Compensation and Employers' Liability policies; (v) cause its insurance to be designated as primary and to provide for thirty days' minimum prior notice of cancellation to Koala-Kangaroo; (vi) at Koala-Kangaroo's request, furnish evidence of insurance from a locally licensed insurance provider reasonably acceptable to Koala-Kangaroo; and (vii) require its Supply Chain to maintain, at a minimum, the same coverages and limits required of Supplier.

D. Publicity. Neither Party will issue a public statement about this Agreement without the other Party's prior written consent.

E. Records and Inspections. Upon request, Supplier will provide to Koala-Kangaroo copies of any records related to this Agreement and required to be kept by law. Koala-Kangaroo, upon written notice, also may inspect and audit Supplier's premises, records, processes, and physical assets regarding Products, Services, claims, or Supplier's performance of this Agreement.

F. Remedies. Except to the extent stated in this Agreement, no remedy is intended to be exclusive or in lieu of other remedies available at law or in equity.

G. Relationship. Supplier is an independent contractor. Nothing in this Agreement is intended to be inconsistent with that status. Supplier's personnel are not Koala-Kangaroo's employees or agents. This Agreement does not constitute or create a joint venture, partnership, or formal business organization of any kind.

H. Severability. If a provision of this Agreement is held to be unenforceable, this Agreement will be construed as if the unenforceable provision was not present, and so as to affect the intent of the parties.

I. Subcontracting. Supplier will not subcontract any portion of this Agreement without Koala-Kangaroo's written consent.

J. Successors. This Agreement is binding upon, inures to the benefit of, and is enforceable by, the Parties and their respective successors and permitted assigns. This agreement does not create rights in any third party.

K. Waiver. Failure of either Party to insist upon the performance of any term, or to exercise any rights under this Agreement, is not a waiver of the future enforceability of the term.

Exhibit A - Supplemental Compliance with Laws and Standards [# 4 and 5 under review]

1. Supplier represents and warrants that Supplier, in activities related to this Agreement, will comply with the following:

2. Ethical Conduct, Anticorruption and Unfair Business Practices. Supplier will: (a) not engage in corrupt practices, including public or private bribery or kickbacks; (b) maintain transparency and accuracy in corporate record keeping; (c) act lawfully and with integrity in handling competitive data, proprietary information, and other intellectual property; and (d) comply with legal requirements regarding fair competition and antitrust, and accurate and truthful marketing.

3. Antidiscrimination and Humane Treatment of Workers. Supplier will:

A. Employ workers on the basis of their ability to do the job, and not on the basis of their personal characteristics or beliefs.

B. Assure that Product, including parts, and Services will not be produced, manufactured, mined or assembled with the use of forced, prison, or indentured labor, including debt bondage, or with the use of illegal child labor in violation of International Labor Conventions for minimum age (C138) and child labor (C182). If Supplier recruits contract workers, Supplier will pay agency recruitment commissions and not require workers to remain in employment for any period of time against their will. If Supplier provides housing or eating facilities, Supplier will assure the facilities are operated and maintained in a safe, sanitary, and dignified manner.

C. (i) Operate safe, healthy, and fair working environments, including managing operations so levels of overtime do not create inhumane working conditions; (ii) where there are no applicable local laws, not routinely require workers to work in excess of six consecutive days without a rest day; (iii) pay workers at least the minimum legal wage or, where no wage law exists, the local industry standard; and (iv) assure that workers are free to join, or refrain from joining, associations of their own choosing, unless otherwise prohibited by law.

4. Environmental Protection.

A. Supplier will have an implemented, functioning Environmental Management System (EMS) in accordance with ISO 14001 or equivalent. Third-party registration is recommended but not required.

B. Supplier certifies on, that Product and their parts do not contain and are not manufactured with a process that uses any Class I ozone-depleting substances (as identified in 40 CFR Part 82 Appendix A to Subpart A, or as subsequently identified by the US Environmental Protection Agency as Class I ozone-depleting substances).

5. Import/Customs. (a) For Product sourced outside the United States Customs Territory, Koala-Kangaroo has the option of being the Importer of Record. Supplier will furnish an invoice containing the following information: (i) port of entry; (ii) name and address of Supplier and of Koala-Kangaroo entity purchasing the Product; (iii) name of shipper (if different from Supplier); (iv) country of export; (v) detailed description of Product in English; (vi) quantities and weights; (vii) actual purchase price, including elements of the amount paid or payable by Koala-Kangaroo; (viii) the currency in which the sale was made; (ix) charges, costs, and expenses associated with the Product, including freight, insurance, commission, containerization, and packing, unless the cost of packing, containerization, and inland freight are already included in the invoice price; (x) rebates or discounts; (xi) the country of origin (manufacture). (b) Supplier will make timely, accurate representations concerning the importation of goods into Australian Customs Territory and other applicable jurisdictions, including representations regarding entry requirements, classification, valuation, preferential treatment, duty drawback or trade terms (INCOTERMS).

6. Export Restriction. Supplier will not export or re-export, directly or indirectly, any of Koala-Kangaroo's Confidential Information or Product to any country for which any applicable government, at the time of export or re-export, requires an export license or other governmental approval, without first obtaining the license or approval.

7. Utilization of Small Business Concerns. If applicable, Supplier will comply with (i) the provisions of FAR 52.219-8 that pertain to Utilization of Small Business Concerns and (ii) other state, and local small and other business utilization laws.

VI. Discussion

1. Why is it easy for Chinese students to translate an English-version contract into Chinese? Why is it very difficult for most Chinese students to translate a Chinese-version contract into English?

2. What is the best way for you to improve your writing in English?

Unit Nine

Terms of Payment

Introduction

In recent years, large amount of overdue debts have occurred in China's foreign trade. Owing to bad management and the disadvantage of enterprise's system, many exporters suffer from failing to recover their foreign exchange. So, every exporter shall pay close attention to terms of payment.

The traditional modes of payment in international trade can be classified into three categories as follows:

A) remittance

B) collection

C) letter of credit

Remittance has three kinds mentioned below:

1) mail transfer (M/T)

2) telegraphic transfer (T/T)

3) demand draft (D/D)

Collection has two kinds mentioned below:

1) documents against payment (D/P)

2) documents against acceptance (D/A)

An L/C is a tool or instrument of payment, and the payment is guaranteed by a bank. It is usually called "an open letter of request", because the opening bank requests the negotiating bank to advance money or give credit to the beneficiary, and promises that he will reimburse or repay the same to the negotiating bank against a draft accompanied by the relative shipping documents.

There are many different kinds of L/C as follows:

1) Sight L/C,

2) Time or usance L/C,

3) Irrevocable L/C,

4) Unconfirmed and confirmed L/C,

5) Transferable and divisible L/C,

6) L/C without recourse,

7) Documentary and clean L/C,

8) Anticipatory L/C and packing credit,

9) Revolving L/C, etc.

L/C is mostly commonly used by Chinese exporters because it is regarded as the safest mode of payment. In fact, the average rate of bad debts was up to 3%-6% in the first five years of the 21 century, while it was only 0.25%-0.5% in the developed countries. Furthermore, the most commonly used mode of payment is commercial credit, which accounts for 95% of all the business transactions there.

Unit Nine Terms of Payment

Small-medium exporters can also take advantage of Factoring, Forfeiting and Export Insurance to reduce business risks.

The domestic enterprises should avail themselves of debt collection agency for recovery of overdue debts if they got into troubles in collection.

Business Letters

Email 1

To: lihua88@alibaba.com
Subject: L/C No: CN611

Dear Henry,

We are pleased to inform you that our L/C No. CN611 for 1×40' of Model FRB51-682 has been opened by our bank, the Pacific Wellington Bank Ltd. on December 3,201*.
Details read as follows:
Unit Price: USD92.00
Quantity: 160 sets
Total Amount: USD14720.00, CIF Putaruru
Brand Name: Super-Yak
Model: FRB51-682
To: Pudong Development Bank, Shanghai and confirmed by our Bank as requested
Latest shipment date: October 15, 200*
Expiry date: October 31, 200*
We hope you will get our L/C very soon, and ship the goods as soon as you finish. We will place regular orders with you for more machines if your first shipment proves to be satisfactory, and we shall be much obliged if you can execute this order within 20-25 days.
Our down payment for your Model FRB50-689 will be remitted to you next week, to the amount of USD2000.00 which accounts for 10 % of the contract. Please start production.

Yours faithfully,
Blair Donaldson
General Manager

First Tool Ltd
1** Domain Road,
PO Box 56*,
Putaruru
New Zealand

Tel: (64) 07885 1***
Fax: (64) 07885 1***
Email: firsttool@online.net.nz

Email 2

==

From: damai-SALES(163) damai-sales@vip.163.com
To: angela <angela@ttry.com>
Cc: haomai-service <haomai-service@vip.163.com>
Subject: EMERGENT AND IMPORTANT COOPERATION
Date: 201*/1/12 15:09:18

==

Dear Angela,

After discussing with our production department, we have decided to give your order the top priority in production after Spring Festival. And we will purchase the raw materials and accessory in this week. After the holiday, we can produce the items and you arrange SGS inspection. We will make shipment after your approval.

Your cooperation

Attached please find the P/I for your required order quantity. In order to save our two sides' time, I send you two versions for your confirmation. Please be noted: if you could pay by T/T, please use "P/I FOR 09DQ001-TT.PDF" as the sales contract arranges 30%T/T ADVANCE.

If you could make payment by L/C, please use "P/I FOR 09DQ001-L/C.PDF" as the sales contract arranges issuing L/C.

If you adopt T/T terms, please arrange the 30% ADVANCE immediately.

If you adopt L/C terms, please leave the last date of shipment and validity of L/C with long time so as to avoid extra cost for L/C amendment! That is, Last date of shipment: 201*0315; validity of L/C: 201*0330.

SHIPMENT

The earliest estimated date of shipment will be the end of Feb.

If you confirm this order by sending us your "signed P/I" within 2 days, we will arrange the order in this week!

Please check and confirm immediately! This is the fastest way we could work for you. Thanks for your cooperation and understanding.

Best Regards,
Jim
Manager
Export & Client Dept.

Unit Nine Terms of Payment

Email 3

Original Message -----
From: RETTO MACHINE INC.
To: Mr. SUN
Sent: Thursday, October 15, 201* 1:12 PM
TO: sun@alibaba.com
SUBJECT: NO CONFIRMATION IS OK?

DEAR MR. SUN,

TOMORROW WE ARE GOING TO OPEN THE COVERING L/C IN YOUR FAVOR. BUT WE NOTICED THAT YOUR PROFORMA INVOICE MENTIONED "CONFIRMED BY HK+SHANGHAI BANKING CORPORATION LTD. SHANGHAI BRANCH". WE THINK THIS POINT WILL CAUSE SOME TROUBLES TO OUR BANK AND OURSELVES. SOMETIMES, OUR BANK HAS NO CONNECTION WITH YOUR CONFIRMING BANK, THEN IT WILL BE IMPOSSIBLE TO BE CONFIRMED BY THIS BANK.

BY THE WAY, WE HAVE CONTACTED EACH OTHER FOR SEVERAL ORDERS. FOR EVERY ORDER WE NEED NO CONFIRMATION ON OUR L/C AND THERE IS NO PROBLEM AT ALL. MOREOVER, CONFIRMATION CHARGE IS VERY EXPENSIVE. THEN, CAN WE OPEN OUR L/C WITH NO CONFIRMATION? PLEASE REPLY ASAP.

WE THANK YOU FOR YOUR COOPERATION.

BEST REGARDS,
PETER THOMAS
IMPORTER COORDINATOR
RETTO MACHINE INC.

2** Industrial Boulevard
Sauk Rapids, MN 5637* USA
PHONE: 320-656-28**
FAX: 320-656-28**
E-MAIL: peter@retto.com

Email 4

Original Message -----
From: BAILLIE HARDWARE SUPPLIER LTD
To: Mr. Peter Thomas
Sent: Friday, October 15, 201* 2:12 PM
Subject: CONFIRMATION FOR L/C

DEAR MR. THOMAS,

THANK YOU FOR YOUR E-MAIL ONE HOUR AGO.

IF YOUR OPENING BANK HAS NO RELATIONSHIP WITH OUR REFERRED CONFIRMING BANK, THEN PLEASE ASK YOUR BANKER TO CONFIRM THE L/C THROUGH A BANK WHO HAS BRANCH IN CHINA.

AS IT IS AN L/C AT 60DAYS' SIGHT, THE CONFIRMING CHARGES WILL BE FOR OUR ACCOUNT.

YOU MAY REST ASSURED THAT OUR PRODUCTS WILL BE TO YOUR ENTIRE SATISFACTION.

WE LOOK FORWARD TO YOUR FULL COOPERATION!

BEST REGARDS,
CHANGLIN SUN
GENERAL MANAGER

Shanghai Lihua Imp. & Exp. Co., Ltd.
Rm. 606 Plaza Building,   Fax: 86-21-642578**
1302 Meilong Road, 200237   Tel: 86-21-642578**
Shanghai, People's Republic of China   E-mail: lihua88@alibaba.com

Email 5

From: damai-SALES(163) damai-sales@vip.163.com
To: angela <angela@ttry.com>
Cc: haomai-service <haomai-service@vip.163.com>
Subject: Urgent Shipment for DQ027!
Date: 201*/4/23 14:42:17

Dear Angela,

What happened to your forwarder? They told us that they would arrange shipment by vessel on Apr. 30th! This means when the vessel leaves Shanghai, the shipping company will take at least 3 working days to issue the B/L. And from May 1st to 3rd we will have Labor Holiday, and on 4th we will have Youth Holiday. And then your forwarder will issue the invoice for us to pay them the domestic transportation cost, and then they will send us the original B/L. So the B/L will arrive at our side very late absolutely after 7th. However this is the expired date for L/C!

Besides, your L/C says that the expired place is in your country, so even we could send documents through our bank on 6th, it takes at least 3 days to deliver by TNT to your bank!

For this order, we have finished production, inspection earlier within the validity and last date of shipment. But it was your forwarder who delayed again and again.

In the beginning, we thought that since we are old friends with many years cooperation, it is not a

Unit Nine Terms of Payment

big problem even such delay caused discrepancy for us against L/C and caused some unnecessary and extra bank cost. But now, it is too much delay and even causes expiry of L/C! We could not accept such things happening!

So kindly please urgently extend your L/C for last date of shipment to "before May 1st" and the expiry date of L/C to "May 15th", and expired place is in Shanghai, China!

FUTURE COOPERATION

In future, for L/C terms, please:

  1) leave enough days for last date of shipment;
  2) leave enough days for L/C validity;
  3) stipulate expired place of L/C is in "Shanghai, China"!

  Otherwise, we will always meet such headaches and problems, which is not our fault!

Best Regards,
Jim
Manager of Export & Client Dept.
Shanghai Lihua Imp. & Exp. Co., Ltd.

Pattern H of Business Letters

As an exporter, you have to make your foreign buyers understand your aimed terms of payment.

When replying, you acknowledge it if the terms of payment are exactly in compliance with your request, and assure the buyer of your high quality and quick delivery; if not, you can make some adjustments or just decline it so as to avoid bad debts arising from dishonest importers.

Relevant Terms

remittance 汇付	collection 托收
Telegraphic Transfer 电汇	Mail Transfer 信汇
Demand Transfer 票汇	Documents against Payment 付款交单
Documents against Acceptance 承兑交单	Factoring 保理
Banker's Letter of Guarantee 银行保函	Sight L/C 即期信用证
Time or Usance L/C 远期信用证	Transferable L/C 可转让信用证
back-to-back L/C 背对背信用证	Revolving L/C 循环信用证
Reciprocal L/C 对开信用证 1	Anticipatory L/C 预支信用证
Standby L/C 备用信用证	irrevocable L/C 不可撤销的信用证
confirmed L/C 保兑的信用证	Divisible L/C 可以分割的信用证
L/C without recourse 不可追索的信用证	Documentary L/C 跟单信用证

续表

Clean L/C 光票信用证	packing credit 打包信用证
amendment 修改，修改件	bearer 持票人
Bill of Exchange 汇票	endorsement 背书
discrepancies 不符点	date of issue 签发日
date of expiry 到期日	Sight Draft 即期汇票
presentation 提示	dishonor 拒付
negotiation 议付	the opener (buyer, applicant) 开证人(买方，申请人)
the issuer (the issuing, opening, establishing bank) 签发人(开证行)	the advising bank (notifying bank) 通知行(通知行)
the drawer (seller, beneficiary) 出票人(卖方，受益人)	the drawee (buyer) 受票人，付款人(买方)
the negotiating bank 议付行	the reimbursing bank 偿付行
remitting bank 寄单银行	collecting bank 托收银行

Useful Phrases

make an exception of sb./sth. 把某人(事)当作例外	pave the way for 为……铺平道路
to one's disappointment 使某人失望	to be in exact accordance with 与……完全一致
to be ready for dispatch 备妥待运	at one's earliest convenience 在某人方便的第一时间
cause sb. much inconvenience 给某人带来诸多不便	fail to 未能
draw a draft on sb. 给某人开出汇票	in due time 在适当的时候
owing to 由于	wholly rest with sb. 完全取决于某人
according to 按照	take immediate action to 立即采取行动
take sth. into account 把某事考虑进去	in all seriousness 非常严肃地
arising from 产生于	as follows 如下
under such circumstances 在如此的环境下	go through 经历，检查，浏览
at the latest 最迟	apply for 申请
on examination 经检查	on perusal 经审阅
amend sth. to read 将……修改为	make necessary amendments 做必要的修改
extend A & B to C & D respectively 将A和B分别延展到C和D	result in 导致
result from 起因于	to our mutual satisfaction 相互满意

Unit Nine   Terms of Payment

Summary

The traditional modes of payment in international trade include remittance, collection and letter of credit. Chinese exporters prefer to accept payment by L/C, which is not as safe as our imagination.

Small-medium exporters can also take advantage of Factoring, Forfeiting and export insurance to reduce business risks.

A debt collection agency is helpful to recovery of overdue debts.

Exercises

I. Questions for review

1. What are the three categories of mode of payment in international trade?
2. Why do we think L/C is not so safe as our imagination?

II. Choose the best answer

1. Now we have two modes _____ payment when we transact with clients in your country.
   A. on   B. to   C. of   D. in

2. First, they use foreign exchange outside their country to advance 30% _____ T/T, then we start to produce.
   A. on   B. into   C. by   D. with

3. After shipment is effected, we will email the B/L, INVOICE and PACKING LIST to the client _____ confirmation.
   A. on   B. to   C. for   D. in

4. Then the client should pay the remaining 70% by T/T. When we receive remittance, we will send all documents _____ courier as soon as possible.
   A. by   B. into   C. in   D. with

5. Second, they can also inform us _____ the total amount of the L/C before its establishment.
   A. on   B. to   C. of   D. in

6. After their government approves it, the client can issue the L/C _____ our favor.
   A. on   B. to   C. of   D. in

7. But government's approval needs much time and a lot of procedures. _____, the second mode is much more inconvenient.
   A. Beside   B. Besides   C. Expert   D. Therefore

8. If you have better method _____ payment, please do not hesitate to tell us. We await your final confirmation.

      A. on   B. to   C. of   D. in

9. Thank you for your E-mail of Sep. 3. We will have to wait for one more week for the Government's issuing authorization _____ foreign exchange.

      A. in   B. for   C. at   D. to

10. In case we fail to receive the authorization, we will use our own funds in USA to make payment. We trust that there will be no problem _____ all.

      A. in   B. for   C. at   D. to

11. The designs are agreeable _____ the taste of this market.

      A. in   B. on   C. at   D. to

12. That three of managers in our company will go to the fair _____ certain.

      A. was   B. were   C. are   D. is

13. We've got only a few sewing machines in stock, because all the rest _____ .

      A. is sold out   B. has been sold out

      C. have been sold out   D. are sold out

14. The manager does not allow _____ the prices.

      A. to cut down B. cut down C. us cut down D. cutting down

15. The shirts _____ in polythene bags or in cartons at seller's option.

      A. are to be packed   B. will be packed

      C. are packed   D. were packed

16. It's too late to go to the negotiation now; _____ I am very tired.

      A. beside   B. besides   C. expert   D. except for

17. We wish to thank you _____ the end-users.

      A. to the interest of   B. for the benefit of

      C. on behalf of   D. to the advantage of

18. They buy these goods _____ quantities.

      A. on   B. to   C. to   D. in

19. Your price is somewhat _____ the high side as compared with those of the rival goods.

      A. in   B. at   C. on   D. of

20. We propose to turn the whole lot over to you, once for all, with a 20% discount _____ their list price.

      A. in   B. at   C. off   D. from

III. Translate the following sentences into Chinese

1. In order to let us finish our production schedule in time, please open the L/C before May 12, 201*. We will keep you informed of the progress of your order.

2. Because this is the first transaction concluded between us, we can only accept payment on sight L/C basis at the present. After several smooth and satisfactory transactions, we may take D/P or other flexible terms of payment into consideration.

3. Yesterday I did remit you USD3,000 and will remit you USD 5,000 shortly. The

Unit Nine Terms of Payment

balance I would try to remit you on time.

4. Can you accept L/C at 60 days' sight for our duplicate order?

5. We regret to note that our draft drawn on you on the terms of D/P 30 days after sight was dishonored.

6. As an exceptional case, we are prepared to accept payment for your first order on a D/P basis.

7. Payment: By 100% confirmed & irrevocable L/C to be available by sight draft, reaching the seller 30 days before the month of shipment, remaining valid for negotiation in China for another 21 days after the prescribed time of shipment, allowing partial shipments.

8. We have carefully examined the terms and conditions stipulated in your L/C, but we regret to inform you that we found some mistakes in the L/C which you have to instruct your banker to make the following amendments.

9. We hope the amendment to the L/C can reach here before July 6, 201*. Otherwise, shipment can't be effected as requested.

10. You can select Bank Transfer/Internet Banking as your method of Payment. Our bank account details are as follows... Bank transfer funds are usually received within 2 working days. Goods will be dispatched upon receipt of payment.

Optional part

11. As we discussed on phone, your terms of payment is too strict for us because we have been accustomed to establishing an L/C at 60 days' sight while you requested for a sight L/C.

12. I am sure you still remember that Croesus and Eddington showed you, during their visit to your factory in Nanjing, a list of our Recent Transactions, in which you could find that all our suppliers in your area allow us to make payment by an L/C at 60 days' sight.

13. In fact, we enjoy a very good reputation of paying fully and promptly. As you know, we are a really big dealer from EU. I'd like to remind you that a sight L/C would cause us much inconvenience.

14. Considering our further cooperation in future, would you please also allow us the same conditions as our other suppliers? We hope that you will be able to accept our suggestion.

15. As for the pricing, we can adopt L/C during the first six months, but thereafter, we shall change the mode of payment that we have discussed during our meeting.

IV. Translate the following sentences into English

1. 鉴于我们之间的友好合作，我们准备接受60天远期付款交单的支付条件。
2. 在这个促销阶段我们愿意接受付款交单的支付条件，但不接受承兑交单。
3. 我们遗憾地通知你方我们的惯例是不接受承兑交单的支付条件。
4. 该跟单信用证凭下列单据提示可兑付。
5. 请务必尽早开立相关信用证，以便使我们能够在规定的时限内安排装运。
6. 装船日期日益临近，但我们至今仍未收到相关信用证，请立即给我们回复。
7. 你方第118号订单项下的货物备妥待运已有相当时日，你方立即开出相关信用证是明智的。否则，你们将不能在圣诞节前拿到这批货物。

8. 我们已经收到相关信用证，但是我们发现有以下不符点：

9. 我们的售货确认书规定本次交易允许的佣金是 3%，但我们发现你们信用证要 5% 的佣金，所以要求你方通知银行修改信用证。

10. 请将装船期和你方第 CHW 118 号信用证的有效期分别延展到 7 月 15 日和 8 月 2 日，并安排好修改通知要在 6 月 15 日之前到达我方。

V. Case Study

Case One

From: wick@yahoo.com [mailto: lihua88@alibaba.com]
Sent: Saturday, September 2, 201*,11:13 AM
To: Lily
Subject: DISHONOUR

Dear Lily,

Bank has already rejected the documents and is waiting for our confirmation for making payment.

Following are the options to solve this problem——

1. As your invoice for 1% Free spare parts is USD1682.40 (instead of USD 2843.20); we can request bank to release payment by deducting the difference of US$1682.40. This is the simplest way of solving it. But we don't want to do that.

2. You may request your bank to call back for the wrong docs and submit new docs with correct invoice.

Then you will get full payment, but you must prove that you have sent spare parts worthy USD2843.20. If you have sent less spare parts, you should arrange to ship out short qty in next lot.

Regards,
Wick Walker

From: lihua88@alibaba.com [mailto: wick@yahoo.com]
Sent: Saturday, Sept.2, 201* 8:13 PM
To: Wick Walker
Subject: Re: Free of Charge Spare Parts

Dear Wick,

On going into the matter we find that a mistake was indeed made in the invoice value for the FOC spare parts. However, the fact is that we had sent you the spares amounting to even more than USD2843.20. You can count the quantity of the spare parts. As you took delivery of the spare parts, please check it tomorrow. I am sure you need the actual spare parts, instead of a piece of an invoice. Of course, I will contact our bank and let them give you the right invoice tomorrow.

We are preparing the goods for your next two orders. In consideration of our long-term friendly business relations, kindly please let your bank make payment right after you check it.

We are looking forward to your favorable reply as soon as possible.

Yours sincerely,
Lily

Case Two

----- Original Message ----- A
From: lihua88@alibaba.com
To: Wick Walker
Sent: Thursday, August 25, 201* 3:21 PM
Subject: SHIPMENT & PAYMENT

Dear Friend Wick Walker,
PAYMENT FOR GR586
We have shipped the GR586 on August 9.

As there is a discrepancy between the date of shipment and the stipulations in the covering L/C, and you have promised to accept this discrepancy, and we also did not ask you to amend your L/C accordingly, so kindly please contact your bank to accept it.

All the documents have been sent through our bank to your opening bank. And your opening bank should have received all documents. Please contact them immediately. Also the goods should arrive at the port of destination.

We appreciate your close cooperation!
Best wishes,
Henry

----- Original Message ----- B
From: Wick Walker
To: lihua88@alibaba.com
Sent: Friday, August 25, 201* 4:08 PM
Subject: Re: SHIPMENT & PAYMENT

DEAR HENRY,
PLEASE DON'T WORRY. WE WILL ACCEPT THESE DOCUMENTS AND MAKE PAYMENT ALTHOUGH DISCREPANCY IS FOUND. PLEASE FEEL FREE TO CONTACT US AT ANY TIME. WE WILL FOLLOW THESE DOCUMENTS UNTIL YOU GET THE MONEY.
BEST REGARDS,
WALKER

----- Original Message ----- C

From: huali88@alibaba.com
To: Wick Walker
Sent: Thursday, August 28, 201* 8:21 AM
Subject: SHIPMENT & PAYMENT

Dear Walker,

PAYMENT FOR GR586

Thanks for your e-mail dated August 25. Today I have just come back from an international fair in Dalian. Fortunately, our products meet a warm reception from Russian and Korean customers.

Thanks for your confirmation on accepting the discrepancy and payment. We will contact the bank for the payment. I trust our mutual understanding and support will surely lead to further development of our cooperation. Thank you very much indeed.

Best Regards,
Henry

VI. Discussion

How to reduce the risks of debt collection for exporters?

Unit Ten

Packing

Introduction

Except from bulk cargo and nude cargo, most cargos need to be packed in a proper way. Adequate packing prevents the goods from being damaged during transit, and a well packaged cargo facilitates handling and transportation. Packing also conveys substantial information to customers.

According to the function of packing, it can be divided into two kinds: transport packing and sales packing.

Transport packing is also called large packing or outer packing, i.e. packing for transportation. There are many packing containers used in international market, such as carton, sack, wooden case, crate, corrugated carton, skeleton case, wooden drum, iron drum, plastic cask, gunny bag, cloth bag, paper bag, plastic bag, bundle, bale, box, can/tin, carboy, pallet and container, etc. On the outer packing, you can always find the shipping mark, indicative mark and warning mark as well as weight, measurement and place of origin.

Sales packing is also called small packing, inner packing or immediate packing, on which you can always find product code.

The packing clause is an important one in a Contract in international trade. The exporter shall make delivery in exact accordance with the requests of packaging set forth in it.

Business Letters

Email 1

To: quew@163.com
Subject: PACKING

Dear Mr. Jack Pittman,
Now we are manufacturing the products against your Order No. 562. But we are confused with the sales packing of box. Which color should we use for the model of QT-3628 & QT3632, with RED & BULE or RED & BLACK? Please inform us of your requirement as soon as possible.
Besides, we made a mistake on the final page of P/I for QT-3628. The correct total quantity is 86,350 instead of 85,350. We are sorry for the inconvenience arising from our negligence.

Yours sincerely,
Henry
Sales Manager

Shanghai Lihua Imp. & Exp. Co., Ltd.

Unit Ten Packing

Rm. 606 Plaza Building,   Fax: 86-21-642578**
1302 Meilong Road, 200237   Tel: 86-21-642578**
Shanghai, People's Republic of China   E-mail: lihua88@alibaba.com

+*

This e-mail is private and confidential, it is for use only by the intended recipient(s). It may contain privileged information and should not be forwarded, copied or disclosed in any manner to any person without the express consent of the sender/author. If this message is not addressed to you or if you are not responsible for the delivery of this message to the addressee. PLEASE DELETE THIS MESSAGE. We would be grateful if you would notify us of your receipt and deletion of this message.

+

Email 2

To: peter@retto.com
Subject: Carton

Dear Henry,

We need a better design for this batch of cartons, because attractive designs will be good for sales promotion. We hope you will be able to send us your improved designs for these cartons within three weeks. It's a good idea for you to send us your new designs by email. You can take several pictures first and then send them for our consideration.

For this order, please make 300 sets in beige and 150 sets in white for the machine body. In the meantime, please make the transparent lid and control panel in light blue.

Your full cooperation is appreciated.

Best wishes,
PETER THOMAS
IMPORTER COORDINATOR
RETTO MACHINE INC.

2** Industrial Boulevard
Sauk Rapids, MN 5637* USA
PHONE: 320-656-28**
FAX: 320-656-28**
E-MAIL: peter@retto.com

Email 3

To: peter@retto.com
Subject: Packing for Wind Musical Instruments

Dear Peter,

In reply to your email of Oct. 20 inquiring about the packing of our wind musical instruments, we wish to answer as follows:

Our Trumpets are packed in strong polythene bags, one bag for one trumpet, a dozen of trumpets to a carton, 200 cartons to a 20' container. Mouth organs are packed in boxes, one box lined with stout, damp-resisting paper for one mouth organ, 80 boxes to a carton, 220 cartons to a 20' container. Your required shipping mark is also stenciled on the package. If you have any good ideas in this respect, please let us know ASAP so as to improve our packing for the next shipment. The first two containers will be shipped out from Shanghai by the end of this month.

Best wishes,
Henry
Export Manager

Shanghai Lihua Imp. & Exp. Co., Ltd.
Rm. 606 Plaza Building,   Fax: 86-21-642578**
1302 Meilong Road, 200237   Tel: 86-21-642578**
Shanghai, People's Republic of China   E-mail: lihua88@alibaba.com

Email 4

To: nobel88@ni.co.nz
Subject: Improving Our Packing

Dear Donald,

I was out when you called me this morning. I understand you attach great importance to our packing. Now I am glad to tell you that we are prepared to improve our packing as follows:

1) Model-251: Header Card is used. We will design the HEADER CARD especially for you, and print your brand name on the HEADER CARD. If you use the inner packing, the price will be increased by USD0.12/PC for extra packing charge.

2) Model-253: We confirm it is 220PCS/CTN. Your order is 2,200PCS, 10 cartons in total.

3) Model-256: As for the color of the box used, please send us your photos by email for our reference.

We are looking forward to your early reply.

Best wishes,
Henry,
Export Manager

Shanghai Lihua Imp. & Exp. Co., Ltd.
Rm. 606 Plaza Building,   Fax: 86-21-642578**
1302 Meilong Road, 200237   Tel: 86-21-642578**
Shanghai, People's Republic of China   E-mail: lihua88@alibaba.com

Unit Ten Packing

Email 5

From: henry66 (163) <henry66@vip.163.com>
To: steve88@codetel.net.do
Cc: hardwaresales@vip.163.com
Subject: Packing Problem
Importance: High

Dear Steve,

Thank you for your feedback on the packing.

However, for your information, we are a factory specializing in business in the South America market. All of our no-brand packages have Spanish Description. They are very popular in Venezuela, Mexico and Panama, etc.

So if you need the packages only with English Description, we will have to open new package edition. Usually, the packing factory will charge us RMB500 for each new edition. In your orders, there are 6 items to be opened. Totally it will be RMB3,000.

Because they will be the new editions, we would like to design them only for you. You may tell us the style you like. We will send you the design very soon for your confirmation.

On the other hand, last week, I just informed Angela that these orders are going to be finished soon, probably in the beginning of July. Our workers are making the final examination and packing. All the inner packages and outer cartons have been ready. And we will have to change the inner box. We estimate the manpower cost will be USD100. So totally, please add USD 500. into the remaining T/T of these orders.

Also please remember to inform us of the new packing style ASAP, because we will finish the design very soon in order to avoid delay in the shipment.

Thank you for your cooperation.

Best Wishes,
Henry
Export Manager
Shanghai Lihua Imp. & Exp. Co., Ltd.
Rm. 606 Plaza Building,   Fax: 0086-21-642578**
1302 Meilong Road, 200237   Tel: 0086-21-642578**
Shanghai, People's Republic of China   www.betterhardware.com

---

Pattern I of Business Letters

An importer shall make the exporter understand his requirements for inner packing or outer packing so as to avoid the subsequent disputes, vice versa. Such business letter should mention the following particulars unless both sides have reached a consensus on it before:

a) what the packing container is;

b) what the marking on export package looks like;

c) what kind of directions or warnings regarding manner of handling, loading, lifting, etc. is used;

d) who will be responsible for faulty packing, if any.

Relevant Terms

packing list 装箱单	Indicative Mark 指示性标志
Warning Mark 警示性标志	neutral packing 中性包装
inner packing 内包装	selling packing 销售包装
outer packing 外包装	transport packing 运输包装
batch number 批号	gunny bag 麻袋
cloth bag 布袋	iron drum 铁桶
wooden case 木箱	plywood case 三夹板箱
veneer case 薄板箱	crate 板条箱，柳条箱
tin 罐	carboy 大玻璃瓶
stuffing material 填充材料	wood shavings 刨花
Packing Clause 包装条款	Inspection Certificate 检验证书

Useful Phrases

during transit 在运输途中	to have sth. packed in 将某物装入
to be packed in 装入	to be lined with 用……做内衬
to have an inner lining of 有……做内衬	pile up 堆积
shift one's responsibilities 推卸责任	on the wharf 在码头上
make necessary improvements 作必要的改进	assure sb. of sth./that… 向某人保证……
on account of 因为	at this end 在我们这头
at your end 在你们那头	for one's perusal 供某人审阅

Summary

Packing is a sensitive subject, which often leads to trade disputes. An exporter shall make delivery in exact accordance with the requests of packaging set forth in the relative contract.

Both transport packing and sales packing are very important to smooth execution of an order.

Unit Ten Packing

Exercises

I. Questions for review

1. What is the function of packing?
2. What are the kinds of packing according to its function?

II. Choose the best answer

1. We are one ____ the largest distributors of ceramic products and building materials in the Brazilian Market and also one of the largest wholesalers in Latin America.
   A. for   B. at   C. of   D. with

2. Fortunately, we have received a great demand ____ your products, so we ask you to kindly email us more details of your relative products along with price lists and pictures and weight of each quoted item if possible.
   A. for   B. at   C. of   D. with

3. Enclosed please find the pictures of the products our clients are currently handling, these are the specific specifications we are searching ____.
   A. for   B. of   C. with   D. in

4. Please be so kind to send the digital pictures of the referred products so that we can manage to go ahead presenting your products ____ the clients.
   A. for   B. at   C. on   D. to

5. As regards the outer packing for our products, we will change the color ____ blue and white, and also make adjustment for the description accordingly.
   A. for   B. at   C. on   D. to

6. We are able to put code bar to each item and do French labels. Enclosed please find the packing design ____ your confirmation. If you have any suggestions, please let us know as early as possible.
   A. for   B. at   C. on   D. with

7. Please contact the agent below and if possible try to deliver the goods to their warehouse ____ the end of the week. Thank you in advance.
   A. of   B. before   C. onto   D. with

8. For the consignment by air, please send it ____ DHL.
   A. for   B. of   C. with   D. by

9. Please do not forget to keep the attached invoice ____ the package, so that it can be used by custom clearance in BULGARIA.
   A. of   B. before   C. onto   D. outside

10. As regards the rest of the order, could you please tell us when you will be ready to ship the order ____ sea?

        A. for   B. of   C. with   D. by

11. All of our products are ____ first quality.
    A. for   B. at   C. of   D. with

12. We should be pleased to send you our samples for your consideration, ____ our own expense.
    A. for   B. at   C. on   D. to

13. We produce decorative fabrics ____ different kinds.
    A. for   B. of   C. with   D. in

14. _____ came to the fair.
    A. A customer of Tom's   B. Tom's a customer
    C. A Tom's customer   D. A customer of Tom

15. ____ please find our price list.
    A. Enclose   B. Enclosed   C. Enclosing   D. Be enclosed

16. We don't know that canned goods ____ the scope of your business activities.
    A. meet   B. fall within   C. reach   D. get into

17. We hope that you will dispatch the goods ____ us before Aug. 15.
    A. reach   B. reaching   C. reached   D. to reach

18. We should appreciate it if you would let us have an ample ____ of samples for free distribution.
    A. supply   B. quantity   C. amount   D. sum

19. Type 26 is ____, so it's price is considerably higher than that of last year.
    A. in short supply   B. in free supply
    C. out of supply   D. for supply

20. We spent a ____ sum of money on samples.
    A. considerate   B. considerable   C. considering   D. consideration

III. Translate the following sentences into Chinese

1. The continued increases in freight costs force us to seek improved packing methods. Could you suggest a more economic packing method for our products?

2. In addition to the production of standard packing material, we also engage in individual and special packing.

3. We hope that you can make some improvements in the packing. Attractive sales packing would help us sell the goods.

4. We are glad to know that you have developed a new packing method whereby breakable items are protected from damage through envelopment in chemical foam. Please give us more details.

5. As far as the outer packing is concerned, we will pack the goods 10 dozen to a carton, gross weight around 25 kilos a carton.

6. Further testing is required before we can recommend a new packing unit to you. Only

after successful results are obtained can we give you a unit price.

7. Apparently, there are special regulations applying to the use of wood packing to certain countries. Could you give us more detailed information on the subject?

8. When you pack, please put 2 or 3 different designs and colors in each box.

9. Chemical foaming represents a new method in the field of packing. Enclosed please find a brochure from which you will learn more about the possibilities of application.

10. We usually do the labeling ourselves as we are responsible for the brand labels of our own products.

Optional Part

11. Each sweater should be packed into an individual polybag, 5 dozens to a carton bound with two iron straps outside.

12. We think that the result of packing in cartons proved to be satisfactory, you may continue using such packing in future.

13. Can you tell me how you usually pack your toys when you export them?

14. We think that these cartons are well protected against moisture by plastic lining.

15. We trust that you will give special care to the packing in order to avoid damage in transit.

IV. Translate the following sentences into English

1. 我们对每一副护腿采用一个聚乙烯包装袋。
2. 我们想把纸板箱包装改为金属箔材料包装。
3. 对这批玩具我们想用硬纸板箱包装。
4. 我们专营塑料包装材料的开发。
5. 我们希望你们采取措施用金属条加固这种纸板箱。
6. 这样的包装方便我们分拨给零售商。
7. 我们将感谢你们对改进包装提出的建议。
8. 包装时请考虑到下面两种情形：这些盒子在我们这边很可能遭遇野蛮装卸；它们必须能承受在糟糕的路面上运输。
9. 我们将衬衫包装在塑料做内衬的防水的纸板箱内，并且用金属条加固。
10. 这种又轻又结实的箱子能节约舱位，并且便于储存和分拨货物。

V. Case Study

Case A

To: lihua88@alibaba.com

Subject: Packing

Dear Sirs,

I'm very glad to receive your email dated September 15, but I didn't receive any quotation, can you re-send it? I hope we can start a long and good relationship with you and your company.

I would like to know if you could email me some pictures of your products, since I tried to see your products at your website, but I can't. I don't know whether there are some problems with the site or not, but it will be easier if you send me the pictures by email together with the quotation, also I appreciate it if you send me an illustrated catalogue for all the products you can offer us, because I want to see your sales packing which is important to our sales promotion. I have some questions: what kind of materials do you use in your package? Are you able to develop new designs based on our requirements? Please let me know about all these matters.

We are looking forward to early reply.

Yours sincerely,
Michael

Case B

To: aloha@online.com.fr

Subject: Improving Our Packing for Artificial Flowers

Dear Philips,

As regards the outer packing for our products, we will change the color to blue and white, and also make adjustment for the description accordingly.

We are able to put code bar to each item and do French labels. Enclosed please find the packing design for your confirmation. If you have any suggestions, please let us know as early as possible.

We hope that our new packing will meet your approval.

Best wishes,
Henry

VI. Discussion

1. Give an example to show the importance of outer packing.
2. Give an example to show the importance of inner packing.
3. How to reduce the cost of inner packing while making it more attractive?

Try to make a list of different materials used for inner packing and outer packing in international trade.

Unit Eleven

Insurance

Introduction

Whatever mode of transport is adopted, there will be many risks to cargo at any stage of the transit. So, exporters or importers need to cover insurance on their goods with insurance companies against different risks.

Cargo transportation insurance falls into the category of property insurance. There are basically six principles that shall be sought after in such insurance: Insurable Interest Principle, Bona Fide Principle, Immediate Cause Principle, Subrogation Principle, Indemnification Principle and Share Principle.

Cargo transportation insurance can be classified into ocean marine cargo insurance, overland transportation insurance, air transportation cargo insurance and parcel post insurance.

The ocean marine cargo insurance mainly includes ocean transportation cargo insurance, ocean transportation cargo war insurance, ocean transportation frozen cargo insurance and ocean transportation wood-oil bulk insurance.

The overland transportation insurance chiefly consists of overland transportation cargo insurance, overland transportation cargo war insurance and overland transportation frozen cargo insurance.

The air transportation cargo insurance is made up with air transportation insurance, air transportation all risks and air transportation cargo war risks.

The parcel post insurance refers to parcel post risks, parcel post all risks and parcel post war risks.

Business Letters

Email 1

To: lihua88@alibaba.com
Subject: INSURANCE ON ORDER NO.152

Dear Henry:

With reference to our Order No.152 for 585 cartons of hardware, we'd like to request you to effect insurance on them for us at your end.

As our order is placed on a CFR basis, we shall be much obliged if you agree with us. The main reason why we changed our mind is that we found the People's Insurance Company of China charges premiums at lower rates. So, we ask you to cover our Order against All Risks for 110% of the invoice value with the PICC.

We will remit you the premium by T/T right after you finish it. Of course, we hope that our future transactions will be concluded on the basis of CIF.

Unit Eleven Insurance

We are very sorry for the inconvenience arising from this email.

Yours truly,
PETER THOMAS
IMPORTER COORDINATOR
RETTO MACHINE INC.

2** Industrial Boulevard
Sauk Rapids, MN 5637* USA
PHONE: 320-656-28**
FAX: 320-656-28**
E-MAIL: peter@retto.com

Email 2

To: peter@retto.com
Subject: INSURANCE ON ORDER NO.152

Dear Peter:

We have received your email of Oct.18, requesting us to arrange insurance on your Order No.152 for your account.

We are pleased to advise you that we have insured your goods with the PICC against All Risks for USD12100.00. The insurance policy is to be sent to you after five days. Please remit the premium to us by T/T upon receipt of our Debit Note.

For your information, this batch of goods has been ready for shipment. The liner will leave for your port as scheduled. We will send you a Shipping Advice very soon.

Best wishes,
Henry
General Manager

Shanghai Lihua Imp. & Exp. Co., Ltd.
Rm. 606 Plaza Building,   Fax: 86-21-642578**
1302 Meilong Road, 200237   Tel: 86-21-642578**
Shanghai, People's Republic of China   E-mail: lihua88@alibaba.com

Email 3

To: lihua88@alibaba.com
Subject: INSURANCE ON ORDER NO.163

Dear Henry,

We are glad to know that our Order No.163 for your washers has been ready for shipment. According to our Contract No. 257, the goods should be insured against All Risks. However, the current situation in the Middle East is becoming more complicated and dangerous. We think that we need to cover this order against War Risk too. Of course, the extra premium will be for our account. Please forgive us for troubling you so much.

We are looking forward to your close cooperation.

Your sincerely,
Wick Coacher
Tom Consumption Group

5**, Sayem Aldaher Street
Golail Industrial Zone
P.O. Box 9**
Jeddah, 21421
Saudi Arabia
Tel: 0096626823*** Ext: 3**
Fax: 0096626826***
Email: wick@ qwev.net
Web sites: www.qwev.net

Email 4

To: maggrett@t&einsurance.com
Subject: Ask for Favorable Rate

Dear Ms Maggrett Coacher,

We are going to ship two 40' Containers HQ to Stockholm, in which Accordions and Mouth Organs are contained. They are to be shipped by M/V "Yuanfan" which leaves Shanghai on Aug. 3 and is estimated to arrive at the destination on Sept.1.

Enclosed please find the particulars of this consignment, which is to be insured against All Risks from port to port. We shall be much obliged if you could quote us a favorable rate.

We are look forward to your reply at your earliest convenience.

Best regards,
Henry Cai
General Manager

Unit Eleven Insurance

Shanghai Lihua Imp. & Exp. Co., Ltd.
Rm. 606 Plaza Building,   Fax: 86-21-642578**
1302 Meilong Road, 200237   Tel: 86-21-642578**
Shanghai, People's Republic of China   E-mail: lihua88@alibaba.com

Email 5

To: philips@163.com
Subject: the relevant documents to be submitted

Dear Sir or Madam:

We are sorry to know that you will have to file a claim with our insurance agent in your city. However, our company enjoys a high reputation in settling claims promptly and equitably. So, we are pleased to inform you that you are required to submit the following documents in presenting a claim to our agent:

    a) Original Policy or Certificate of Insurance, original or copy of B/L, Invoice and Packing List;

    b) Certificate of Loss or Damage and/or Short-landed memo and Survey Report;

    c) Statement of Claim.

We'd like to draw your attention to the fact that an insurance claim should be submitted to our agent as promptly as possible so as to provide the latter with ample time to pursue recovery from the relative party in fault.

We hope that everything will go smoothly. For further information, please contact us or our agent in your city directly.

Best wishes,
Maggrett Coacher
Director

Customer Service Dept.
T & E Insurance Co.,Ltd.

Pattern J of Business Letters

    Generally speaking, the following information should be stated clearly in a letter covering insurance, such as subject matter, insurance coverage, insurance amount, insurance premium, insurance rate, the insurer, etc.

Relevant Terms

F.P.A. (Free from Particular Average)平安险	W.A. / W.P.A (With Average or With Particular Average) 水渍险
All Risks 一切险	War Risk 战争险
Risk of Leakage 渗漏险	Risk of Rust 锈蚀险
Risk of Shortage 货差险	T.P.N.D. (Theft, Pilferage & Non-delivery) 偷窃、提货不着险
Export Credit Insurance 出口信用保险	Subject Matter Insured 保险标的
Sum Insured 保险金额	Insurance Agent 保险代理人
Insurance Policy 保险单	Insurance Certificate 保险凭证
Open Policy 预约保险单	insurance premium 保险费
insurance claim 保险索赔	insurance clause 保险条款
reinsurance 再保险	

Useful Phrases

to meet one's approval 得到某人的批准	for one's account 记在某人的账上
in the presence of 在某人在场	in advance 预先
at lower rates 以更低的费率	to effect insurance on sth. against/with/at/for 投保
to provide insurance 投保	to take out insurance 投保
to arrange insurance 投保	to cover insurance 投保
to enjoy high prestige in 享有很高的声誉	to submit an insurance claim 提交保险索赔
to settle claims 理赔	to compensate for 补偿
usual practice 惯例	to vary with 随……而变
for 110% of the invoice value 按发票金额的110%投保	to get in touch with 与……接触，联系
to go contrary to 违背	to have no objection to 不反对

Summary

Cargo transportation insurance falls into the category of property insurance. There are basically six principles that shall be sought after in such insurance.

Cargo transportation insurance can be classified into ocean marine cargo insurance, overland transportation insurance, air transportation cargo insurance and parcel post insurance.

Importers and exporters have to arrange insurance on their goods against different risks for their own interest.

Exercises

I. Questions for review

1. What are the main insurance principles?
2. What are the types of cargo transportation insurance?
3. What do the basic risks cover?
4. What do the additional risks cover?
5. What does the general additional risk cover?
6. What does the special additional risk cover?
7. What are the six insurance coverages of Institute Cargo Clauses?

II. Choose the best answer

1. We will cover insurance on this batch of our products _____ 110% of the invoice value against All Risks.
    A. for   B. to   C. on   D. in
2. Your Order No.112 for our Silk Stockings will be covered _____ the PICC.
    A. for   B. with   C. on   D. in
3. The rate of premium _____ War Risk is 0.04%.
    A. for   B. with   C. on   D. against
4. The extra premium will be _____ the buyer's account.
    A. for   B. with   C. on   D. in
5. Samsung Fire & Marine Insurance Company (China), LTD. charges premium _____ a reasonable rate, so it is to your advantage to have your products insured with them.
    A. for   B. at   C. as   D. in
6. As your Order No.258 for our Silk Handkerchiefs was booked _____ CIF basis, insurance will be arranged at this end.
    A. for   B. with   C. on   D. in
7. As your Order No. 359 for our Pearls Necklaces, Bracelet and Earrings is placed on CFR basis, insurance will be arranged _____ your end.
    A. for   B. at   C. as   D. in
8. We can get a favorable rate of premium if we take _____ insurance with this insurance company.
    A. for   B. at   C. as   D. out
9. This batch of products is to be insured _____ All Risks based on warehouse to

warehouse clause.

    A. for   B. with   C. on   D. against

10. As the Gulf War broke out, the insurer had to charge all the insured _____ a higher rate.

    A. for   B. at   C. as   D. in

11. I sent out the samples _____ .

    A. four days   B. four days before

    C. four days ago   D. for four days

12. _____ Mr. Smith told me, he would import garments from China in the near future.

    A. According as   B. According with

    C. According to   D. In according with

13. His design is not acceptable _____ the buyer.

    A. for   B. to   C. on   D. in

14. Please _____ us of the name of the liner.

    A. advise   B. to inform   C. advising   D. give

15. We will give the factory _____ ten days to complete their production plan.

    A. the other   B. others   C. another   D. other

16. We rely on receiving your reply _____ .

    A. by return   B. in return   C. with return   D. on return

17. In _____ to your suggestions, our manufacturer has made improvement in the packing of the spare parts.

    A. reply   B. response   C. answer   D. respond

18. _____ be satisfactory to our customers, we can assure you that repeat orders will be placed.

    A. Would this trial order   B. This trial order should

    C. Should this trial order   D. This trial order would

19. We think your price is offered _____ high level.

    A. on the   B. at a   C. on a   D. at the

20. Nowadays art has become a _____ .

    A. merchandise   B. goods   C. commodity   D. cargo

III. Translate the following sentences into Chinese

1. How long is the period from the commencement to termination of insurance? The cover shall be limited to sixty days upon discharge of the insured goods from the seagoing vessel at the final port of discharge.

2. We enjoy high prestige in settling claims promptly and equitably. You are advised to insure your goods with us.

3. We adopt the warehouse to warehouse clause which is commonly used in international insurance.

4. For the coverage of All Risks, the insurance company shall be liable for total or partial

loss on land or sea of the insured goods within the period covered by the insurance.

5. If the goods, after arrival at the port of destination, are to be transported immediately to an inland city or other port, we may cover the inland insurance on your behalf and debit you with the additional premium.

6. If we conclude the business on CIF basis, what cover will you take out for the goods? We will only insure W.P.A.

7. Risk of breakage is classified under extraneous risks. We can cover the Risk of Breakage for you. Who will pay the premium for the risk of breakage? The additional premium is for the buyer's account.

8. As requested by you, we shall arrange insurance on the goods against All Risks and War Risk for 110% of the invoice value, which is our usual practice accepted by most of our customers.

9. As our order was placed on a CIF basis and you took out insurance, we should be grateful if you would take the matter up for us with the insurance company.

10. Please see to it that the above-mentioned goods are to be shipped before Sept. 16 and insured against All Risks for 130% of the invoice value. We know that, according to your usual practice, you insure the goods only for 110% of the invoice value, therefore, the extra premium will be for our account.

Optional Part

11. We will effect insurance against All Risks, as requested, charging the premium to the consignee.

12. For goods sold on CIF basis, insurance is arranged against All Risks & War Risk for 110% of the invoice value. If broader coverage is required, the extra premium involved will be for buyers' account.

13. Once the cargo is sent off, it is insured instantaneously.

14. Should any damage to the goods occur, a claim may be filed with the insurance agent at your end, who will undertake to compensate you for the loss sustained.

15. Since the premium varies with the insurance coverage, extra premium is for buyers' account should additional risks be required.

IV. Translate the following sentences into English

1. 请给我们为附页上列出的货物办理保险。
2. 我们是按 FOB 价达成交易的，所以由你方去投保。
3. 我们应按发票金额的 110%投保水渍险。
4. 对于按 CIF 价成交的货物，由我方按发票金额的 110%投保一切险。
5. 你们想投保什么险别？这次我们想要水渍险。
6. 你们保险公司通常承保什么险别？
7. 这批玩具将按仓至仓条款向中国人民保险公司投保一切险。
8. 我们已将 20 公吨的棉花按发票金额的 110%投保了一切险。

9. 我们附上一份检验证书和船运代理的声明，并希望上述索赔金额达 5000 美元的理赔不会产生困难。

保险索赔应尽早提交给保险公司或其代理人，以便使保险公司或其代理人有足够的时间向相关过失方追偿。

V. Case Study

Please calculate the CIF value of this order according to the following information:
Subject Matter Insured:
Order No.0626 for 200 cartons of electric toys
Sum Insured:
CFR value: USD6200.00 + 10% of the invoice value
To be covered against All Risks and War Risk
Rate of Premium: All Risks---0.65%, War Risk---0.05%

VI. Discussion

1. What should the insured do after he has chosen a kind of insurance coverage?
2. How does the insured make claim against the insurer?

Unit Twelve

Shipping Instructions and Shipping Advice

Introduction

There are many modes of transportation in international trade, such as seaway transportation, airway transportation, road transportation and railway transportation.

Seaway transportation is a widely accepted mode of transport and a majority of international trade is conveyed by maritime transport. Basically there are two types of ocean freight according to the assorted shipping vessels used, that is, liner business and tramp business.

Airway transportation plays a more important role in international conveyance of cargo for its many advantages over maritime transport, such as high speed, low risks, simplified documentation system, elimination of storage and capital tie-up. Of course, employment of air freight is still restricted due to its many weak points, such as limited carriage capacity and high expense.

Roadway transport, dissimilar to the other modes of transport, has its own distinctive features. Normally road vehicle can provide a door-to-door service without intermediate handling. Road transport has a spacious flexibility in that should circumstance demand a change in routing or a blockage of shipping services. It can also provide a reliable service with high quality.

Railway transportation is a mode of transportation through which the cargo is conveyed through railway. It is not affected by bad weather. Therefore, normal operation through the whole year is guaranteed. This mode of transport benefits from its large transport capacity and high transport continuance.

The most commonly used mode of transportation is seaway transportation because of its low freight cost.

If a transaction is concluded on CIF basis, the exporter needs to book shipping space or charter a ship. Of course, this complex process shall usually be handled by a professional shipping and forwarding agent. The exporter shall send a Shipping Instruction to the shipping company through the forwarding agent before goods are loaded. After goods are loaded on board, the exporter shall inform the foreign importer of particulars covering the shipment by sending a Shipping Advice.

Business Letters

Email 1

To: lihua66@alibaba.com
Subject: Arrangement before Shipment

Unit Twelve Shipping Instructions and Shipping Advice

Dear friend:

Thank you very much for your information covering the date of shipment. I hope everything will be perfect for both of us then we can do business for long term. So I need your help in making double check in some points as follows before shipment:

Please make sure there is no Chinese character on any print material. Please make sure there will be no grammatical mistakes with English words on print material. The origin and capacity should be marked as our design and should not be written anywhere else on other print material such as the control panel.

Please make sure all payments and shipping documents, such as contract, bill of lading, commercial invoice, packing list, country of origin, certificate of origin, certificate of quality and quantity, will be made correctly as indicated:

The brand name is "SUPER-YAK"

Model: M58JP, capacity: 5.0 kg.

We'd like to draw your attention to the fact that all the above notes are very important for our customs clearance because last time we met a big problem when importing refrigerator from the Chinese supplier. as we imported 120L refrigerator, unfortunately, they sent us model 132L. So we stuck in custom for quite a long time and finally had to pay a big penalty.

We hope everything will be ok with our first shipment and them we can start with next order soon.

Best regards,
Joerg Nordsieck
Area Manager

Email 2

To: lorna@southiland.co.nz
Subject: by sea, pls

Dear Lorna,

We are really very sorry for the further delays, but have to tell you what we could do and let you be clear about the actual situation.

We thank you very much for all the delivery extension for some of the products, but for those goods which you asked for air shipment, please help to check and see whether you could agree to do in this way: we still ship them by sea ASAP. We will treat them as special shipment, and put them into FCL containers. We could instruct our forwarder to clear out the goods within 18-19 days in emergency case, then arrange our warehouse staff to put on the stickers, deliver the goods directly to buyer's place from the warehouse. Our warehouse staffs are very experienced, so they could finish and deliver out the goods within two days after arrival.

In this way, we only need to keep 21 days. If we ship the goods by air, we also need to take around 12-15 days before we get the goods as our forwarder is not so quick on customs clearance by air shipment, then need to take another 5-7 days for delivery from the warehouse to the airport. It also takes around 20 days. So would you please have a further discussion with your customer and give us your close cooperation?

We are looking forward to your favorable reply. Thanks in advance!

Best regards,
Henry
Export Coordinator

Shanghai Lihua Imp. & Exp. Co., Ltd.
Rm. 606 Plaza Building,   Fax: 86-21-642578**
1302 Meilong Road, 200237   Tel: 86-21-642578**
Shanghai, People's Republic of China   E-mail: lihua88@alibaba.com

Email 3

To: purchasemanager1@emirates.net.ae
Cc: importmanager@emirates.net.ae
Subject: Ocean Freight from Shanghai to Dubai

Dear Bennett,

As requested, we offer you the following rates at the most favorable prices we can give:

1) Carrier: Zim
   Ocean Freight: USD2450/20', USD3550/40' & 40'HQ
   Peak season surcharges: USD225/20', USD300/40', USD340/40'HQ Effective: from 1 June, 200*
   Other Charges: RMB370/20' , RMB560/40' & 40'HQ
   Doc: HKD115 per bill

2) Carrier: APL (Excluded commodity: Garments / Textile / Fabric)
   Ocean Freight: USD2250/20', USD3450/40', USD3550/40'HQ
   Peak Season Surcharges:USD225/20', USD300/40', USD340/40'HQ Effective: from 10 June, 200*
   Other Charges: RMB370/20' , RMB560/40' & 40'HQ
   Doc: HKD115 per bill

3) Carrier: CMA
   Ocean Freight: USD3300/40', USD3400/40'HQ
   Other Charges: RMB370/20', RMB560/40' & 40'HQ
   Doc: HKD115 per bill

We hope you can make decision as soon as possible. Should you have any questions, please feel free to let me know.

Unit Twelve Shipping Instructions and Shipping Advice

Yours sincerely,
Michael Sparks
Customer Service Dept.
Far East Shipping Ltd.

Email 4

SHIPPING ADVICE

Contract No: YR/06/85.316

L/C No: LC77E0068/06

To: Tom Consumption Group

5**, Sayem Aldaher Street

Golail Industrial Zone

P.O. Box 9**

Jeddah, 21421

Saudi Arabia

From: Shanghai Lihua Imp. & Exp. Co., Ltd.

Rm. 608 Plaza Building,

1302 Meilong Road, 200237

Shanghai, People's Republic of China

Commodity: Trumpets and Mouth Organs

Packing: Trumpets are packed in strong polythene bags, one bag for one trumpet, a dozen of trumpets to a carton, 200 cartons to a 20' container. Mouth organs are packed in boxes, one box lined with stout, damp-resisting paper for one mouth organ, 80 boxes to a carton, 220 cartons to a 20' container, in 2x 20'containers.

Conditions: As called for by the L/C

Quantity: 2400 Trumpets, 17600 Mouth Organs.

Gross weight: 7800 kg

Net weight: 6500 kg

Total value: USD415189.00

Please be informed that these goods have been shipped from Shanghai to Jeddah by M/V APL.

Shipment date: October 21, 200*.

B/L No.   LYR821008022

We herewith certify this message to be true and correct.

Shanghai Lihua Imp. & Exp. Co., Ltd.

as beneficiary

Shanghai, October 22, 201*.

Email 5

To: Evelyn
Cc: donald@aol.com
Subject: Arrange Shipment

Evelyn,

We can arrange shipment within this week for all the items except for KOM-6523-DD. Owing to the late arrival of the raw materials, there are still 15,500pcs under production. So, we have to ask you for your accepting partial shipment.

We can let you know the weight before we arrange shipment. Since we will make shipment by L.K. Int'l on freight collect basis, please let me know whether we still need to check the freight charge before we ship out the goods.

The Shipping Advice will be sent to you by email very soon. If you have any questions, please do not hesitate to contact us as soon as possible.

Best wishes,
Reht
Export Coordinator

Shanghai Lihua Imp. & Exp. Co., Ltd.
Rm. 608 Plaza Building,   Fax: 86-21-642578**
1302 Meilong Road, 200237   Tel: 86-21-642578**
Shanghai, People's Republic of China   E-mail: lihua88@alibaba.com

Pattern K of Business Letters

After goods are loaded on board, the exporter shall inform the foreign importer of particulars covering the shipment by sending a Shipping Advice which normally covers the following details: Contract No., L/C No., To whom, From whom, Commodity, Mode of Packing, how many of containers (kind included), Terms of payment, Quantity, Gross weight, Net weight, Total value, From which port to which destination by M/V (ship), Shipment date, B/L No., Beneficiary and Date of this advice, etc.

Relevant Terms

Shipping Instruction 装运指示	Shipping Advice 装运通知
shipping expenses 装运费用	liner 班轮
tramp 不定期货船	shipping space 舱位

Unit Twelve Shipping Instructions and Shipping Advice

续表

shipper 托运人，货主	ship owner 船东
partial shipment 分批装运	Freight Prepaid 运费预付
Freight to Collect 运费到付	International Combined Transportation 国际联运
Shipping Order (S/O) 发货通知，装货单	Mate's Receipt (M/R) 大副收据
carrier 运输公司	Bill of Lading 提单
booking shipping space 订舱	chartering a ship 租船
Arrival Notice 到货通知	consignee 收件人
Consular Invoice 领事发票	

Useful Phrases

in that case 在这种情况下	to effect shipment 办理装运
to arrange shipment 办理装运	to make shipment 办理装运
to advance shipment 提前装运	to postpone shipment 推迟装运
to hold oneself responsible for 某人对某事负责	wrong delivery 误交货物
in this regards 就此而言	as regards 关于，至于
referring to 提到，参照	with regard to 关于，至于
to be ready for shipment 备妥待运	to call one's attention 提请某人注意
in urgent need of 急需某物	up to present moment 到目前为止
without further delay 不再拖延	in due course 在适当的时候，及时地
in the immediate future 在不久的将来	to make a partial shipment 分批装运
to let alone 更别提，遑论	time and again 多次，反复
to dispute with sb. over sth. 与某人对某事有分歧	at any cost 不惜任何代价
to serve sb. to one's satisfaction 为某人服务使之满意	by special express 特快
to exert one's best efforts to do sth. 尽某人最大努力做某事	

Summary

There are many modes of transportation in international trade. The most commonly used mode of transportation is seaway transportation because of its low freight cost.

If a transaction is concluded on CIF basis, a Shipping Instruction is sent to a shipping company through a forward agent by an exporter before goods are loaded on board. A Shipping Advice is sent to a foreign importer after goods are loaded on board. If a transaction is concluded on FOB basis, it is the buyer who is in charge of booking shipping space or chartering a ship and sends a Shipping Instructions informing the seller of the name of vessel, the port of loading and the date of delivery, etc.

Exercises

I. Questions for review

1. How many modes of transportation are there in international trade?
2. Which mode of transportation is mostly commonly used in international trade? Why?
3. What is a Shipping Instruction?
4. What is a Shipping Advice?

II. Choose the best answer

1. As the supplement to previous notice "Yangshan Terminal Migration – Europe Service", here I would like to share more information with all of you, _____ the sake of your early acknowledgement.
     A. at   B. as   C. with   D. for

2. There still is uncertainty subject to further confirmation. We will keep you well informed _____ any changes.
     A. from   B. of   C. in   D. to

3. It is said that Yangshan Terminal will open _____ operation from Nov. 20th.
     A. by   B. as   C. like   D. for

4. If so, the first Maersk Sealand Vessel is planned _____ be SL WASHINGTON v.0516, departing from Shanghai on Nov. 27th.
     A. from   B. off   C. in   D. to

5. This company enjoys the fullest respect and unquestionable confidence _____ the business world.
     A. by   B. as   C. like   D. in

6. CIF stands _____ cost, insurance and freight.
     A. by   B. as   C. like   D. for

7. We are willing to renew the agreement on the same terms _____ last.
     A. like   B. as   C. with   D. to

8. We will not be held responsible for any damage which results _____ rough handling.
     A. from   B. off   C. in   D. to

9. Your firm has been recommended to us by DINOSOUR TOY CO., LTD., _____ we have done business for many years.
     A. which   B. with whom   C. whom   D. with which

10. We have made _____ that we would accept D/P terms for your present order.
      A. clear   B. it is clear   C. that clear   D. it clear

11. We regret to say that your price is not _____ the current world market.
      A. on a level with   B. at a level with

Unit Twelve Shipping Instructions and Shipping Advice

        C. in a level with   D. in level with

12. To _____ extent, the information about the Japanese supply is not correct.
    A. the   B. some   C. a   D. in
13. We regret to have to _____ your request.
    A. refuse   B. fail   C. decline   D. obtain
14. We have always _____ you for the accommodation which you offered us.
    A. obliged   B. appreciated   C. thanked   D. been grateful to
15. We look forward to _____ the goods in the fourth quarter.
    A. your deliver   B. delivery   C. deliver   D. delivery of
16. The goods are urgently needed. We _____ hope you will deliver them immediately.
    A. so   B. in the case   C. therefore   D. for
17. _____ our regret, we are unable to accept your price.
    A. On   B. With   C. For   D. To
18. It sells fast because of the heavy demand _____ the limited supply in the market.
    A. with   B. for   C. on   D. of
19. The increasing demand will result _____ the prices being raised.
    A. for   B. from   C. to   D. in
20. You may avail yourselves of this special offer if you will send us your order _____ two weeks.
    A. for   B. of   C. within   D. after

III. Translate the following sentences into Chinese

1. We have arranged shipment for Article No.TN563 on May 12th.
2. We will send you the B/L, Invoice, Packing List through the fax and e-mail for your confirmation. Thanks for your cooperation!
3. We have no any appointed courier. You can arrange shipment via A.K. LTD which will provide us with door-to-door service, but please advise us of the freight charge in advance.
4. When the goods are ready for shipment, please send us your shipping advice by e-mail to facilitate our necessary arrangement.
5. Now we are ready to ship the cargo. The forwarder is the same with your last order. But we hope you can find a shipping company who will charge lower freight.
6. As our traditional Spring Festival holiday is approaching, it will be very difficult for us to book space.
7. To make it easier for us to get the goods ready for shipment, we hope that partial shipment is allowed.
8. If you cannot get the goods ready by the time the ship chartered by us arrives at the port of loading, you will be responsible for the losses thus incurred.
9. As stipulated in the contract, you should inform us by email, 30 days before the month of shipment, of the contract number, the name of the commodity, quantity, loading port and the

estimated date when the goods would reach the port of loading.

10. You should advise us by email, 12 days before the date of loading, of the name of ship, expected lay days, loading capacity, contract number and the shipping agents.

Optional part

11. We regret that we are unable to consider your request for payment under D/A terms, we generally ask for payment by L/C.

12. Up to date, we haven't received your L/C. We shall be glad if you look into the matter and let us have a reply without delay.

13. The undersigned seller and buyer have agreed to close the following transaction according to the terms and conditions stipulated below.

14. How about 50% by L/C and the rest by D/P?

15. It will be easier for us to make the necessary arrangement if your L/C can reach us 15 to 30 days before delivery.

IV. Translate the following sentences into English

1. 买方负责租船或订舱。
2. 兹通知你方，我们已经指示他们与贵公司联系以协调与这批船货有关的一切事务。
3. 最后我们想通知你方，由于一项新的政府规定，这批货物必须在6月6日前运出。
4. 现在我们要求按照我方第3112号合同交货。
5. 这批货物将由马士基(中国)有限公司[Maersk (China) Shipping Co. Ltd]运出，应该在今年12月12日当天或左右到达你方港口。
6. 由于以下原因我们正停止交货：所需货款尚未支付，并且你们撤销了购货合同。
7. 如果你们觉得这份订单能等三周，那么请告诉我们；我们将很高兴按你们期待的低价把货物装运给你们。
8. 我们深信该货物将准时到达你方，并使你们完全满意。
9. 你们可能还记得，我们一再强调准时装运的极端重要性，因为这些商品将在9月16日昆明举行的一个国际展览会上展出。
10. 我们很高兴通知你们第116号售货确认书项下的这批货物已由华盛顿号轮船运出，它于201*年8月29日驶往横滨。

V. Case Study

Case A FCL or LCL?

==

From: damai-SALES(163) damai-sales@vip.163.com

To: angela <angela@ttry.com>

Cc: haomai-service <haomai-service@vip.163.com>

Subject: P/I FOR NEW ORDER DQ066

Date: 201*/2/24 14:58:38

==

Unit Twelve Shipping Instructions and Shipping Advice

Dear Angela,

Thanks for your waiting!
NEW ORDER QTY
According to your quantity, total volume is about 18CBM.

If you want to make the container full to minimize the freight proportion rate among whole import cost, it's better for you to increase some items' quantity up to about 25CBM.

Of course, you can keep the original quantity for the order, but you need to let us know whether you use FCL(full container load) to ship the order or to use LCL(Less than container load) to ship the order. You choice will affect the extra cost for palletizing and packing...

Usually, 18CBM will be regarded as LCL, so you could find we have added the extra cost into the P/I.

So the P/I amount will be:

1) if you choose LCL, order amount is USD12,271.00, 18CBM is the total space before palleting. After palleting the total space will be about 24CBM, which is almost full container load.

2) if you choose FCL, order amount is USD11,850.00, 18CBM is the total space and there is no extra packing cost if you do not need pellets. But you may waste the 25-18 = 7CBM space, which is not fully used.

Please compare with the freight from your forwarder between the FCL and LCL cost, plus the extra palleting cost.

And let us know your decision for whether increase quantity? FCL or LCL?

Best Regards
Jim
Manager
Export & Client Dept.

Shanghai Better Hardware Trade Co., Ltd
ADD: No.1991, Meilong Road West, Humin Plaza Shanghai, #200237
TEL: 0086-21-642503**/642532**/642508** (ext.208)
FAX: 0086-21-642503**
Website: www.betterhardware.com

Case B Inquire about the Lowest Freight

Dear Leanne,

Thanks for your email dated Oct. 21.

Now we'd like to avail ourselves of this opportunity to inquire about your lowest freight as follows:

1) 20' / 40' / 40'HQ (FCL)
2) ETD/SHA
3) following ports:

SHA / LA GUAIRA(VENEZUELA)	4 × 8 40' OR 40'HQ /MONTH
SHA /GUAYAQUIL(ECUADOR)	1× 40' OR 40'HQ / MONTH
SHA /LONG BEACH (USA)	2 × 20' OR 40'HQ /MONTH
SHA /MIAMI (USA)	2 × 4 20' OR 40' /MONTH
SHA /MULAN BOMBAY (INDIA) or SHA /NHAVA SHEVA	4×8 20',40' OR 40'HQ /MONTH
SHA / BUENAVENTURA	1 × 20'/MONTH
SHA / ALEXANDRIA	1 × 20'/MONTH

We are looking forward to the reply at your earliest convenience.

Best Regards,
David

VI. Discussion

Try to make an investigation in the fluctuations of freight rates during the past two years from your local port to European ports, West America or East America.

Unit Thirteen

Trade Disputes and Settlement

Introduction

It is very normal for dealers to meet trade disputes. There are many ways in the settlement of an international trade dispute. Normally, amicable settlement or conciliation is the first choice because it saves time and cost while maintaining good business relations. If amicable settlement does not lead to a satisfactory result, the party concerned may seek for arbitration in which the arbitration award shall be final and binding to both parties. It is more flexible compared with a legal suit.

A complaint may result from wrong delivery, unsatisfactory quality, damaged goods or being overcharged, etc.

If a complaint has to be made, your letter should:

a) express your regret;
b) inform the receiver of the subject matter, such as order/contract number and its date;
c) tell him directly why you are not satisfied;
d) give your suggestions and hope for an early reply.

If you receive a complaint, you should make an investigation. If the complaint is reasonable, just admit it readily and send a reply as follows:

a) Thank him for his complaint and admit a mistake is made at your end;
b) Promise that you will take actions to put it right;
c) Say you are sorry for the inconvenience caused;
d) Assure him that more care will be taken in the future.

If the complaint is not reasonable, tell him that it is not your responsibility and give your suggestions if possible.

Business Letters

Email 1

From: Steve McCurry <Steve McCurry @concordia88.bg>
To: DAMAI-SALES(163) <damai-sales@vip.163.com>
Cc: service of damai <damai-service@vip.163.com>
Subject: RE: BG--Steve--SGS inspection finished
Date: 201*/4/11 0:43:37

Dear Jim,

The situation as reported by SGS and yourself is very serious. As you have seen in the QC checklists according to our quality criteria, the lot is to be rejected!

Unit Thirteen Trade Disputes and Settlement

These criteria are mandatory for us to observe as they guarantee our company to keep free from compromising its end product quality and brand image. Having studied the reports of SGS, our Quality Assurance and R&D departments also require rejection of the goods.

Now the only acceptable action plan I can suggest is:

We will prepare extra staff and equipment to check and sort out the bad quality goods on site by the production line (the goods will be inspected and sorted before their implementation into the end product).

I see no other reasonable variant because:

1) We cannot wait for your workers to sort out and rework the lot. The order was planned to be received long ago and any further delay is equal to cancellation to our production flow;

2) Checking the goods at once immediately after the reception of the lot is not possible because the water pressure test (for leakage of the shower head) requires special equipment and much time.

As you can imagine this will cost us extra costs and lower productivity, so I would like to ask you for a 15% discount on the L/C amount. This discount might not sufficient to cover our expenses but it will at least show your responsible position and liability for your quality and will give me grounds to ask our QA and R&D to give permission for acceptance of the goods.

I stand by to receive your earliest reply.

Best regards,

Steve McCurry

Purchasing Manager

Water Heating Division

Email 2

===

From: DAMAI-SALES(163) <damai-sales@vip.163.com>

To: Steve McCurry <Steve McCurry @ concordia88.bg>

Cc: service of damai <damai@vip.163.com>

Subject: BG-- Steve --SGS inspection finished

Date: 201*/4/11 11:02:07

===

Dear Steve,

Thanks for your reply dated April 11.

First of all, we are sorry for such defects and inconvenience in this order. However, as you can see, we have tried our best to meet your target price with close quality.

I think you still remember this project was discussed throughout almost one year and finally after we finalized this order with price and technical dimensions and confirmed order and L/C, we received your inspection requirement——which is later discussed. This kind of way, relatively speaking, is not fair. I have to say, because new criteria are added after price is fixed!

Does it mean if you add much stricter and impossible requirement after price is confirmed and L/C is opened, we still have to finish this impossible mission?

I understand your viewpoints, and understand your situation and your company's strategy in protecting and develop a company brand. But no matter who is the supplier and who is the buyer, it is always the same criteria over the world, that is, to balance between the price and quality.

I have to say under this price, we could only do that level of quality; and under other higher or lower price, the quality is different. I think you understand this point and also understand our situation.

Secondly, I want to say, although there are many discrepancies found by SGS inspectors, most of them are very tiny points. For any products, if people want to inspect very carefully and strictly, there will be always defectives.

As regards the chroming, the defects discovered by SGS are very small, and most are on the back side of the soap holder, which does not affect the whole appearance or out-looking of the set;

About the curve of the tube, SGS just use a coin to check the height of the end, as reported as 2MM-3.5MM, but you can see in close distance that it is very hard to find it is curved because the distance is very tiny.

About the spraying types, most of the sprays is good, and 2PCS are with one line cross but does not affect the function and not easily to be noticed when using.

As to the leakage, we are sorry for 3PCS problem, but we promise to replace them after-sale. If you'd prefer to have spare one earlier, we can send you 10PCS through UPS.

Thirdly, about your suggestion for 15% discount for the solution, it is really hard for us to accept, because the average quality of this order is good. We did not produce garbage for you. The products are still quite good. We use the fresh new ABS raw material to injection, use the same raw material as per your drawings, use the high quality brass raw material to make the spout. Everything is good except for some small discrepancies and low percentage of the defectives.

SOLUTION

There is no need to re-check Item No.CI1583 (3-way diverter); CI1585 (wall holder), CI1586 (sliding bar), CI1584 (hose) one by one from your side, because we could guarantee you 99.5% of these items are good.

Item CI1786 (brass spout) only cannot produce perfect water flow in spraying. The water flow type is like (II) defined in my WORD file in last email. And there is no function problem. Besides, the inspection is on basis of $8kg/cm^2$ pressure, while during your clients' using it at home it is at most $2kg/cm^2$. So the water flow will be much better than inspection results. Furthermore, the result of water flow is also due to the designing structure, which we think is not very ideal design, and therefore we hope you could accept these items and understand our situation.

With reference to CI1584 (A93 showerhead), we admit that there are serval leaking showerheads, but we are sure there are no more than 10PCS among all.

Anyway, to show our cooperation, we would like to grant you a discount of 5% on the showerhead price (USD1.87 x 2800 x 5% = USD261.80). And we also confirm you could get replacement from us if your clients return this showerhead to you. We are looking forward to your reply.

Best Regards,
Jim
Manager
Export & Client Dept.

Shanghai Better Hardware Trade Co., Ltd
ADD: No.1991, Meilong Road West, Humin Plaza Shanghai, #200237
TEL: 0086-21-642503**/642532**/642508** (ext.208)
FAX: 0086-21-642503**
Website: www.betterhardware.com

Email 3

From: Steve McCurry <SteveMcCurry@concordia88.bg>
To: DAMAI-SALES(163) <damai-sales@vip.163.com>
Cc: service of damai <damai-service@vip.163.com>
Subject: RE: BG--Steve--SGS inspection finished
Date: 201*/4/13 0:27:48

Dear Sirs,

I find your reply truly upsetting. You can apparently write very well and elaborately but I prefer to be very concise and clear. Let me comment below:

1. Giving excuse for your poor quality by referring to price is not a serious position of a reliable supplier. This is what people call blackmailing. When we research the market for suppliers we always look for both price and quality, not either! We selected you as our supplier on the base of samples approval. Your samples were satisfactory – no leakages and just some minor visual defects and the correction of which was agreed on our personal meeting in Zhucu in 201*. Now it turns out that you can no longer sustain the agreed quality because of the prices? I am sorry but I cannot accept such manner of price negotiations.

2. I do not want you to classify the defects. We have set our quality standard and it is to be conformed with! Qualifications as "very tiny points" are useless. For us, what you call "very tiny points" are actually huge quality issues, so please do not take the liberty to give arbitrary qualifications to the findings of SGS! All in all, you seem to be trying to persuade me that 1) our quality standard is unduly stringent and 2) the findings of SGS were actually not as important as we think. Please excuse me but this is not the way we work. A quality issue is a quality issue.

There is no place for elaborate rhetoric when it comes to business.

3. SOLUTION: in your point titled "SOLUTION" I found no suggestion for solution. Your offered compensation of USD261.8 is merely upsetting! I would not lose my time writing e-mails for petty change. We need to negotiate agreeable solution together asap; otherwise I will have to turn to our domestic market for a quick supply of decent quality goods.

I already told you if we pick up your lot I will have to appoint 100% QC at our premises and this will surely cost us much. I expect to learn how you are willing to contribute to mitigate the negative consequences for us as result of the quality fault. You say you guarantee that 99.5% of the goods are good but unfortunately they are not. The inspectors already proved that. The defect ratio is disturbingly high (you can calculate it for each item). I am waiting to learn your reasonable proposal in shortest term!

Best regards,
Steve McCurry
Purchasing Manager

Email 4

----- Original Message -----
From: Concordia
To: DAMAI-SALES(163)
Sent: Thursday, February 21, 201* 4:24 PM
Subject: RE: REASONABLE ADJUSTMENT

Dear Jim,

The national holidays are very important, but the business is business. You promise us that the goods will be ready in the end of February. The delay of 20 days is too bad news for us. This means that our manufactory will stop for one month or more and we cannot receive our salaries. We paid you two months before receiving the goods and in the last moment we find out that the delivery of the goods will be delayed one more month.

These facts are very unfavorable for me personally, because when the owner of our group finds out that his factory will have to stop for one month I will probably be thrown out of work.

We hope that you understand this very unpleasant situation and we are looking forward to your proposal.

Regards,
Concordia
Purchasing Manager

NGS GROUP CO., LTD.

Unit Thirteen　Trade Disputes and Settlement

P. O. BOX 576**
DUBAI - UNITED ARAB EMIRATES
TEL: + 971 - 4 - 3525***
FAX: + 971 - 4 - 3525***
MOBILE: + 971 - 50 – 669****
EMAIL: Concordia88@emirates.net.ae

Email 5

==

From: DAMAI-SALES(163) <damai@vip.163.com>
To: Concordia <Concordia88@emirates.net.ae >
Cc: DAMAI-SERVICE <damai -service@vip.163.com>
Subject: REASONABLE ADJUSTMENT
Date: 201*/2/21 16:59:23

==

Dear Concordia,

Thanks for your email dated February 21.

Kindly please be noted that this delay is beyond our control, which is due to the long national holiday and your late confirmation of orders.

Enclosed please find some past email records:

　　1) As far as I could remember, Item No.GT005 was discussed ever since Jan. 11th, 201*. However, your boss did not confirm it until Jan. 31th. And we've already informed you that we will soon have a long holiday. If you need order you must arrange T/T ASAP. But we were blocked in the terms of payment for such a small order.

　　2) And on Jan. 21th, we've already informed you that due to your delay on confirmation, we already received 4 orders from other clients, and even if you place order immediately, your products will be arranged after theirs. We must follow the principle *one by one* for fair treatment. And we also informed you that:

　　Due to the Spring Festival from Feb. 23th to 16th when all factories in China will be closed, our production will actually be activated after 16th.

　　At present, we have already received 4 orders, yours will be arranged from the end of Feb. And it takes about 20 days for these items. (most time-consuming is on the chrome-plating). After that we need to arrange your SGS inspection, which needs booking at least 1 week in advance. Finally, shipment can be made. So it is estimated that the date of shipment will be around March 22th to 26th.

　　3) And then your accounting dept. even delayed to arrange the T/T on Feb. 4th rather than Jan. 31th.

　　The records says:　Settlement Amount　　*32 A : Date 1*0204 Currency USD Amount 232,800.00

4) Between the traditional long holidays, usually local people who work in office always have 7-day holiday, but in the factories located in rural areas with workers coming from nearby or remote provinces, they will always have very long holidays from Jan. 20th to Feb. 15th.

This causes such phenomenon that even urban citizens have finished their holidays, there is still no worker at all in the rural areas!

No workers, no accessory factories opening, no chrome plating factories working, no raw material suppliers...only holiday before Feb. 15th!!!

Now you could get to know such a traditional holiday, during which people are keen to stay with family members for re-union! That's why it is called mission impossible for us to arrange production during this period.

Even in the port and export warehouse, there is no labor force, fork drivers working for you. No one makes pallets, loading containers for you!!! You could do nothing but wait. This is the very long tradition which is beyond our and your control! I think you may explain well to your boss for his understanding!

Right now, we are hurrying up to help you. We will try to finish production ASAP. But the date of shipment is still around Mar. 15th.

Even if you had placed your order on Jan.15th, 16th, 17th, 18th, 19th, 20th...it would made no sense because at that time workers have already gone! We would still have no chance to ship the order in Feb. and make you receive it in March! So please check and understand this situation!

SUGGESTION

Try to place big orders to make your storage lasting longer.

Try to choose the convenient mode of payment in advance, e. g. T/T.

Best Regards,

Jim

Manager

Export & Client Dept.

Shanghai Better Hardware Trade Co., Ltd

ADD: No.1991, Meilong Road West, Humin Plaza Shanghai, #200237

TEL: 0086-21-642503**/642532**/642508** (ext.208)

FAX: 0086-21-642503**

Website: www.betterhardware.com

Pattern L of Business Letters

If a complaint has to be made, your letter should:

a) express your regret;

b) inform the receiver of the subject matter, such as order/contract number and its date;

Unit Thirteen Trade Disputes and Settlement

c) tell him directly why you are not satisfied;
d) give your suggestions and hope for an early reply.

If the complaint is reasonable, just admit it readily and send a reply as follows:

a) Thank him for his complaint and admit a mistake is made at your end;
b) Promise that you will take actions to put it right;
c) Say you are sorry for the inconvenience caused;
d) Assure him that more care will be taken in the future.

Relevant Terms

claim 索赔	penalty 罚款
breach of contract 违约	claimant 索赔者，原告
jurisdiction 管辖权，审判权	litigation 诉讼，起诉
adjudication 判决，裁定	Force Majeure Clause 不可抗力条款
penalty clause 处罚条款	amicable settlement 和解
arbitration 仲裁	arbitration agreement 仲裁协议
costs of arbitration 仲裁费用	arbitral award 仲裁裁决

Useful Phrases

to take delivery of 接受，提取	to be in good condition 情况良好(毫无破损)
to check sth. with sth. 与某人核实某事	at one's disposal 受其管理，由其随意支配
at the current price 以目前的价格	at the prevailing price 以目前的价格
to make a complaint about 就某事投诉	in consequence 结果，因此
to ask for a compensation 要求补偿	to file a claim against sb. for sth. 就某事向某人提出索赔
to make a claim with sb. for sth. 就某事向某人提出索赔	to lay a claim on sb. for sth. 就某事向某人提出索赔
to render a claim against sb. for sth. 就某事向某人提出索赔	to bring up a claim upon sb. for sth. 就某事向某人提出索赔
to set up a claim against sb. for sth. 就某事向某人提出索赔	to accept a claim 接受索赔
to admit a claim 接受索赔	to entertain a claim 接受索赔
to handle a claim 处理索赔	to settle a claim 解决索赔
to dismiss a claim 驳回索赔	to reject a claim 拒绝索赔
to withdraw a claim 撤回索赔	in good order 情况良好
in an amicable way 以友好的方式	to start with a clean slate 重新开始

续表

in attractive designs 设计吸引人	in proof of 证明
to make a minute investigation 做详细调查	to settle by arbitration 用仲裁解决
to go counter to 违背	to run counter to 违反
to haggle over 争论不休，讨价还价	

Summary

There are many ways in the settlement of an international trade dispute. Friendly communication is the first choice because it saves time and cost while maintaining good business relations. Sometimes arbitration is also necessary, which is more flexible compared with a legal suit.

An exporter should treat every complaint in all seriousness and try to solve it as soon as possible.

Exercises

I. Questions for review

1. What are the methods of settlement in an international trade dispute?
2. How to make a complaint?
3. How to reply to a reasonable complaint?

II. Choose the best answer

1. I am told that you haven't received the rest 80% of the machine value up to now _____ the machine you provided is still working.

   A. for   B. after   C. before   D. while

2. So, I think you might need a local lawyer who will be able to investigate it and obtain evidence _____ you in Shanghai.

   A. for   B. with   C. on   D. to

3. If so, please do not hesitate to tell me and I'll recommend a capable lawyer _____ you.

   A. with   B. within   C. to   D. until

4. Steve told me that you are interested _____ establishing a joint venture in Shanghai.

   A. for   B. in   C. at   D. until

5. As regards this, I will have a lot of suggestions _____ your reference.

   A. for   B. within   C. at   D. until

6. Please note that our quotation remains valid _____ Dec. 30.

   A. for   B. within   C. at   D. until

Unit Thirteen Trade Disputes and Settlement

7. To be candid _____ you, we like your new products.
   A. for   B. with   C. to   D. of
8. We suggest that you make some allowance, say 5% _____ your quoted prices.
   A. for   B. with   C. on   D. in
9. Some parcels from New York have been sold here _____ a much lower price.
   A. for   B. at   C. on   D. in
10. We have indicated those articles that are available _____ stock.
    A. for   B. with   C. on   D. from
11. We are _____ the opinion that the quality of the Spanish goods is far from being comparable to that of ours.
    A. as   B. of   C. with   D. for
12. We quote you as below and hope to be favored _____ your orders.
    A. for   B. with   C. at   D. in
13. Now the market is weak and all economic indicators point _____ a fall in prices.
    A. for   B. to   C. at   D. in
14. The contract will be ready _____ in a week.
    A. to be signed   B. for signing   C. for sign   D. to sign
15. What you are doing does not accord _____ your promise.
    A. from   B. to   C. for   D. with
16. We find your quotation _____, therefore, we place an order with you now.
    A. attracting   B. to be attractive
    C. attract our attention   D. attractive
17. As a result _____ the exchange of letters between us, we have now come to a conclusion.
    A. in   B. of   C. for   D. on
18. Kindly give the above your consideration and let us know whether our proposal is _____ you.
    A. agreeable to   B. agree by   C. agreed to   D. agreeably to
19. The second point concerns the currency to _____ in pricing and making payment.
    A. base   B. be based on   C. basis   D. base on
20. We would appreciate your _____ attention to the question.
    A. prompt   B. instant   C. first   D. immediately

III. Translate the following sentences into Chinese

1. The woolen sweaters you delivered do not match the sample we provided. I would like to talk with someone in charge.

2. I have brought one sample to our quality controller to check and try to find where the real problem is.

3. The washing machine makes great noise and shaking, after a while of spinning, the washer

moves aside due to great shake.

4. We think the problem results from two reasons: The quality of springs and 4 hanging steel panel is not as good as before, and opposition weight panel is not heavy enough to make the tub not shake.

5. Our retailers wanted to return all this lot to us if we cannot provide right solutions. Please send us spare parts to fix these machines along with our next container.

6. We will keep this machine if you agree to refund the difference between the two models.

7. We have been receiving many complaints from our customers about your Model Se-09. They have not been satisfactory and, therefore, we have had to refund the purchase price on many of them. The trouble seems to be with the last shipment.

8. This product before seemed sufficient and we did not have any complaints from our customers. Please check to see if there was an error in making these batch of machines. We would also like to suggest that you check to see if they are being packed with enough protection for shipping.

9. We would like to have you send us a replacement shipment as soon as possible because it is in urgent need by our customer.

10. We are prepared to solve this problem in an amicable way by paying you a rebate of 6% so as to start with a clean slate.

Optional Part

11. We are sorry for the delay, which was due to circumstances beyond our control.

12. We hope that with your valuable support and cooperation we can still further develop the business to our mutual benefit.

13. We have duly received the 50 cases you sent, but we regret to find that two of them have been wholly damaged in transit.

14. We have to inform you that the quality of your wheat is far inferior to the sample you sent us last month.

15. We regret to tell you that your tins of lobster have caused numerous complaints from our customers.

IV. Translate the following sentences into English

1. 我们感谢你方的直率，你们指出了第 35 号纸板箱并没有装入你们所订的商品。

2. 让我们失望的是，我方第 268 号订单的货物缺重 58 公斤。

3. 我们已经要求我们的服务部门对该投诉做彻底的调查。

4. 我们很遗憾不得不对 10 月 12 日所订货物迟交之事进行投诉，因为正如你们所知，准时装运对我们非常重要。

5. 因此，我们认为向生产商索赔是比较困难的。

6. 我们希望我方的理赔将会使你们完全满意。你方认为怎样才算公平？

7. 由于你方未能在所要求的时间内装运，我们就此取消订单，同时保留我们拥有的进一步追偿的权利。

8. 货物离开我们仓库时完好无损，显然损坏是在转运途中发生的。
9. 我们的货物应该包装在纸板箱里，而不是塑料容器中。
10. 我方对这一问题已做让步，希望你们对此满意。

V. Case Study

----- Original Message ----- (A)

To: henry@alibaba.com

Subject: The Wrong Brand Name

Dear Henry,

With reference to your Items No.YL-66 & SN-88, I deeply regret to inform you that all the 2000 boxes containing these items were stenciled with the wrong band name ABSOLUTE instead of SUPER-YAK we designated for this order.

For your information, enclosed please find hereunder pictures of the boxes received in our warehouse for these items.

Besides, I would like to remind you that another 500 boxes against our Order No.568, which was shipped out three days ago as scheduled, also includes 1000 pieces of Item No. YL-66. Therefore, we urgently need to know which brand name you printed on these boxes.

In case, this new shipment has this item packed in ABSOLUTE boxes, we need you to send us by courier 2500 boxes with our SUPER-YAK brand for us to repack as long as goods are received in our warehouse. Additional 100 boxes are requested to be sent at the same time for possible delivery damage.

Meanwhile, we are buying locally 2000 white boxes to repack the items to solve this problem quickly so that it does not impact our sales. We will send you a copy of invoice covering the cost of replacement boxes for you to issue and send a check to our account in USA.

As for the labor charges caused for the repacking process and the expenses incurred for the courier service, we will absorb them, but this is the last time we do it.

As a matter of fact, I am thinking that the best way to avoid these problems is to buy from other suppliers whatever items you sell. You must know we are deeply disappointed. Please send us the new boxes, which should be duly approved by us in advance. We look forward to your reply.

Best regards,

David

----- Original Message ----- (B)

To: david@southiland.co.nz

Subject: The Wrong Brand Name

Dear David,

Thanks for your email of Oct. 22. We are terribly sorry for the inconvenience caused to you!

After investigation, we find that we made mistakes on the inner boxes containing Items No.YL-66 & SN-88. Please replace the wrong boxes by yourselves first and inform us how much your total cost for replacement is, we will pay it by T/T very soon.

Furthermore, we will immediately make new design for the box with SUPER-YAK brand name on it as per your requirement and then send samples for your approval. After that, we will send you 2600 SUPER-YAK branded boxes through the courier for you to replace.

We have troubled you so much! We will immediately have a meeting for better management and avoid any further mistakes of this kind. If this happens again, we promise, we accept any punishment.

For the already-happened mistakes, we again apologize for our mistakes and wish to have your understanding and kindness.

Your cooperation and forgiveness are appreciated!

Best Regards,

Henry

Export Manager

Shanghai Lihua Imp. & Exp. Co., Ltd.

VI. Discussion

How to solve this problem if you were Mr. Qi?

===

From: vip.163.com <damai-sales@vip.163.com>
To: Concordia <Concordia@ttry.com>
Cc: =dm <damai-service@vip.163.com>
Subject: COMPLAIM ABOUT YOUR APPOINTED FORWARDER
Date: 201*/6/25 14:16:35

===

Dear Concordia,

We have to complain about your appointed forwarder as follows:

1) Your appointed forwarder could not provide us with a warehouse which should be located in the west part of Shanghai. Usually any forwarder could always provide the suppliers with either the warehouse located in the west part or the east part of Shanghai.

We would like to have a warehouse in west part because it will be much more convenient for our Shanghai office to arrange pallets, second checking before shipment, and supervision for loading. But your forwarder only gives us a very distant place in the far east part! Anyway, we have to accept it considering saving time.

2) Your appointed forwarder does not provide pallets-packing service!

Usually any forwarder and warehouse could provide this normal service, but your forwarder do not provide. Their excuse is that they do not have enough labor force!

And they also refuse to use our purchased and delivered STANDARD "IPPC" pallets for packing! These "IPPC" certified pallets are the international standard pallets which we always purchase from our pallets supplier.

Now they refuse to use them, and told us they only accept their own pallets, which cost 4 times than normal cost! This is almost "ransom" or "blackmail"!

This forwarder is even the worst compared with your past different forwarders! Very bad service!

We strongly need your help to ask them to provide us with the pallet packing service with normal packing cost!

Due to their problems, we have to again delay your vessel by one week because we could not arrange shipment without packing.

We are looking forward to your earliest reply!

Best regards,
Jim Qi

Unit Fourteen

Sales Promotion

Introduction

Sales promotion is absolutely necessary for exporters in international trade. The following business letters fall within the scope of promotion letters, that is, Sales Letter, Reviver and a Follow-up Letter.

Sales Letter is a kind of business letters which is to find new customers so as to expand business. A good Sales Letter should be able to:

a) arouse buyers' interest;
b) create buyers' desire;
c) convince the readers of the seller's comments;
d) lead to customers' action.

A Reviver is another kind of business letters which is to retain or regain former customers. Such letter is written under such circumstances in which the writer has had substantial business with the receiver, but recently there has been no business concluded at all for a long time. So, such letter is to revive their cooperation. It usually contains the following elements:

a) Review previous good cooperation;
b) Add a favorable comment on the goods;
c) Offer a generous discount;
d) Look forward to receiving a new order.

A Follow-up letter is also a kind of business letter which is to discreetly inquire into the reason why the offeror has not received an order from the offeree. That is, the buyer has made an enquiry to the seller, and the seller also has sent him a quotation, but he has not had the pleasure of hearing from the buyer. Under such circumstances, the seller sends a follow-up letter to the potential buyer. Such letter should include the following aspects:

a) Refer to the buyer's inquiry and the seller's quotation;
b) Express regret that no order has been received and assume some possible reasons so as to push sales;
c) Point out some new selling-points and add a favorable comment on the goods;
d) Expect to receive an order from the importer.

The above-mentioned three kinds of business letters could be sent out by means of traditional letter, Fax or email.

Business Letters

Email 1

To: lebrauda@aol.net
Subject: Stone Products

Unit Fourteen Sales Promotion

Gentlemen:

Shanghai Fast East Stone Trading Co., Ltd., established in 1991, is located in Xinzhuang Town, south-east of Shanghai. It's only 30 kilometers to Shanghai port and only 10 kilometers to Hongqiao International Airport. We specialize in the export business of stone and crafts. Its registered capital is CNY 2,000,000.00.

We are dealing in processing and exporting various stone products, such as granite tiles, big slabs, long strip slabs, kitchen top, garden sculpture, and tomb stone, etc. Most of our products are made of high-quality China granite and marble, and part of them are imported from Italy. In virtue of its high standard of craftsmanship, our products have become very popular in EU, US, the Middle East and ASEAN. A latest illustrated catalog is enclosed for your reference.

We take the liberty of writing to you with a view to establish direct business relations with you. If there is anything in which you are interested in our catalog, please do not hesitate to contact us. You are also welcome to visit our homepage (www.granitemarble.com).

Sincerely,
Henry Cai,
General Manager

Shanghai Lihua Imp. & Exp. Co., Ltd.
Rm. 606 Plaza Building,   Fax: 86-21-642578**
1302 Meilong Road, 200237   Tel: 86-21-642578**
Shanghai, People's Republic of China   E-mail: lihua88@alibaba.com

Email 2

To: kato@alibaba.com.cn
Subject: Cooperation

Dear Sir or Madam:

We are pleased to introduce our organization as manufacturer, exporter and trader of all types of sports goods as well as martial arts and its allied equipment. We specialize in judo and karate uniforms, which are well-known in Asian countries. Having been working in this field for more than twenty five years, we are well-organized business organization having skilled workers and competitive professionals.

Currently, we are focusing on enhancing coordination and understanding with valuable organizations and buyers, who intend to have long-lasting business tie-ups with us.

Our organization warmly invites you or any representative of your organization to have dialogues on business opportunities and to explore the possibility of establishing business partnership for the days to come. We would appreciate it if you let us have the detailed specifications of your goods, which would enable us to quote you accordingly. So, please feel free to contact us for any information.

We are looking forward to your cooperation.

Yours sincerely,
Henry Cai,
General Manager

Shanghai Lihua Imp. & Exp. Co., Ltd.

Rm. 606 Plaza Building,   Fax: 86-21-64257***

1302 Meilong Road, 200237   Tel: 86-21-64257***

Shanghai, People's Republic of China E-mail: lihua88@alibaba.com

Email 3

To: peter@aol.com

Subject: A Generous Discount

Dear Peter,

We noted that your esteemed company was our valuable customer during the last three years. You placed regular orders with us for our ceramic products in large quantities. But, to our disappointment, we haven't had the pleasure of hearing from you during the last six months.

We think you may be interested to know that recently we have developed many new makes. In order to promote the sales of these products, we are going to allow our valuable buyers a generous discount as follows. Say,

  Tableware Art. No. Y6658

  3 % for an order for 1000 sets to 1999 sets

  6 % for an order for 2000 sets to 2999 sets

  9 % for an order for 3000 sets and above

on the prevailing price of USD 19.90-per set CIF San Francisco. Enclosed please find the new design of the item. Our offer is subject to your reply reaching us on or before Oct.30.

At present, our discount on new products is given only to established customers. We hope that you will take it into your consideration.

We look forward to your favorable reply at your earliest convenience.

Yours sincerely,
Henry Cai,
General Manager

Shanghai Lihua Imp. & Exp. Co., Ltd.

Rm. 606 Plaza Building,   Fax: 86-21-642578**

1302 Meilong Road, 200237   Tel: 86-21-642578**

Shanghai, People's Republic of China   E-mail: lihua88@alibaba.com

Unit Fourteen Sales Promotion

Email 4

To: david@christinacostume.com.uk
Subject: Your Enquiry Dated March 23

Dear David,

We sent an email on March 25 in reply to your enquiry dated March 23 for our Tangzhuang, attire of traditional Chinese style. However, up to now, we haven't had the pleasure of receiving an order from you.

Perhaps you have not found your aimed customers in your area. As you know, our costumes are specially designed for the high-end customers, such as CEOs, presidents, vice presidents, owners, partners, general managers and diplomats. It is also probable that you are looking for the latest styles.

For your information, we will attend the forthcoming Paris Fashion Show, which will be held during May. 15-18. We will have a booth No. 6G16 there. Our new designs will surely suit the fondness of those persons in the business circle having tight ties with China. We are confident of the prospect of our goods in the up-market.

Meantime, we hope to discuss the possibility of signing a Distributorship Agreement with you. If you agree, you can sell our unique costumes in UK on the basis of Sole Distribution in the future. You are warmly welcome to visit us at the fair so that we could have a talk face to face.

If you have any questions, please feel free to contact us promptly.

Yours faithfully,
Henry
General Manager

Shanghai Lihua Imp. & Exp. Co., Ltd.
Rm. 606 Plaza Building,   Fax: 86-21-642578**
1302 Meilong Road, 200237   Tel: 86-21-642578**
Shanghai, People's Republic of China E-mail: lihua88@alibaba.com

Email 5

To: ivan@southiland.co.nz
Subject: Thanks for Your Trial Order

Dear Mr. Hansen,

We are glad to know you have received our samples and catalogue. We are also much honored to welcome you to become our new customer!

Due to the small quantity for this order, we would like to ask you to make payment by T/T as per the following procedures:

a) We send you our pro forma invoice by e-mail for your confirmation and you remit 30% of the total amount of this order by T/T in advance.

b) We start production and send you the copies of the B/L, COMMERCIAL INVOICE, PACKING LIST by e-mail for your confirmation and you remit 70% of the total amount of this order by T/T.

c) Upon receipt of the payment in the bank, we immediately send you all original documents through "DHL" courier.

It is our usual practice to deal with small orders when L/C is not economical. For big orders, payment by 30% T/T + 70% D/P AT SIGHT is also accepted.

We'd like to draw your attention to Item No. 1258, which is of high quality and competitive price as your ordered item. Samples will be sent to you upon receipt of your request.

We are confident that the first shipment will prove to be satisfactory and look forward to your more bigger orders.

Yours faithfully,
Henry
General Manager

Shanghai Lihua Imp. & Exp. Co., Ltd.
Rm. 606 Plaza Building,   Fax: 86-21-642578**
1302 Meilong Road, 200237   Tel: 86-21-642578**
Shanghai, People's Republic of China   E-mail: lihua88@alibaba.com

Pattern M of Business Letters

A good Sales Letter should be able to:
a) arouse buyers' interest;
b) create buyers' desire;
c) convince the readers;
d) lead to customers' action.

A Reviver usually contains the following elements:
a) review previous good cooperation;
b) add a favorable comment on the goods;
c) offer a generous discount;
d) look forward to receiving a new order.

A Follow-up letter should include the following aspects:
a) refer to the buyer's inquiry and the seller's quotation;
b) express regret that no order has been received assume some possible reasons so as to

Unit Fourteen Sales Promotion

push sales;
c) point out some new selling-points and add a favorable comment on the goods;
d) expect to receive an order from the importer.

Relevant Terms

sales letter 推销信	reviver 振兴信
follow-up letter 随访信	80/20 rule 80/20 法则，二八原理
wholesaler 批发商	retailer 零售商
corporate chain 公司连锁店	price discrimination 价格歧视
consumer goods 消费品	cultural symbol 文化符号
cross-cultural analysis 跨文化分析	dumping 倾销
global competition 全球竞争	international marketing 国际营销
sales management 销售管理	ultimate users 最终用户
trademark 商标	

Useful Phrases

to be of great value 有很大价值	to make an investment in 投资于
to clear the stock 清仓	to be aware that 意识到
up to the present 至今	to lead to 导致
to preclude sb. from doing sth. 阻止某人做某事	it is quite probably that 很可能
to conclude transactions 结束交易	by virtue of 由于
for one's inspection 供某人检查	to be superior in quality 质量优异
to be moderate in price 价格适中	to have an advantage over 有优势
to have good reasons 有很好的理由	to heavy backlog of orders 订单积压多

Summary

Sales promotion is absolute necessary for exporters in international trade.

When you try to find new customers, you need to send sales letters. When you try to retain or regain established customers, you need to send a reviver. When you try to retain the potential buyer who has made enquiry to you, you need to send a follow-up letter.

These different kinds of business letters could be sent out by means of letter, fax or email.

Exercises

I. Questions for review

1. What is a Sales Letter?
2. What is a Reviver?
3. What is a Follow-up Letter?

II. Choose the best answer

1. Our company is a privately owned company governed _____ a board of directors.
   A. on   B. to   C. by   D. in
2. A dedicated and enthusiastic management team works in conjunction _____ a skilled and stable work force.
   A. in   B. with   C. on   D. of
3. We own 2,200 hectares _____ timber plantation, which ensures ongoing consistent supply.
   A. in   B. with   C. on   D. of
4. Our sawmill produces 72,000 m³ _____ sawn timber output per annum.
   A. in   B. with   C. on   D. of
5. We satisfy our customers' needs by producing and marketing JINJIN branded Fir _____ primary processed form from secured log resource.
   A. on   B. to   C. in   D. by
6. We are much honored to introduce ourselves to you. Our company, established 15 years ago, is a wholesaler and a commission house. We enjoy a big share _____ this line in the local market.
   A. on   B. to   C. in   D. by
7. Therefore, we are always looking _____ new suppliers and competitive prices.
   A. in   B. for   C. on   D. of
8. With reference to your offer we received today, we note that your prices are much higher than that _____ similar goods in our market.
   A. in   B. with   C. on   D. of
9. We attached the photos of the goods we are importing _____ India, please compare the quality and price with yours.
   A. on   B. from   C. in   D. by
10. If you really want to sell your goods in our market, please quote us your best prices. We'd like to tell you that we are also interested in other items, such _____ black Teflon and gate valve.
    A. on   B. as   C. by   D. in

Unit Fourteen Sales Promotion

11. _____ the increased demand for our products, we wish to appoint an agent.
    A. With   B. In view of   C. But for   D. Despite
12. This price is entirely due to increase _____ freight cost.
    A. in   B. with   C. on   D. of
13. As there is a crowd of enquires for Chinese machine tools, it is advisable for you to _____ your orders.
    A. rush   B. strike   C. cancel   D. make
14. It is not difficult for us to book the necessary shipping space _____ this end.
    A. on   B. to   C. at   D. in
15. All the models you saw _____ the fashion show are obtainable.
    A. in   B. at   C. on   D. from
16. We_____ your terms satisfactory and now send you our order for your products.
    A. believe   B. find   C. think   D. suppose
17. We were told that the consignment would be sent _____ to reach the final destination by the end of December.
    A. so as   B. in order   C. in time   D. as
18. In this case, the buyer _____ cancel the contract.
    A. could   B. may have to
    C. has the right to   D. reserve the right to
19. We _____ you that all your enquiries will receive our prompt attention.
    A. ensure   B. assure   C. insure   D. guarantee
20. Our stocks are _____ low.
    A. falling   B. running   C. becoming   D. going

III. Translation

Part A Translate the following sentences into Chinese

1. With high quality, competitive prices, timely delivery and excellent after-sale services, we have obtained high reputation in the international market.

2. We seek cooperation with foreign buyers who are interested in China-made Handicrafts.

3. We are familiar with Home Furniture/Furnishings; Holiday Decorates; Floral Arrangements &/or Components; Fashion Hats & Bags.

4. We are interested in joint venture with any manufacturer of quality leisure wear for summer for the US and European markets.

5. Only serious companies who can meet international standard need to contact us. Please send details of product in price indication.

6. We are prepared to clear the stock by allowing you a generous discount. Say 12% for an order for 100 units on the prevailing price of USD112.00-per unit CIF New York.

7. We emailed you on Aug. 29 in reply to your enquiry for our new makes. However, up to now, we have not had the pleasure of hearing from you. Your silence leads us to think that there

must be something that precludes you from making further enquiries.

8. Now we enclose our latest illustrated catalogue for your consideration. These new articles command ready sales for their durability and energy-saving property.

9. As these items are in great demand in the Gulf areas, I am afraid we cannot wait for new orders for a long time. So, may we suggest, you will send us your repeat order as soon as possible. We assure you that we will serve you to your entire satisfaction.

10. If you are interested in any one of the items in our catalogue, please do not hesitate to contact us. We will make offers upon receipt of your specific enquiries. We sincerely hope to conclude some satisfactory transactions with your esteemed company in the near future.

Part B   Translate the following paragraphs into Chinese

Paragraph One

From pants to dresses, skirts, blouses and shirts, SELFWOMEN blends the best colors, linen, cotton, silk, and other fabrics to create the inner confidence a modern woman should feel at work and on social occasions. Our blended textures, patterns and shapes combine to create a bit oversized and loose fitting "dressed-up" casual style, which is uniquely brand "SELFWOMEN". To accomplish the best quality goals and supply ability, SELFWOMEN has a modern plant facility and a staff of experienced stylists that work hard to reflect the Asian diversity and the most recent American and European fashions trends. SELFWOMEN began from a single small facility in Shanghai in 1984, supplying quality women clothing to wholesalers all over the country. Today, we have a national well-known brand and our sales have grown to significant values since we are also exporting. The range too has expanded somewhat from that original production. It now covers women casual clothes, handbags, footwear, accessories, etc- all created to the same high quality and unbeatable value as those first pieces of basic clothing.

Paragraph Two

With its entry into WTO, China will gradually remove its tariff and non-tariff trade barriers. China is opening its door to the rest of the world. A huge market is emerging in the east of the world; a dragon is wakening...

DHB International intends to explore the international trade opportunities between the United States and China, both import from China to USA and export from USA to China.

Our advantage lies in our understanding of both the USA market and the China market. We have several closely connected branches across the Pacific Ocean, some in the USA and others in China. Most of our members have academic and professional background in international trade and export/import practice. Our closely connected team will provide more trade opportunities to local suppliers and more exotic products to local market. Meanwhile, we are exploring more worldwide opportunities in Mexico, Japan, etc. If you want to recommend your products or have any suggestions, please contact us.

Unit Fourteen Sales Promotion

IV. Translate the following Use Direction into English

产品使用说明

1. 将专用电线与身体取暖饼相连。当它接通插座时，指示灯即亮，加热开始。十分钟后储热停止，指示灯灭，同时电流自动切断。拔出电线即可使用。

2. 该产品采用进口特殊储热材料，故一次通电即可供热持续五小时。

3. 该产品达到国家五类绝缘材料安全标准。

注意事项：

1. 本产品不可浸泡；
2. 本产品不可当体育用品使用，避免敲打；
3. 本产品不可用火加热。

天寒地冻时，它给您带来温暖。

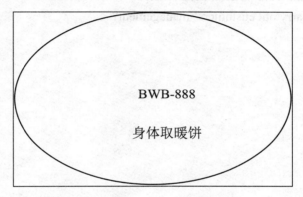

给年长者以温馨；
　　给孩子们以关爱；
　　　　让学生学习专心；
　　　　　　给您的旅途带来方便。

V. Case Study!

Dear Mr. Grabher,

Many thanks for your e-mail of Sept. 2.

We are very pleased to know that you and your general manager will attend the Canton Fair. I will stay in Guangzhou from Oct. 10 to 20, so we hope you can visit our booth during this period. Our booth No is 3.1C1*. Please inform us before your arrival in Guangzhou, so we can help you book your room if necessary. On the other hand, we have told you that our best price for Electric Shaver GT66 is USD68.00, please believe that this price is our lowest price. We can't reduce it any more. For the price of Electric Shaver GT68, our best price is USD76.00 as it is the newest model. So, please note that our quotations are listed as below:

Model　　　　　　　　Unit Price (CIF DUBAI)
GT66　　　　　　　　 USD68.00

GT68　　　　　　　　　USD76.00

The terms of payment we can accept are by sight L/C, but we are prepared to accept L/C at 60 days' sight only after we have established reliable business relations with your company. As you know, we are a very famous manufacturer in China. It is possible for you to find cheaper prices. But our Electric Shaver is priced at this level because of our high quality.

Your early reply is appreciated.

Best Regards,
Henry Cai
General Manager

VI. Discussion

1. How can you find your potential customers?
2. How can you carry out customers' management?

Unit Fifteen

Expos

Introduction

Participating in fairs is one of the most important marketing modes for enterprises and it is also their first choice to develop new markets. A fair is a neutral place where the seller or buyer can negotiate with each other on the basis of equality. Besides, it can make the buyers recognize the exhibits thoroughly.

There are some basic objectives for enterprises to participate in fairs:

a) establish and maintain enterprise's image;
b) look for new customers;
c) introduce new products or services;
d) choose selling agents and wholesalers;
e) study the local market and its trend.

Many researches conducted by governments or enquiry agencies show that more than fifty percent of enterprises regard exhibition as a very important means of marketing.

In the past 20 years, many private enterprises in East China, especially from Zhejiang, Jiangsu and Fujian Provinces, go abroad to participate in various international fairs.

Nowadays, there are many famous fairs in the world, such as Chicago Tools Expo, Milan Fashion Expo, Hannover Fairs, and Chinese Import and Export Fair (also once called Canton Fair, Guangzhou Fair). Normally, the more famous the fair is, the more exhibitors and buyers there will be, of course, the more possibilities of transaction there will be.

Business Letters

Email 1

==
From: vip.163.com <damai-sales@vip.163.com>
To: concordia < concordia @memo.net>
Cc: xinshidai@globalsourcing.com < xinshidai@globalsourcing.com>
Subject: VISIT
Date: 201*/2/28 12:53:49
==

Dear Concordia,

Welcome you to China!

As we are good friends, if you need someone pick you up at the airport, please tell us. As the hotel is very hard to find during the Canton Fair, we will book one room for you in advance. Please do not worry!

Unit Fifteen Expos

If everything goes smoothly, we will check in the same hotel so as to communicate easily. Enclosed please find the address and keep it with you. We will stay in Zhong Han Hotel. You can visit the website: http://zhonghan68.com. It is a 4 star hotel.

Maybe on Apr1.11th, 201* Jim will arrive at Guangzhou for decorating the booth, so if you need assistance, you can call:

    0138********   Jim's mobile
    0131********   Henry's mobile

We are looking forward to your visit in Guangzhou.

PAYMENT FOR HOTEL

We will pay the cost for booking, please do not worry anything.

NEW ORDER

Because the raw material prices increased too much, we have to adjust the prices. Many of clients like BBAMETAL, LATOVE, all accepted our new prices. So the prices in Venezuela may be increased a lot in the market.

If some items you think are too expensive, please tell us which item, and we will cooperate with you as much as possible. But we are always sure our prices are very competitive, especially after the prices of the raw materials increased, our prices are reasonable.

Kindly please send us the details of your order ASAP. Any delay may cause the past efforts and quotation in vain, because the prices of the raw material will not stop advancing in these months. Please study and make final decision.

PHOTO

When you enter the Canton Fair, you need to register, which will need some small photos of yourself. The size is 3.5CM x 5.0CM, just like the ID card's photo. Please do not forget to take with you. Of course you can take the necessary photo here at the Canton Fair, but maybe expensive than usual.

Best Regards,
Jim
Manager
Export & Client Dept.

Shanghai Better Hardware Trade Co., Ltd.
ADD: No.1991, Meilong Road West, Humin Plaza Shanghai, #200237
TEL: 0086-21-642503**/642532**/642508** (ext.208)
FAX: 0086-21-642503**
Website: www.betterhardware.com

Email 2

    To: lorna@southiland.co.nz
    Subject: Chinese Import and Export Commodities Fair (Canton Fair)

Dear Lorna,

We are glad to inform you that we will attend the forthcoming Chinese Import and Export Commodities Fair (Canton Fair), which will be held from April 15th 201* - 21th 201*.

Information covering our booth number was told just a moment ago as follows:

    Hall: 18

    Floor: 1st Floor

    Aisle: E

    Booth Number: 18.1E25--29

    Person attending: Henry, Lily, Snowen

    Mobile phones of Person attending: 136****8888, 138****8888, 130****6666 (respective).

Our new makes will be at display in which, we trust, you will be interested. We sincerely hope that you will be able to find time to visit us and view our new products.

We are looking forward to your early reply.

Best wishes,
Henry
General Manager

Shanghai Lihua Imp. & Exp. Co., Ltd.

Rm. 606 Plaza Building,   Fax: 86-21-642578**

1302 Meilong Road, 200237   Tel: 86-21-642578**

Shanghai, People's Republic of China   E-mail: henry@alibaba.com

Email 3

    To: wick@pyramidcomerce.com.sy

    Subject: Chinese Import and Export Commodities Fair (Canton Fair)

Dear Mr. Coacher,

We attend the Chinese Import and Export Commodities Fair (Canton Fair) twice a year. Today we send you some information about this largest fair in China as follows:

Canton Fair: 2 times each year (divided into Spring and Autumn ones), with 2 Phases each time.

    Spring Canton Fair:

    First Phase: from 04/15th--to 04/20th, each year. Hardware, Garments can be found.

    Second Phase: from 04/25th--to 04/30th, each year. Arts & Crafts, various commodities can be found.

    Autumn Canton Fair:

    First Phase: from 10/15th--to 10/20th, each year. Hardware, Garments can be found.

    Second Phase: from 10/25th--to 10/30th, each year. Arts & Crafts, Various commodities can be found.

We always attend Spring and Autumn Canton Fair each year for the second phase. We hope that you will attend this year's autumn fair. Our booth number will be sent to you as soon as we are informed.

Best regards,
Lily Cao
Sales Manager
Shanghai Lihua Imp. & Exp. Co., Ltd.

Rm. 606 Plaza Building,	Fax: 86-21-642578**
1302 Meilong Road, 200237	Tel: 86-21-642578**
Shanghai, People's Republic of China	E-mail: lihua88@alibaba.com

Email 4

To: lihua88@alibaba.com
Subject: Chinese Export Commodities Fair (Canton Fair)

Dear lily,

Thank you for your email of September 6 inviting us to attend the 1**th Chinese Export Commodities Fair in October.

We take pleasure in informing you that we are going to pay a visit to this Canton Fair. We will be in Guangzhou from October 16 to 20 and will certainly visit your booth.

We will discuss our pending order with you and place new orders with you for your new products as long as your prices are competitive and the quality is assured.

Reviewing the past three years, we think both of us are satisfied with the transactions concluded. We have to say your products have become popular and enjoyed a high reputation in our area. Our company is benefiting from the prosperous China economy. Thank you very much indeed! Meanwhile, we are very confident about our future cooperation.

We look forward to meeting you in Guangzhou.

Best Regards,
Wick Coacher
Tom Consumption Group

5**, Sayem Aldaher Street
Golail Industrial Zone
P.O. Box 9**
Jeddah, 21421
Saudi Arabia
Tel: 00966268***** Ext: 3**
Fax: 00966268*****
Email: wick@qwev.net

Email 5

To: richard@aol.com

Subject: 2*th East China Fair

Dear Richard,

We take pleasure in informing you that the 16th East China Fair (201* Shanghai) will be held in Shanghai New International Expo Center from March 1 to 6, 201*.

The exhibition halls are to be divided into four parts as Garments, Home Textiles, Art Deco Gifts and Consumer Goods, covering an area of 103,500 square meters and having about 3,500 exhibitors with more than 5,300 standard booths in the fair. It is estimated to receive more than 23,000 merchants from overseas.

We are pleased to advise you that we will have a booth there. The booth number will be sent to you right after we are told. We sincerely hope that you can come and find your interested goods. For your selection, we will show you many new designs of our products.

Place: Shanghai New International Expo Centre. (near the Long Yang Road Station of Metro Line No.2)

Helen will pick you up at the Pu Dong International Airport if you inform us of your flight number in advance. Helen is a very good driver now. She bought a BMW for herself six months ago.

Your favorable reply is appreciated.

Best regards,
Henry
General Manager

Shanghai Lihua Imp. & Exp. Co., Ltd.

Rm. 606 Plaza Building,	Fax: 86-21-642578**
1302 Meilong Road, 200237	Tel: 86-21-642578**
Shanghai, People's Republic of China	E-mail: lihua88@alibaba.com

Pattern N of Business Letters

If you want to invite your prospective importers to visit your booth at an international fair, you should mention the aspects as follows:

    a)   you are much honored to invite your customer to attend a forthcoming fair;

    b)   inform him of the name of the fair, address, date, hall, floor, aisle, booth number, person attending, mobile phones of persons attending, etc;

c) you will have many new items at display, which are attractive in design, excellent in quality and competitive in price;

d) ask him whether he needs your help if the fair is held in your own country;

e) you are looking forward to meeting him.

Relevant Terms

exhibitor 参展方	participant 参与人
participator 参与人	applicant 申请人
exhibit 展览品	pavilion 展馆
sponsor 主办者，赞助人	co-sponsor 协办方
admission 入场券	complimentary ticket 免费门票
aisle 通道，侧廊	a booth/stand 一个展位
booking deadline 订位截止期	rental fees 租赁费
indoor floor space 室内地面空间	outdoor exhibition area 室外展区

Useful Phrases

on show 展览，陈列	on display 展览，公开展出
to aim at 针对，瞄准	to be aimed at 针对，瞄准
to play a role in 发挥作用	in contact with 接触，交往
to communicate with 与……交流	in disagreement with 与……不一致
in one's own interest 为自己的利益	to inquire into 调查，探究
to inquire of 询问	workable price 可行的价格

Summary

Fairs are good channels for exporters to find new importers. At a fair, a buyer and a seller can negotiate equally. It is also easier for a buyer to find new products at a fair. Many regular exhibitors benefit from their participating in fairs globally. The expo industry is developing rapidly in the 21 century.

Exercises

I. Questions for review

1. What are the main functions of participating in foreign fairs?

2. How do the small and medium-sized enterprises develop the international market by participating in foreign fairs?

3. How do the exporters choose a right fair agent?

4. How do the exporters choose a right foreign fair?

5. What should the exporters prepare before participating in a foreign fair?

6. What should the exhibitor do during the exhibition period?

7. Why do we think it important for an exporter to continue participation in foreign fairs even if the first participation fails to bring many orders?

8. What should the exhibitor do after he comes back from the foreign fair?

II. Choose the best answer

1. The home improvement industry had its first face-to-face buying and selling Show. And _____ a result, the National Hardware Show became an instant success.

    A. on   B. at   C. to   D. as

2. Today we were told that our Order No.HM088 was randomly selected by the Customs _____ random inspection.

    A. at   B. to   C. on   D. for

3. Exhibitors were again mentioning high costs and lower attendance _____ other inconveniences.

    A. in   B. on   C. among   D. during

4. Due _____ this inspection, shipment will be delayed until to next month.

    A. on   B. at   C. to   D. as

5. The new venue allows him to significantly lower or eliminate a wide range _____ costs associated with exhibiting (booth space, drayage, labor, hotel).

    A. by   B. of   C. with   D. through

6. The National Hardware Show in Las Vegas is the only housing after-market show, bringing together manufacturers and resellers _____ all products used to remodel, repair, maintain and decorate the home and its surroundings.

    A. by   B. of   C. with   D. through

7. We received the goods at our warehouse and unfortunately we were very badly impressed _____ the fact that the container was only 50% filled.

    A. on   B. at   C. to   D. by

8. This time we will afford the fees together with you. We hope USD100 _____ each side could be the final solution.

    A. at   B. to   C. of   D. for

9. On the other hand, we ask you to send us the price CIF Caucedo or Haina port _____ 5% commission.

    A. at   B. to   C. on   D. with

10. After careful consideration and talking with Clients, we have decided that it is best to

cancel this order _____ your production has failed to pass the shipping inspection.

  A. at   B. but   C. since   D. in

11. We hope you will effect shipment _____ the earliest possible date.

  A. in   B. on   C. at   D. during

12. Please make us your lowest _____ firm offer.

  A. possible   B. probable   C. likely   D. liable

13. We accept your order _____ condition that your buyer accepts October shipment.

  A. for   B. in   C. at   D. on

14. The best we can do is to allow you a discount of 2% _____ our quotation.

  A. at   B. off   C. in   D. from

15. No other buyer has _____ higher than this price.

  A. bid   B. quote   C. offer   D. quota

16. Please quote us your lowest price, FOB London, stating the best discounts and _____ particulars of weight and measurement.

  A. complete   B. all   C. full   D. detailed

17. They must be quite new _____ design.

  A. on   B. at   C. to   D. in

18. Our commodities have _____ the competition well.

  A. stood   B. met   C. from   D. by

19. Please feel assured that we will abide _____ our promise.

  A. by   B. of   C. with   D. through

20. You should adapt your terms of trade _____ the new circumstance.

  A. at   B. to   C. of   D. on

III. Translate the following sentences into Chinese

1. Fill in the application form for participating in the exhibition and send it by post or fax to the organizers.

2. Please remit by T/T the exhibition cost (50% down payment or full payment) to the organizer within 7 days after making the application. The balance should be paid off before Feb 20. We will issue a receipt after we receive all the exhibition cost.

3. The exhibitors submitting application form after Feb 20 201* should pay the exhibition cost in full amount at one time.

4. Principle for allocating exhibition site: "First applying, first making payment and first making arrangement"; for double entrance booth, plus 20% charge.

5. The exhibitors should fax the bank bill to the organizer after remitting the full amount of the cost.

6. The exhibitors can have the ordered exhibition site reserved only after they have paid the 50% down payment within the stipulated period.

7. The organizer will send application manual to exhibitors not later than January 21, 201*

after receiving the application form and payments.

8. Attendees include CEOs, presidents, vice presidents, owners, partners, buyers, operations, logistics, merchandising, and marketing professionals from retailers, wholesalers & distributors and importers & exporters. Retailers are represented from home centers, mass, specialty, grocers, chain drug stores and wholesaler clubs.

9. Exhibitors include: manufacturers of home-related products including hand and power tools, electrical and plumbing, housewares, paint and home decor, lawn and garden, outdoor living and global sourcing.

10. The manufacturers that exhibit at the National Hardware Show are represented in the following areas: Hardware & Tools, Housewares, Lawn & Garden, Paint & Home Décor, Electrical & Plumbing and Global Sourcing.

Optional Part

11. We have decided to have a sole agent in your area in order to take advantage of the growing demand there for our products.

12. Mr. Tang's place has been taken by Mr. Li, who will have the pleasure of calling upon you next week with our samples for the coming season, when we believe you will favor us with your new order.

13. We have received your samples and quotation sheet. The quality is satisfactory, but your prices are considerably above our usual figures.

14. The garments on display at the fair were attractive, especially their fashionable styles interested the attendee.

15. We intend to extend our export trade in the wines produced in this area, and enclose a complete price-list for your consideration.

IV. Translate the following sentences into English

1. 我们将参加201*年10月15日的广交会。如果你方能有时间来访，我们将会非常高兴。

2. 我们很高兴告知你方我们的建筑材料专业展是与世界展会集团联合主办的。

3. 我们每年在中国成功主办50多个展会。请尽管与我们联系索要详细信息。

4. 我们已经决定参加于9月22日至25日在大连举行的第十届大连国际建筑材料展。

5. 请告知我方你们的联系人姓名、职务、地址、电话、传真、邮件地址、网址及经营产品。

6. 如果你方对我们的展会更新信息不感兴趣，那么就请以"移除"为主题发回邮件，以便我们把你方的地址从我们的邮寄清单上去除。

7. 该展览中心位于上海中央商务区的中心地带，自从2000年10月开业以来吸引了全球范围的注意。它每年主办50多个世界级的展览。

8. 目前，该展览中心有9个展览大厅，室内展览面积达125,500平方米，还有90,000平方米的室外展览面积。

9. 我们的网页旨在为国际买家和国内供应商提供一个更有效的在线交易平台。

10. 展览大厅分为四个部分，即服装、家纺、艺术装饰礼品和消费品，面积达105,200平方米，有3,652个参展商，5,556个标准展位。

Unit Fifteen Expos

V. Case Study

Case A: Contacting your customer after Canton fair

-----Original Message　1　-----
From: DUOMAI-SALES(163) [mailto:duomai-sales@vip.163.com]
Sent: Monday, November 06, 201* 9:43 AM
To: Concordia
Cc: service of duomai
Subject: brass spout & control valve project
Importance: High

Dear Concordia,

How are you? Hope everything is fine at your side.

We are very busy these days in arranging many shipments, applying for brands' registration, Visas to France, Venezuela, Ecuador, Peru...

It was such a delight to meet you again at the Canton Fair, and we are very glad to invite you to visit our factory in Yueguo.

According to our discussion, we are now making improvement on brass spout and control valves. We will send you the final sample later.

As regards the BRASS SPOUT, we quote you again as per the present raw material situation:

　　FOB Shanghai
　　BRASS SPOUT as per drawings and sample:
　　USD1.415/PCS　　minimum qty.: 6000PCS

We look forward to receive your early reply.

Best Regards,
James
Manager
Export & Client Dept.

Shanghai Better Hardware Trade Co., Ltd
ADD: No.1991, Meilong Road West, Humin Plaza Shanghai, #200237
TEL: 0086-21-642503**/642532**/642508** (ext.208)
FAX: 0086-21-642503** Website: www.betterhardware.com

-----Original Message　2　-----
==
From: Steve McCurry <Steve McCurry @concordia88.bg>
To: DAMAI-SALES(163) <damai-sales@vip.163.com>
Cc: service of damai <damai-service@vip.163.com>
Subject: MEETING MINUTES Oct'06
Date: 201*/11/9 3:39:57
==

Dear Friend,

It was a pleasure to visit your plant and have the chance to discuss the pending issues with you in person. I am convinced our meeting was very fruitful and you understood our requirements well.

I am sending the attached meeting minutes. Let us both follow the open issues recorded therein and give each other updates on the progress.

I look forward to receiving your confirmation and your additions if any to all the topics.

Best regards,
Steve
Purchasing Manager

Case B: Contacting your customer after Canton fair

Dear Mr. Smith,

We were very pleased to meet you at the Canton Fair last week. We really hope that you could have a happy journey in China.

We have over 20 years' experience in manufacturing and supplying sanitary fittings and relative hardware for many markets, especially in South America and Caribbean area. Our products enjoys quite good reputation in Venezuela, Ecuador, Peru, Colombia, Panama, Argentina, Brazil, Uruguay, Dominica, Jamaica, Costa Rica, Mexico. Our products are of high quality and competitive in prices.

At the Canton Fair, you showed your interest in our newly developed products. Enclosed please find our latest catalogue for your consideration. We sincerely hope to start our cooperation this year.

By the way, we are glad to inform you that we will attend the Costa Rica Hardware Fair in the next April. We will tell you our booth number after we know it.

We are looking forward to your specific enquiry.

Best Regards,
Henry Cai
Export & Client Dept.

Case C: Attending a local fair

Exhibition industry is developing rapidly in China. Every year there are always many fairs held in some big cities. For example:

1. China Import and Export Fair (Canton Fair)
2. East China Fair
3. China International Import Expo

Try to attend a local fair and share what you see and learn with your classmates.

VI. Discussion

What can we learn from the true story mentioned below?

广交会体会

很荣幸有机会可以参加第***届中国出口商品交易会(广交会)，在4月25—30日这6天时间中，作为一个参展商，我有幸亲身体验了中国最大的商品交易会的盛况，也让我在工作中学习到了很多东西，其中有工作经验，也有生活经验，更有对学习和人生新的认识，下面就是我的一些体会。

首先，广交会作为中国最大的商品交易会，随着中国市场的扩大，吸引了越来越多的参展商和采购商参与，于是在广交会上的第一印象就是外国人特别多。第一天参加广交会时，由于是菜鸟，对业务流程和样品材质不是很了解，再加上头一次见到那么多奇装异服者，一时间不知所措，整天都在手忙脚乱，而且还有很大的心理障碍，不敢开口说话，虽然心中已经盘算好了对话的内容，但是真到了采购商的面前，还是会紧张得忘记要说什么，看看其他业务员，虽然学历不一定很高，口语也不一定很好，但是在面对客商时一点也不怯，可以大方地交流，再加上肢体语言，一样能够很好地进行业务交流。这对我的触动很大，学习了那么多时间的英语却不能和别人交流，等于没有学过。于是在老业务员的帮助和自己的努力下，第二天和第三天起我便开始渐渐放开自己，也不担心会犯错，保持着微笑，有些不明白不懂的地方就用肢体和表情来表示，同样也能达到效果，而随着我的逐渐放开，客商也逐渐愿意与我洽谈，得到的机会和意向也越来越多了。我认为，虽然我的口语并没有在这段时间提高多少，但是这短短的六天却让我突破了害怕开口说话的一个瓶颈。

其次，我认识到想要做好一件事情就一定要拼尽全力，不能给自己留任何退路，否则就会半途而废。第一天到达广州，由于是头一回一个人出那么远的门，周围所有的一切都是陌生的，也没有朋友和同学，一切都只能自己摸索。但也是这样的环境让我没有任何偷懒的机会，于是把自己所有的注意力都放进了广交会，这样才可以那么快地适应这个节奏。在工作中，如果想要好的业绩和成果，同样也要投入120分的努力，从早上9点开始站在摊位前对着来往的客商微笑招呼，直到2点半左右才有时间吃饭，要拉住一个潜在的客户就更加困难，要主动地向他们推荐一些被他们忽视的样品，虽然这样会比简单地按照他们的需要报价累许多，但是如果看到他们产生浓厚的兴趣并且表达了订货意向的时候，这种成就感也是敷衍了事不能比拟的。

最后就是我终于体会到了学生生活的美好和幸福，没有压力，没有强迫，可以做许多自己想做的事情，不用那么累，可以随便看看自己喜欢的书，也认识到了专业课的重要作用，过去为了考试而学的想法是相当幼稚的，也是不可取的，只有真的学到了东西以后在工作中才可以随心地使用。学生时代真的应该好好学一些东西，因为在工作之后就根本没有充裕的时间和精力再去学习再去提高，只有依靠自己的基础进行一些修补，要像在大学里一样飞速进步是绝对不再可能了。或许我知道这个道理也不是很早了，但是至少还是有些时间的，可以趁着最后的时间做一些有意义的事情。

以上就是我去广交会的一些随想和感受，也许比较肤浅，但是的确是最真实和印象最深刻的，感谢老师阅读。(彭亮, May 19)

Unit Sixteen

Flexible Trade (I)

Introduction

The mode of trade means the practice by which a business transaction is concluded.

Nowadays, many different modes of trade are prevailing in the international market. From the exporters' point of view, except for individual transactions, such modes of trade are also adopted, as distribution, agency, consignment, auction, fairs and sales, invitation to tender, submission of tender, counter trade (barter, compensation trade, counter purchase, offset trade, international trading certificate) and processing trade, etc. Furthermore, establishing a joint venture has also been regarded as a flexible mode of trade in globalization.

Every mode of trade has its advantages and disadvantages. Exporters should choose the suitable mode with low risks. Generally speaking, to select which mode of trade depends on the nature of goods, the foreign buyer's situation and the usual practice in different countries and regions.

What is a Sole Agency?

A supplier can list their goods with as many agents as they wish, but the only one agent listed is not necessarily a sole agency. Authority for the agent to sell as the "sole agent" must be given by the supplier, in written form. A specified time period for the sole agency should be clearly defined.

A sole agency precludes all other agents from working on the sale of the goods, although another agent may approach the sole agent if they have a suitable client. Even then the sole agent would tie up the deal.

The main benefit of a sole agency is the obligation it places on the agent to provide a sale. The agent is bound to work harder to sell the goods and, according to a code of ethics, to exert his best efforts. If an agent is unable to perform in this manner then the sole agency should not be accepted.

Business Letters

Email 1

To: lihua88@alibaba.com
Subject: Sole Agent

Dear Henry,

I hope you are enjoying your holiday in Hainan Island.

Up to now, all big suppliers from China, such as Midea, Haier, Kelon, Jinling, Little Swan…after long time's dealing with Cyprus market since early 1990s', now are applying benefit-sharing

Unit Sixteen Flexible Trade (I)

policy with Cyprus buyers. One model of a product will be given to only one buyer in Cyprus and they are getting successful because of that policy.

For your refrigerator, the same policy should be applied as you can see consequence soon if you try to sell to so many buyers here. Because nobody gets profit as Cyprus is a small market with total population and area that just equals to a medium-sized city in your province. And we think that the two constant buyers you have kept are enough for your business because competition now is really fierce. Please consider it carefully and we hope that you can have policy to protect reliable and long-term buyers like us. If possible, please entrust us as your sole agent in our market as soon as business develops to our mutual satisfaction.

After your holiday, we will place more orders with you for about 2-3 containers and we are trying to place regular orders with you. We hope that by this way we can keep business for a long term.

Best regards,
Joseph Epaminondas
Import Manager

Consumption Goods Marketing International

Email 2

To: lihua88@alibaba.com
Subject: Represent You in Germany

Dear Mr. Cai,

From the internet, we have come to know that your esteemed company specializes in silk products, such as silk thread, silk paper, silk stockings/socks, pure silk scarf, and silken garments (Tangzhuang, attire of traditional Chinese style included). We'd like to tell you that we are greatly interested in representing you in Germany for the sale of your unique products.

We take the liberty of writing to you in the hope of offering our services as your agent in Europe. For your information, our company, established 15 years ago, specializes in special local products from Asia in Europe. We have excellent marketing channels with high efficiency. Our annual turnover reached EUR10.00 million last year.

To our much encouragement, we know that you will attend the forthcoming Hamburger Fair next month. Of course, we will visit your booth. At the first stage, we think, we shall place a trial order with you for your new products at the fair and discuss a draft agreement based on the possible sales volume. Once the time is mature, a Sole Agency Agreement shall be considered.

We look forward to meeting you with much interest next month.

Best regards,
Clemens

Alps Marketing GmbH
Littenstrasse 5** 1017* Berlin
Tel: +49 (0) 30 240**
Fax: +49 (0) 30 240**
Email: clemens@alpsmarketing.de

Doc. 1

Exclusive Agency Agreement

This agreement is made and entered into by and between the parties concerned on Sept. 6, 20** in Shanghai, China, on the basis of equality and mutual benefit to develop business on terms and conditions mutually agreed upon as follows:

1. The Parties Concerned

  Party A:
  Add:
  Tel:
  Fax:

  Party B:
  Add:
  Tel:
  Fax:

2. Appointment

Party A hereby appoints Party B as its Exclusive Agent to solicit orders for the commodity stipulated in Article 3 from customers in the territory stipulated in Article 4, and Party B accepts such appointment.

3. Commodity

4. Territory

5. Minimum turnover

Party B shall undertake to solicit orders for the above commodity from customers in the above territory during the effective period of this agreement for not less than USD 1,000,000.00 every year.

6. Price and Payment

The price for each individual transaction shall be fixed through negotiations between Party B and the buyer, and subject to Party A's final confirmation.

Payment shall be made by confirmed, irrevocable L/C opened by the buyer in favor of Party A, which shall reach Party A 30 days before the date of shipment.

7. Exclusive Right

In consideration of the exclusive rights granted herein, Party A shall not, directly or indirectly, sell or export the commodity stipulated in Article 4 to customers in Australia through channels other than Party B; Party B shall not sell, distribute or promote the sales of any products competitive with or similar to the above commodity in Australia. Party A shall refer to Party B any enquiries or orders for the commodity in question received by Party A from other firms in Australia during the validity of this agreement.

8. Market Report

In order to keep Party A well informed of the prevailing market conditions, Party B should undertake to supply Party A, at least once a quarter or at any time when necessary, with market reports concerning changes of the local regulations in connection with the import and sales of the commodity covered by this agreement, local market tendency and the buyer's comments on quality, packing, price, etc. of the goods supplied by Party A under this agreement. Party B shall also supply party A with quotations and advertising materials on similar products of other suppliers.

9. Advertising and Expenses

Party B shall bear all expenses for advertising and publicity in connection with the commodity in question in Australia within the validity of this agreement, and shall submit to Party A all audio and video materials intended for advertising for prior approval.

10. Industrial Property Rights

Party B may use the trade-marks owned by Party A for the sale of the Plastic items covered herein within the validity of this agreement, and shall acknowledge that all patents, trademarks, copy rights or any other industrial property rights used or embodied in the Plastic items shall remain to be the sole properties of Party A. Should any infringement be found, Party B shall promptly notify and assist Party A to take steps to protect the latter's rights.

11. Validity of Agreement

This agreement, when duly signed by the both parties concerned, shall remain valid for 12 months from _____ to _____, and it shall be automatically extended for another 12 months upon expiration unless notice in writing is given to the contrary.

12. Termination

During the validity of this agreement, if either of the two parties is found to have violated the stipulations herein, the other party has the right to terminate this agreement.

13. Force Majeure

Either party shall not be held responsible for failure or delay to perform all or any part of this agreement due to flood, fire, earthquake, draught, war or any other events which could not be predicted, controlled, avoided or overcome by the relative party. However, the party affected by the event of Force Majeure shall inform the other party of its occurrence in writing as soon as possible and thereafter send a certificate of the event issued by the relevant authorities to the other party within 15 days after its occurrence.

14. Arbitration

All disputes arising from the performance of this agreement shall be settled through friendly negotiation. Should no settlement be reached through negotiation, the case shall then be submitted for arbitration to the China International Economic and Trade Arbitration Commission (Beijing) and the rules of this Commission shall be applied. The award of the arbitration shall be final and binding upon both parties.

Party A: Party B:
(Signature)   (Signature)

Doc. 2

NONDISCLOSURE AGREEMENT

This Agreement (hereinafter referred to as "Agreement") made and entered into this ___ day of _____, by and between_____ (hereinafter referred to as "Recipient"), and QQD (hereinafter referred to as "Proprietor").

WHEREAS, QQD represents and warrants that it is the owner and possessor of certain Proprietary Information relating to QQD Products. This includes Proprietary Information provided to Recipient in oral or written form or learned by Recipient during any inspection of QQD facilities (hereinafter referred to as "Proprietary Information"), and;

WHEREAS, it is desirable that QQD disclose certain of the Proprietary Information to Recipient, and;

WHEREAS, it is the mutual desire of both parties hereto to preserve the secrecy and confidentiality of the Proprietary Information;

NOW THEREFORE, in consideration of the disclosure and other undertakings giving rise to such disclosure, it is hereby agreed as follows:

1. Purpose

QQD will deliver and/or disclose certain of its Proprietary Information to Recipient for the purpose of Soliciting Bids. All information QQD delivers to Recipient is Proprietary Information hereunder.

2. Recipient's Obligations

Except as authorized by this Agreement or as otherwise authorized in writing by QQD, Recipient agrees that:

    a.   It will not disclose the Proprietary Information or any portion thereof to others;

    b.   It will not use the Proprietary Information or any portion thereof for its own account or purpose other than for the purpose stated above, or to serve the purposes of any other person or entity;

    c.   It will be responsible for strictly maintaining the secrecy and confidentiality of the Proprietary Information or any portion thereof disclosed to it;

    d.   It will take reasonable measures and exercise its best efforts to prevent unauthorized disclosure of the Proprietary Information or any portion thereof;

　　e.　It will disclose the Proprietary Information or any portion thereof only to such of its employees or professional advisors as are necessary to carry out the purposes of this Agreement, and make such persons aware of the obligations of confidentiality and use contained in this Agreement.

　　3.　Exceptions to Recipient's Obligations

The obligations in paragraph 2 above shall not apply to:

　　a.　Information which is in the public domain as of the date of the execution of this Agreement;

　　b.　Information already known to Recipient at the time of disclosure to Recipient, which was not received from a source obligated under a nondisclosure agreement;

　　c.　Information which comes to Recipient from a bona fide third party source having the right to disclose such information to Recipient;

　　d.　Information required to be disclosed pursuant to any statute, law, rule or regulation of any governmental authority or pursuant to any order of any court of competent jurisdiction; provided however, Recipient will: (i) immediately notify QQD of such request or demand; and (ii) at least ten (10) days prior, or as soon as possible to making any such disclosure of Proprietary Information, provide QQD with a written, detailed description of the matter pertaining to the requestor demand.

　　e.　Information developed internally by Recipient entirely independent of any relationship with QQD or access to Proprietary Information.

　　4.　No License or Waiver

None of the provisions of this Agreement shall be construed as a grant of a license of the Proprietary Information to Recipient by QQD, or as a waiver of the rights and remedies afforded by the patent, trademark and copyright laws of the _____(Country).

　　5.　Term

Notwithstanding the above, all obligations of Recipient hereunder shall terminate ten (10) years from the date of execution by QQD.

　　6.　Governing Law

The parties hereto expressly agree that all disputes, controversies or claims arising hereunder, and the interpretation of any of the provisions or the performance called for hereunder shall be governed and determined by the laws of the _____, excluding any conflicts or choice of law rule or principle that might otherwise refer construction or interpretation of this Agreement to the substantive law of another jurisdiction. Any suit or action at law or in equity involving a dispute, controversy or claim arising hereunder shall be brought and maintained by either party in the appropriate court located in, _____, or if jurisdiction will so permit, in the ** Court of _____. Recipient consents to personal jurisdiction over itself in such courts.

7. Remedies

Because of the unique nature of the Proprietary Information, the parties acknowledge that QQD will suffer irreparable harm if Recipient fails to comply with any of its obligations under this Agreement, and monetary damages for such breach would be totally inadequate. Therefore, the parties agree that QQD shall be entitled to injunctive relief for any such breach by Recipient, in addition to any other remedies available at law or equity.

8. Headings

The paragraph headings are for convenience only, and shall not be construed as a part of this Agreement.

9. Return of Information

Upon request by QQD, Recipient shall promptly return to QQD, or destroy if so directed by QQD, all Proprietary Information (including written information and all copies provided by QQD, as well as notes, compilations or other documents prepared by Recipient containing Proprietary Information).

10. Solicitation

Recipient will neither directly nor indirectly solicit for hire any employee of the other party or any of its subsidiaries for a period of one (1) year subsequent to the termination of this Agreement without the written permission of a senior executive officer of QQD; provided, however, that the foregoing provision will not prevent Recipient from employing any former QQD employee who contacts such party at his or her own initiative without any direct or indirect solicitation by or encouragement from such Recipient.

11. Public Statements

Without the prior written consent of the other, neither party will disclose to any person or entity other than on an as-needed basis to immediate advisors such as a lawyer or accountant, the fact that any exchange of information, investigations, discussions or negotiations are taking place between the parties. The parties shall agree the content of any public statement on.

12. Indemnification

Recipient does hereby covenant and agree, at its expense, to pay, and to indemnify and hold harmless QQD, its parent, subsidiary, affiliated corporations and their respective directors, officers, employees, shareholders, representatives and agents (the "QQD Division") from and against any and all, expenses, losses, liabilities, demands, causes of action, costs, damages, expenses, legal and other fees, fines and penalties of every kind and nature including, without limitation, claims for damage to or destruction of any property and injury to or death of any person arising out of or in any way connected with this Agreement and any performance or failure to perform by Recipient of the duties imposed upon Recipient pursuant to this Agreement. The provisions of this paragraph and Recipient's obligations hereunder will survive any termination of this Agreement.

WHEREFORE, the parties hereto have entered into this Agreement on the day and year first above written.

    PROPRIETOR: QQD
    PRINTED NAME: _____
    Signature: _____
    TITLE: Director of Purchasing & Inventory Control
    RECEPIENT: _____
    PRINTED NAME: _____
    Signature: _____
    TITLE: _____
    DATE: _____

Email 3

To: huali88@alibaba.com
Subject: Establishing a Joint Venture

Dear Mr. Cai,

    We supply materials and products for automobiles to a major manufacturer of automobile components in France, who makes starters and other electronic parts.

    Competition in this field gets severer every year, but there is an opportunity to establish and develop a new joint venture to make automobile components and products using advanced technologies owned by medium-sized French specialist manufacturers for sales to automobile manufacturers worldwide.

    Therefore we hope to establish a joint venture to make and assemble automobile components and/or die-cast products and electric components for sale to new clients in France and around the world.

    The aim of such a joint venture would be to reduce manufacturing costs by economy of scale and the use of advanced manufacturing technology in France. We can expect to increase sales to new and established customers around the world.

    We wish to say that we plan to invest USD 4000,000.00, of which 40% in cash, 40% in capital goods, and the rest 20% in technologies. You are expected to invest equal amount as your share of contribution. The investment contributed by you may include the right to the use of a site provided for the joint venture company during the period of its operation.

    Your favorable reply is awaited.
Sincerely yours,
Mr. Gustave Eiffel
C.E.O.
Eiffel Corporation LTD.
Telephone: 33-
Facsimile: 33-
Email: eiffel@online.com.fr

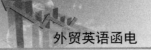

Pattern O of Business Letters

If you are seeking for an opportunity to act as a foreign supplier's agent in a territory, you should state the following aspects clearly:

A) you are greatly interested in representing him for the sales of his competitive goods in your area;

B) you have sufficient means to develop the trade and excellent business connections to reach a reasonable sales volume within a period of time;

C) you hope an agency agreement will be taken into the supplier's consideration when time becomes mature;

D) you hope to have a talk with the supplier personally, if possible;

E) you look forward to his favorable reply as soon as possible.

Relevant Terms

distribution center 分拨中心，销售中心	distributor 经销商，批发商
supplier 供应商	Distributorship Agreement 经销协议
sole distributor 独家经销商	Exclusive Sales 包销
agency 经销商，代理处	agent 代理人，代理商
principal 委托人	consignment 委托，寄售，寄售物
consignor 发货人，委托人	consignee 承销人，收货人
auction 拍卖	auctioneer 拍卖人
English Auction 英式拍卖	Dutch Auction 荷兰式拍卖

Useful Phrases

consignment merchandise 寄售品	to change hands 转手，易主
to call on 拜访，请求	to call the deal off 取消这笔生意
on consignment 寄售方式	of inferior quality 质量差
of superior quality 质量上乘	of no use 无用
nothing different from 没有什么不同	to clear off 清理，摆脱
a wide variety of 各种各样	to lodge a claim against sb. 向某人提出索赔

Summary

There are many different modes of trade prevailing in the international market. Every mode of trade has its advantages and disadvantages. Any trader should find his best mode of trade.

Exercises

I. Questions for review

1. From the point of view of exporters', what are the flexible modes of trade which can be adopted except for traditional individual transaction?
2. What is distribution?
3. What is agency?
4. What is consignment?
5. What is auction?
6. What is fairs and sales?
7. What is compensation trade?
8. What is counter purchase?
9. What is offset trade?
10. What is international trading certificate?
11. What is processing trade?

II. Choose the best answer

1. It is_____ a great privilege and pleasure to answer your letter about Anita & Sons Corp.
   A. at   B. in   C. on   D. with
2. They have been a credit customer _____ ours.
   A. at   B. in   C. on   D. of
3. It has always paid its account _____ time.
   A. at   B. within   C. on   D. to
4. We recommend Australia Trading Co. Ltd. to you _____ no reservations.
   A. at   B. in   C. with   D. to
5. Would you please to let us have a report _____ the reputation and financial standing of the firm?
   A. at   B. in   C. on   D. to
6. We should also like your advice _____ the maximum amount for which it would be safe to grant credit on a quarterly account.
   A. at   B. in   C. on   D. to
7. We should like to know the financial and credit standing _____ the above-mentioned company.
   A. at   B. in   C. on   D. of
8. We should be much obliged if you would tell us _____ the above-mentioned company is

reliable in their dealings with you.

    A. whether   B. in   C. on   D. to

9. We must advise you to regard their request for credit _____ caution.

    A. at   B. with   C. on   D. to

10. Thank you for your enquiry, but we find that some items may be not suitable _____ Panama market.

    A. at   B. in   C. on   D. for

11. We shall write to him _____ his old address.

    A. at   B. in   C. on   D. to

12. As you _____, we are in urgent need of this product.

    A. know   B. would know   C. knew   D. had know

13. _____ the point of currency, it has been our practice to use CNY dollar in our dealings for a long time.

    A. To   B. In   C. On   D. At

14. We thank you for your Fax dated Mar.3, _____ us 3,000 M/T of your new products.

    A. offer   B. offering   C. to offer   D. for offering

15. If the end-user finds it necessary to replenish their stock before the end of this year, we shall _____ you again.

    A. meet   B. contract   C. communicate   D. contact

16. Please let us know as _____ as possible when the certificate is expected to reach us.

    A. sooner   B. prompt   C. quick   D. promptly

17. We find _____ to procure any ship sailing directly to China prior to September.

    A. it impossible   B. we are impossible

    C. impossible   D. difficult

18. The shortage in weight was due to the original bags being short-weighted _____ shipment.

    A. prior   B. prior to   C. prior that   D. previous

19. The market for this product _____ recently, and thus we cannot make a decision right now.

    A. fluctuates   B. has been fluctuating

    C. fluctuated   D. has fluctuated

20. We shall redouble our efforts _____ this business a success.

    A. to make   B. make   C. making   D. made

III. Translate the following sentences into Chinese

1. How about the feedback from your retailers and consumers? Your application for sole agency is now under our careful consideration.

2. We are glad to inform you that we have been appointed the Sole Agent in Shanghai for Tanaka Trading Co., Ltd., Yokohama.

3. Through the courtesy of Mr. Ding Kaixuan, we know that you are looking for an agent in this area, we are pleased to apply for the post.

4. We'll consider appointing you as our sole agent for our boilers for the next two years in your local market. Could we have a personal conversation before signing a contract in order to discuss relative terms and conditions?

5. We are very glad to know that you made application for Sole Agency of our company in South Africa. But we'll leave aside the question of agency until next week when our Exporter Manager visits you. We would like to arrange an interview with you. Please give us a suitable date.

6. In view of your extensive experience in this field, we are glad to appoint you as our agent. We suggest the duration of the contract should be for two years, automatically renewable upon expiration for a similar period unless notice is given to the contrary.

7. As our products have been introduced to your area for only three months, we won't consider agency in your market at present.

8. We have decided to entrust you with the sole agency for our precious stones in your area and look forward to a mutually beneficial association.

9. This agreement is made by and entered into between Shanghai Huali Imp. & Exp. Co., Ltd. (hereinafter referred to as Party A) and Tanaka Trading Co., Ltd., Yokohama (hereinafter referred to as Party B), whereby Party A agrees to appoint Party B to act as its sole agent for carpets in the designated territory on the terms and conditions set forth below.

10. During the valid period of this agreement, Party A shall not make offers of the said goods to any other party in the above-mentioned territory, and Party B shall guarantee not to undertake the agency of, or to handle the sale of, the same kind of goods for any other suppliers.

Optional Part

11. We appreciate your effort in pushing the sale of our products. We'd like to sign a sole agency agreement with you for a period of 3 years.

12. I am afraid we can't agree to appoint you as our sole agent because the annual turnover you achieved last year was too small.

13. You have done very well in fulfilling the agreement. We'd like to renew our sole agency agreement for another two years.

14. I think the annual sale of 100 pianos for a sole agent in your city is conservative. I'm sure that you can sell more this year in light of the market conditions at your end.

15. We would like to receive a detailed report from you every six months on current market conditions and the end-users' comments on our products.

IV. Translate the following sentences into English

1. 我们感谢你方有关独家代理在澳大利亚销售中国旗袍的问询。

2. 有关你方在东非代理中国五金的建议，我们已经决定任命贵公司为我们的独家代理，试用期为一年。

3. 我认为现在讨论代理问题为时过早。但请不要误解我方意见，我们并没有什么不满。

4. 目前阶段我们不得不谢绝你们作为我方独家代理的建议。正如你方所见，你们的年营业额还相当有限。

5. 除非你们的年营业额达到我方满意的程度，否则我们无法指定你们作为我方的独家代理。

6. 我建议订一个专销中国艺术品、收藏品和古玩的为期三年的独家代理协议。

7. 甲方有权根据市场行情修改销售价格，并及时通知乙方。

8. 本独家代理协议将有效期定为两年，自201*年9月2日至201*年9月1日。

9. 我们已经注意到你方想要成为我们在墨西哥城的独家代理，在深入探讨此事之前，我们想知道你们的促销计划以及你们在你方市场可能实现的年销售额。

10. 我们想申请做你方产品在我方当地市场上的独家代理。

V. Case Study

Your company, Shanghai Lihua Imp. & Exp. Co., Ltd., is going to sign an agreement with a domestic buyer, who intends to import a batch of goods from a foreign exporter. Your colleague has drawn it up as follows. In your opinion, is there anything to be refined?

进口代理协议书

甲方：上海****有限公司

乙方：上海利华进出口有限公司

甲、乙双方本着平等互利，共同发展的原则，经友好协商，自愿签订本协议：

一、甲方委托乙方代理进口相关产品。

二、甲方应提前8~10个工作日将进口计划告知乙方，并提供产品的品名、数量、重量、价格、产地、贸易国及产品的HS编码，如需办理机电批文请提前告知以便乙方及时办理。

三、甲方应积极配合乙方做好通关手续(随时提供海关所需资料)。

四、甲方应付给乙方进口代理费，代理费为合同金额的__%，具体费用每单清算。最低每单元人民币。

五、在通关过程中发生的其他费用，按实际发生数与甲方结算。

六、乙方应积极为甲方做好购汇手续。

七、批文费及购汇乙方不再收取手续费。

乙方仅承担代理该商品的义务，对于实际买卖双方发生的争议(如商品品质、数量、交货期等)乙方概不负责。

以上协议经双方盖章后生效。有效期为一年。

甲方：上海****有限公司   乙方：上海利华进出口有限公司

日期：   年   月   日   日期：   年   月   日

VI. Discussion

In your opinion, how can the small and medium-sized Chinese enterprises find a qualified agent in their target market? How do you select the best applicant among many candidates?

Unit Seventeen

Flexible Trade (II)

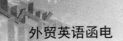

Introduction

Owing to the rapid development of the transportation, logistics, media, e-commerce and the WTO's drive, all the people in the world are facing a faster trend of globalization.

In international trade, the modes of trade are also become complicated and comprehensive. Some new varieties of modes of trade are emerging from time to time. Every enterprise should adapt itself to seize every opportunity to survive the fast-changing environment better.

Business Letters

Email 1

To: meyer@aol.com
Subject: General Agency or Consignment

Dear Mr. Meyer,

This is Helen Xie, Product Manager of Shanghai Home Decoration Co., Ltd., who met you in Hamburg last month.

We are very pleased to introduce ourselves to you. Our company deals in all kinds of imported home furnishings, such as curtains, furniture, sofa, etc. Founded in 1998, our company has emerged to be a leading resource in Shanghai for home furnishings. Superior quality and competitive pricing make us grow faster and become popular in China. Our store, which covers 21,500 square meters, will be expanded to 56,000 square meters by the end of the year. The completion of this expansion will designate Shanghai Home Decoration Co., Ltd. as the largest furnishing store in Shanghai.

We feature thousands of stylish sofas, curtains, and other furnishings and our showrooms are constantly being filled with the newest furniture, ranging from classical to contemporary styles. Our purchasers bring to our customers the finest furnishings in quality and style from all over the world. With one of the largest selections of furniture to choose from, our customers will be sure to find exactly what they're looking for.

As to sofa, through our investigation, we believe we will win a great success together with our suppliers. We have imported some sofas from Europe. In June, we will have a showroom special for imported sofa, covering 2,000 square meters. Now we plan to set up the largest show center for imported sofa in Shanghai, with an area of about 10,000 square meters. We are looking for more sofa suppliers and ready to order. We were strongly impressed on your products in Hamburg and hope to cooperate with you to introduce your products into Shanghai market.

It is our desire to offer our customers the widest and best selection of sofas, and we are therefore always interested in new products that fall within this line. We hope to act as your General Agency in Shanghai or cooperate with you on the basis of consignment.

For more details about our company, you are welcome to visit our website. We are looking forward to your favorable reply at your earliest convenience.

Yours faithfully,

Helen,

Product Manager

Shanghai Lihua Imp. & Exp. Co., Ltd.

Rm. 606 Plaza Building,   Fax: 86-21-642578**

1302 Meilong Road, 200237   Tel: 86-21-642578**

Shanghai, People's Republic of China   E-mail: lihua88@alibaba.com

Fax 1

FAX MESSAGE

Total Pages:1   Date: July 15, 201*

To: Mr. Antonio Pittman   From: Li Ming/Shanghai, China

Fax no: 0049-76**-981***   Subject: Investment or Trade

Dear Mr. Antonio Pittman,

This is Li Ming from Shanghai writing to you. I think you still remember me. I was working for SAMSUNG when you met me in China.

I'd like to know whether you or your friends have a plan to invest in China or handle import business from China. Whatever you do, I think I can do a substantial job for you.

As you know, China is a developing country and has a large market with rich natural resources. The prices of both labor and raw materials are much lower than those in Europe. If we use both the advanced technology from Europe and the cheap labor and raw materials in China to form a joint venture, I think your company shall have a good prospect.

If you or your friends are interested in international trade, I am sure you can always find cheaper products of high quality, which suit the fondness of the customers in your area.

I hope that we will be able to cooperate with each other in the near future. If you have any idea, please feel free to contact me. My fax no. is 0086-21-6424****. My mobile phone is 0086-13*1970***. I am looking forward to your favorable reply.

Best regards,

Li Ming

Fax 2

ROBERT MACHINERY & ELECTRONIC EQUIPMENT CO., LTD.
2nd Fl.1500, Shilong Rd. Shanghai 200237
Tel: 86-21-6453-6***　　Fax: 86-21-6453-5***

DATE：Oct. 5,201*
TO：MR. JOHN HAMILTON
FAX：406-255-9***
FM：LIU RUNNAN

Dear Mr. John Hamilton,

<u>Truck Mounted Stripers</u>[①]

Thank you for your Fax dated Oct. 3.

We've received your 17-page Fax dated 9-9-201*, which has also been accepted by the local government. And the local government has provided all the performance parameters of your truck-mounted stripers to the Ministry of Communication in Beijing. After its examination and approval, we will be able to know the result in November this year. By then, we need to buy bid documents, because the purchase of stripers will use the loans from the World Bank.

We will contact your company if we need more relevant information.

Best Regards,
Liu Runnan
General Manager

Fax 3

ROBERT MACHINERY & ELECTRONIC EQUIPMENT CO., LTD.
2nd Fl.1500, Shilong Rd. Shanghai 200237
Tel: 86-21-6453-62**　　Fax: 86-21-6453-59**

DATE：Nov.17, 200*
TO：Mr. John Hamilton,
　　　HITEC EQUIPMENT COMPANY
FAX：406-255-9***
FM：Liu Runnan

---

① 指公路上施工用的车载画线机。

Dear Mr. John Hamilton,

Thermoplastic Handliners[①] & Truck Mounted Stripers

We faxed to Mr. Peter Shanks on Oct.31 and Nov. 5 and Nov. 11, in which we expressed our hope that you would be able to submit a tender, because one of our clients in Hangzhou is interested in your Model 200 Thermoplastic Handliners and we think your products are competitive in price. We also bought the relative bidding documents. But up to present, we still haven't got any news replies from your company. Could you please give us a reply as soon as possible?

As regards Truck Mounted Stripers, sealed tenders will be opened on Nov. 20, and we have confidence in our victory. Please also let us know whether you will proceed with it.

Your prompt reply is awaited.

Best Regards,
Liu Runnan
General Manager

Doc.1

Agreement on Jointly Operating Shanghai Easy-home Furniture Factory
General Provisions

On the basis of equality and mutual benefit, Shanghai Benefit-all Industrial Company and Shanghai Easy-home Furniture Co., Ltd. reach an agreement after friendly negotiation to co-invest and jointly establish Shanghai Easy-home Furniture Factory. This agreement is as follows:

Clause 1: Two Parties Involved in This Joint Venture

Party A: Shanghai Benefit-all Industrial Company located at 5** Lida Rd., Taopu Town, Putuo District, Shanghai

Legal Representative: Wang Dali

Party B: Shanghai Easy-home Furniture Co., Ltd. located at Touqiao Town, Fengxian District, Shanghai

Legal Representative: Li Wenzhong

Clause 2: Setting Joint Venture: Shanghai Easy-home Furniture Factory

1. The above two parties have made an agreement to jointly establish Shanghai Easy-home Furniture Factory on Zhengcheng Road in Putuo District Industry Development Park.

2. Easy-home Furniture Factory is an independent legal person and registered at Taopu Town of Putuo District. This company must observe the State's rules, laws and relevant regulations and protected by the State's laws.

---

① 指公路上施工用的手动画线机。

Clause 3: Business Scope and Scale

1. Shanghai Easy-home Furniture Factory is mainly designed to produce a wide variety of furniture and office necessities for domestic and overseas market.

2. Shanghai Easy-home Furniture Factory sells its products and it's estimated that the annual output value will reach an amount of about CNY18.00 million and the yearly profit between CNY2 million to CNY3 million.

Clause 4: Total Investment, Registered Capital and Conditions for Cooperation

1. This Factory is a joint venture which is invested by both parties and is undertaken by Party B's legal representative to run.

2. Party A provides factory buildings with 2,800 m^2 and other facilities for office and daily life, total area is 10 mu and the power supply is 80 kV. It's estimated that Party A provides the production facilities with a total value between RMB 1.7 million to 2 million to enable Party B to produce.

3. Party B is responsible for supplying production equipment to the amount of CNY 1 million and in charge of the overall production and operation of this works.

Shanghai Easy-home Furniture Factory possesses registered capital of CNY 3 million in which Party A provides the fixed basic facilities with the amount of 2 million and Party B provides the fixed equipment with the amount of 1 million.

Clause 5: The two parts' Rights and Obligations

Party A:

1. Be in charge of finishing all the registration procedures.

2. Be in charge of preparing all the production facilities required by Party B before Spring Festival and getting ready for use by Party B.

3. Be in charge of coordinating the relations between the works and the local community of Taopu Town covering production and sales so as to make the production smooth.

Party B:

1. Be in charge of providing all relevant documents.

2. Be in charge of the business activities of the factory.

3. Be in charge of undertaking the business in compliance with Party A's co-operation conditions and paying the remuneration stipulated in the agreement.

4. Be in charge of purchasing, installing and testing the equipment in the factory.

5. Be in compliance with the regulations of the local government of Taopu Town covering fire control, environmental protection, labor, security, etc.

Clause 6: Distribution of Profit

In accordance with the above principles, the two parties have made an agreement in distributing profit:

1. Party B should send the factory's monthly financial statement to Party A in time.

2. Distribution of profit is based on the actual proportion of investment, Party A provides capital between CNY 1.7 million to 2 million and land covering 10 mu as co-operation condition and Party B's investment is between CNY 0.425 million to 0.5 million, and Party A should be paid at the end of June and December. (Party A collects profit from the date co-operation conditions for use are provided.)

3. Except tax, the profits or losses of Party B belong to Party B.

Clause 7: Duration

It is agreed temporarily the valid period of the Contract is 15 years, from October 30, 201* to October 29, 201*. If it needs to be extended, Party A should give complete support.

Clause 8: Liquidation after Termination of the Contract

When the contract expires or be terminated in advance, the factory assets should be settled in line with the principles of this Contract: assets from Party A's investment belong to Party A; equipment provided by Party B is returned to Party B. The newly invested fixed assets should be divided according to the proportion of investment.

Clause 9: Responsibilities for Violation

1. As the Contract becomes effective, Party B should pay earnest money CNY 300,000 to Party A as rent.

2. As the Contract goes into effect, the two parties should observe strictly the contracted amount of money. If one Party violates the contract, the relevant party should be responsible for compensating the economic losses resulting from breaking this Contract.

Clause 10: Miscellaneous Items

1. The current capital needed by the factory should be loaned from Taopu Bank if it is accordance with the principles of loan.

2. This Contract is in octuplicate, the two parties keep four of them respectively.

3. A supplement agreement should be reached if there are something unmentioned in this Contract. And it is of the same legal effect as this Contract after co-signature.

4. This Contract is put into effect after signature and stamped by both two parties.

Party A: Shanghai Benifit-all Industrial Company   Party B: Shanghai Easy-home Co., Ltd

Legal Representative (signature):   Legal Representative (signature):

Pattern P of Business Letters

There are many different forms of flexible trade. To cooperate with your prospective partner, you should state clearly what you want to do with your customer, and ask him whether he would accept or not. If approved, then draw the relative contract or agreement.

Relevant Terms

Contract of Transfer of Technology 技术转让合同	Agreement on Trademark License 商标使用许可协议
Contract of Patent License 专利许可合同	invitation to tender 招标
submission of tender 投标	open bidding 公开招标
bidding documents 投标文件	barter 以货易货
compensation trade 补偿贸易	Contract for Compensation Trade 补偿贸易合同
International Leasing Contract 国际租赁合同	

Useful Phrases

on the basis of compensation trade 按补偿贸易方式	to carry out compensation trade with sb. for 为某事与某人开展补偿贸易
to conclude compensation trade agreement 达成补偿贸易协议	to form a joint venture 组建合资企业
to share profits and losses in proportion to 按比例分享利润和亏损	in the form of cash, capital goods or know-how 以现金、资本货物或技术诀窍的方式(出资)

Summary

Except for individual transaction, there are still many different opportunities for enterprises to conclude business. Some business documents concerning agency, consignment, submission of tender, etc, are offered in this unit for the readers' reference. There are still many various kinds of business documents covering flexible trade. If you are requested to draft a certain document, try to study the relative specimen documents first.

Exercises

I. Questions for review

1. What are the differences between distribution and agency?
2. What are the advantages and disadvantages of consignment?

Unit Seventeen Flexible Trade (II)

II. Choose the best answer

1. For your information, we estimate all the products will be finished around December 25. Please inform us _____ the details about your forwarder. Or shall we contact your agent in Hangzhou?

  A. with   B. of   C. as   D. to

2. Please note that this batch of goods will be packed _____ neutral packing, so there should be no information about the manufacture on the box.

  A. on   B. with   C. in   D. to

3. We send you some pictures of the packages we exported _____ Panama. Please have a look at the pictures attached.

  A. on   B. with   C. in   D. to

4. We want to have a look at your box, polybag, carton and head card _____ no information covering your factory printed on them.

  A. with   B. of   C. as   D. to

5. We have received your down payment by T/T this morning. Enclosed pleased find the refined P/I _____ your confirmation.

  A. with   B. as   C. by   D. for

6. Because sending our samples by courier is quite expensive, next time we will send you illustrated e-catalog, _____ the detailed dimensions.

  A. attached   B. enclosed   C. following   D. including

7. Today we received an email from your agent in Ningbo, confirming that the quality _____ our sample is well accepted.

  A. with   B. of   C. as   D. to

8. Considering it is our first cooperation, our boss agreed to accept your order _____ such a small quantity. Please check the P/I for Item No.DF068 in the attachment.

  A. on   B. within   C. in   D. to

9. Your quantity is too small to be acceptable. Please check the minimum Qty. _____ the attached file.

  A. on   B. with   C. in   D. to

10. Please send us the pro forma invoice and samples _____ each item.

  A. with   B. as   C. by   D. for

11. In the meantime, kindly _____ the suppliers to explain the reasons for the delay.

  A. to ask   B. ask   C. contact to   D. to contact

12. As the goods are _____, we believe consumers can afford to buy them.

  A. highly priced   B. moderately priced
  C. priced high   D. priced low

13. You may make the spare parts yourselves, if you consider it _____ or appropriate to do so.

  A. economy   B. economical   C. economic   D. economics

14. Refusal to amend the L/C is equivalent _____ the cancellation of the contract.
    A. with   B. of   C. as   D. to
15. Payment is to be made _____ presentation of the shipping documents.
    A. by   B. upon   C. at   D. to
16. All rights and obligations involved in the agreement shall not be _____ to any third party.
    A. transmitted   B. passed on   C. transferred D. transit
17. We have drawn our draft on you payable ninety days _____ sight.
    A. at   B. on   C. after   D. by
18. Please remit the 15% down payment to us _____ T/T.
    A. with   B. as   C. by   D. up
19. Our terms of payment are by irrevocable L/C payable by draft at sight _____ by shipping documents.
    A. attached   B. enclosed   C. followed   D. accompanied
20. The seller asked for amendment _____ the L/C.
    A. on   B. with   C. at   D. to

III. Translate the following sentences into Chinese

1. It is our desire to offer our customers the widest and best selection possible of furniture, and we are therefore always interested in new products that fall within in this line. We are interested in your products and welcome you as one of our suppliers.

2. Our General Manager and Import Manager have decided to have an European visit from June 14th to 20th, for purchasing sofa. Italy will be their first stop.

3. May I ask you to set another date for meeting us at your factory or other place in which is convenient to you?

4. For your reference, we send you the information of two hotels, which are all close to our company, you can choose anyone as you like.

5. Please inform us the time you have scheduled for your visit. We look forward to meeting you in Ningbo very soon.

6. We will send somebody to pick you up at the airport in the morning on Wednesday and he will accompany you to check in at your hotel.

7. We are very happy that you accept our invitation to visit us. But July is too late for us, as you will understand if we order now, goods will not be received until September. It will be out of season. Your soonest visit will be most helpful for quick processing of orders and catching up the sales midseason.

8. We sincerely hope that you can schedule a time to visit us at the beginning of June. Your visit would help make the discussion of terms and conditions go smoother. We believe that you will have a productive visit.

9. We still want to invite you to visit us at your earliest convenience with a full set of your

leather samples, latest catalogues, informational video CDs, company profiles and price list.

10. The two containers of goods you sent to us have been received. Thank you for your cooperation. The items that have been displayed in our showroom look great! However, they have a strong leather smell that does not go away even after several weeks of being displayed in our store. Please advise us how we can eliminate this smell to avoid any complaints from our customers.

Optional Part

11. We have decided to establish a joint venture with you. Our contribution will be partly in cash and partly in equipment.

12. The Chinese participant is a big private company with more than 20 years' experience in the manufacture of building materials.

13. For the sake of formality, we will hold a board meeting at our end to thoroughly discuss the draft agreement so as to reach a unanimous understanding among the board members.

14. What is your estimation of the volume of trade we can achieve in a joint venture?

15. As there are a lot of pending matters relating to the conclusion of an agreement, we will send representatives to your city for a face-to-face discussion with you.

IV. Translate the following sentences into English

1. 这是对卡帝尔家具配件(上海)有限公司可行性研究报告和章程的回复。
2. 你方要我们审批卡帝尔家具配件(上海)有限公司可行性研究报告和章程的要求已经收到，经研究，正式答复如下：
3. 本公司每年生产6百万套各类家具配件，50%将销往国际市场。
4. 那里现有的厂房是租用的。如果厂房位于规划区内，该公司将不得不无条件搬迁。
5. 收到本答复后，请准备所有相关文件去申请外商投资企业的批准证书，并向工商局办理登记手续。
6. 租赁条件可以与上述两家公司相同。该开发区不允许有污染，请在可行性研究报告中加以说明。
7. 请立即考虑我方意向以便抓住良机，因为有很多商家来我公司寻找合作机会。
8. 为了让你方更好地了解本公司，我们通过号码为 EA56682****CN 的邮政快递寄给你们我方的目录和光盘。
9. 当发生歧义时，应以本协议的中文原文为准。
10. 如果每家工厂都按要求并准备所有上述文件，我们将能获得所有证明程序中需要的文件。

V. Case Study Direcftion

To: tanaga66@fuji.com.jp
Subject: Export Timber

Dear Mr. Suzuki,

We are much pleased to meet you at East China Fair last week, and glad to know that you are a big importer of timber in Japan.

We avail ourselves of this opportunity to introduce Fuzhou Timber Co., Ltd. to you. Our company is a privately owned company governed by a board of directors. A dedicated and enthusiastic management team works in conjunction with a skilled and stable work force. Fuzhou Timber Co., Ltd. owns 2,900 hectares of timber plantations which ensures ongoing consistent supply. Our sawmills produce 92,000 m^3 of sawn timber output per annum. Fuzhou Timber Co., Ltd. makes this commitment to all customers:

---Timber of consistent quality

---Prompt shipment

---Enduring, mutually beneficial business relationships

We satisfy our customers' needs by producing and marketing Double FU branded fir in primary processed form from secured log resource, providing quality employment for our team and giving the maximum long term return on our shareholder's funds. Our company is innovative, proactive and focused on growth strategies in its core business.

Our marketing team operates laptop computers and all e-mails and faxes will be responded within one working day.

For any inquiries for export sales, please contact Dalong (dalong@fuzhoutimber88.com.cn).

We look forward to receiving your specific enquiry.

Best wishes,
Lu Dalong
Sales Manager

VI. Discussion

In your opinion, how should the small and middle-sized enterprises in China take advantage of the flexible trade?

Unit Eighteen

Miscellaneous

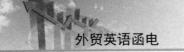

Introduction

Generally speaking, international trade focuses on the exchange of commodities across borders, while international business covers a wide range of business activities. The latter includes not only the exchange of commodities, but also international investment, international finance, international economic cooperation, technical exchange, service export and consultation, etc.

This unit provides some business documents for the reader's reference, such as Contract, Agreement, Plan, Certificate, etc., which are helpful to your business activities.

Business Documents

Contract

Labor Contract of Shanghai Reebok Machinery Equipment Co., Ltd

_____(hereinafter called Party A)
_____(hereinafter called Party B)

According to *The Labor Law of The People's Republic of China* and *The Shanghai Municipal Regulation For Labor Agreement*, the two parties reach this labor agreement on the basis of equality and negotiation.

Article 1: The Duration of This Agreement

1. The validity of this agreement commence from _____ to _____ (of which from _____ to _____ is the probation period).

2. This agreement will end upon expiration. It can be renewed for need after the two parties' negotiation. Procedures will be arranged 7 days ahead for general employee and 30 days ahead for the management before expiration.

Article 2: Positions

1. Based on the work requirement and the intention of the Party B, Party A assigns _____ to Party B.

2. Based on the work requirement and the ability and performance of the Party B, Party A can rearrange the Party B's position. The Party B shall accept it and the treatment shall be adjusted accordingly.

Article 3: Work Condition and Protection

1. Party A carries out the work system for 40 hours per week, with 2 days' rest. Due to the work requirement, the retail section carries out 2 shifts by turns. The schedule is arranged by Party A and Party B expresses their obedience.

2. Party B shall submit to the overtime arranged by Party A for work demand. Party B's compensatory vocation shall obtain Party A's consent in advance. The pay for overtime is carried

out according to the national labor law.

3. Party A furnishes Party B with the work condition which is in compliance with the safe and hygeian standard of the state, ensuring Party B to work under the condition which is safe and no harm to their bodies.

4. According to the work requirement, Party A offers necessary training to Party B.

Article 4: Pay and Welfare

1. According to the state and municipal relevant regulations, Party A makes payment to Party B in the form of CNY monthly. The monthly pay is CNY_____ in probation period and CNY_____ after the probation period.

2. Contributing individual income tax is Party B's duty, so it is deducted from the Party B's wage account by Party A according to the state's regulation.

3. According to the state's regulations, Party A shall arrange insurance for Party B against Endowment and Unemployment insurance on time with the designated organization. Other relevant welfare shall be carried out according to the state's regulation.

4. Party B takes the state holidays, such as the legal holidays and wedding holiday, etc. Party B takes the state's relevant treatment in their wedding holidays and mourning days, women employee also takes the same treatment during their pregnancy, giving birth to a child and lactation period.

5. Party B takes the annual holiday regulated by this corporation. Party B can take a 5-day paying holiday after working for one year, one day more every year afterwards, but no more than 15 days (Party A does not offer holidays for going home to visit their families).

6. It shall be disposed according to this corporation's bylaws when Party B is sick or injured after work, but subject to the state statute when conflicting to them.

7. If this corporation is declared to be disorganized owing to termination or bankruptcy, Party A shall pay off all the labor premium to the labor department.

8. If Party B is injured because of work, Party A is in charge of Party B's therapy and recreation.

9. The Party B's treatment during unemployment and after retirement will be carried out according to the state's law and statute covering social laboring and security.

Article 5: Work Discipline, Rewards and Punishment

1. Party B shall abide by the state's laws and statutes.

2. Party B shall abide by every bylaw and work discipline stipulated by Party A, initiatively obey Party A's administration.

3. According to the relevant bylaws of this corporation, Party A puts a premium on Party B based on Party B's performance and contribution.

4. If Party B violates Party A's bylaws and work discipline, Party A will punish Party B according to the relevant stipulations of this corporation.

Article 6: Alteration, Termination and Relief of This Contract

1. The two parties shall keep their own commitments stipulated by this contract after it is

signed. Any party cannot make bold to change the contract. If it is really needed to be altered, the two parties shall confer with each other on it and then amend it according to the original signing procedure. If the two parties cannot reach an agreement, the existing contract remains valid.

2. This contract terminates upon its expiration or occurrence of the conventional conditions.

3. Party A can rescind this labor contract at any time as long as any of the following cases happen to Party B:

   a) Party B proves to unqualified during the probation period;
   b) Violates seriously the work discipline or bylaws of this corporation;
   c) Serious breach of duty, jobbery, harmful to the benefits of the Party A;
   d) Be to blame for criminal responsibility according to the laws;

4. Party A can rescind this labor contract as long as any of the following cases happen to Party B, but with written notice 30 days in advance:

   a) Party B sickens or medical treatment expires after Party B's injury due to work;
   b) Party B is not competent for the position requirement and still cannot be competent for it after being trained or alteration of the position;
   c) When the environment changes greatly, on which the contract is based, and result in being unable to fulfill the contract, an agreement on alteration of the contract cannot be reached after the two parties negotiate;

5. If Party B requests to cease the contract, written notice is required to be sent to Party A 30 days in advance. If there is any of the following cases, Party B can inform Party A of rescinding the labor contract:

   a) during the probation period;
   b) Party A fails to pay Party B or offer the necessary work conditions according to the labor contract;
   c) the employer's unit threatens by force or illegal means to limit employee's personal freedom to compel employee to work;

6. If there is any of the following cases happened to Party B, Party A cannot rescind the contract:

   a) being sick or during the stipulated period of treatment due to being injured for work;
   b) as Party B is injured because of work, during the period of treatment and recreation (it shall be carried out according to the Bylaw when the employee is confirmed to have lose work ability to some extent by the Labor Identification Committee);
   c) during the period of women workers' pregnancy, confinement and lactation.

Article 7: Compensation for Violation or Rescinding of the Contract

1. This corporation shall make an agreement with these employees when they are paid to be trained for their positions. The employees have to work for this corporation during the duration of the agreement. If the employee violates it, this corporation holds the right to require the

employee to repay the training expenses. If there is no agreement signed when the unit pays the training expenses, and the trained party fails to work for the unit less than five years, the unit can draw in the training expenses based on the descending rate of 20% annually. One certain rate of the traffic and life compensation expenses might be reduced according to specific circumstances.

2. If any of the two parties ceases the contract, which results in economic loss to the other party, the initial party shall reimburse the other party according to *Shanghai Municipal Stipulations for Labor Contract*.

Article 8: Patent, Know-how and Secrecy Obligation

1. The ownership of any invention or new technology obtained from Party B's using Party A's data and equipment during the duration of the labor contract belongs to Party A and shall be registered in the name of Party A.

2. Even not registered, quality control, operation methods and acquired new effective creation fruits also belong to Party A.

3. Party B cannot leak everything obtained during the duration of the contract from Party A's business activities to any other firms, including business methods, know-how and the contents in Article 1 and 2. If such things occur, Party B bears the criminal responsibility and reimburse the economic losses arising from it.

4. Party B cannot reveal or use or furnish others with the commercial secrets which belong to Party A, however Party B leaves this corporation.

5. Party B cannot work for the other firms of the same trade within 2 years after Party B leaves;

6. If Party B offends this secrecy obligation, all the losses arising from it shall wholly rest with Party B.

Article 9: Miscellaneous

1. The two parties think that other items which shall be stipulated include:

Both of the two parties agree to abide by the following stipulations:

a) Occupation Rules of ...

b) Wage Rules of ...

c) Other Rules of...

If there are any discrepancies between the above-mentioned rules and the state's laws, everything shall be subject to the state's laws and statutes. The above-mentioned rules and stipulations are used as the appendixes of the contract, with the equivalent law effect.

2. If there is any dispute between Party A and Party B, it shall be solved by negotiation. If it cannot be settled by negotiation, one party concerned shall apply to the local *Labor Dispute Arbitration Committee* for arbitration. If any party disobeys the arbitration, he can bring an action against the other party within 15 days after receiving the Arbitration Decision.

3. All the articles shall be subject to the state's laws and statutes when they are not in compliance with the latter.

4. This contract is made in duplicate. Both Party A and Party B hold one copy. It comes into force after being signed. The two copies have the equivalent law effect.

Party A: Party B:
Legal Representative or entrusted person: Legal Representative or entrusted person:
Date: Date:

Agreement

Letter of Intent

for

Formulating National Standard of Drawer Slideway[①]

After negotiating on jointly making a national standard of drawer slideway, National Furniture Quality Supervising & Examining Centre and National Furniture Standardization Centre (hereinafter called Party A) and Home-easy Holding AG (hereinafter called Party B) reach the following points:

I. In view of the fact that there is no national standard of drawer slideway in China, which is harmful to improving product quality and restraining the domestic market and promoting exportation, Party A intents to place the standard-making work on the agenda in which the standard will be made and amended in 200*, and invites Party B who possesses advanced producing experience to jointly make the standard.

II. Party B agrees to jointly draw up the national standard of drawer slideway, and bear part of the costs of drafting the standard, amounting to CNY 10,000, which will be remitted to Party A's' account before October, 200*.

III. The two parts agree that the standard-drafting work will be finished before the end of 200* on the basis of the German Standard: DIN 68858 "Furniture Fittings Drawer Slideway; Requirements and Inspection".

Party A (Official seal) NFQSEC   Party B (Official seal) HEHAG

Representative (Signature)   Representative (Signature)

d/m/y   d/m/y

A Plan

A Plan for Formulating the National Standard of Drawer Slideway

Eight steps should be taken while formulating the national standard of drawer slideway:

I. Establish a standard-drafting work group, which consists of those personnel from National Furniture Standardization Centre, furniture study institutes, popular science units, and those

---

① 指抽屉导轨。

enterprises who jointly make the standard;

II. Translate and proofread the German Standard: DIN 68858 "Furniture Fittings Drawer Slideway: Requirements and Inspection";

III. Investigate the present quality situation of those enterprises who manufacture drawer slideway in China, test and verify their products;

IV. Develop relevant testing equipment required by the standard;

V. With reference to the German Standard DIN 68858, a first draft is written out to solicit opinions on the basis of investigation and test, and nationwide sent to relevant units to ask for criticisms;

VI. According to the feedback for the first draft, a further investigation and test is conducted and refine the first draft and make it become a formal draft, which will be examined;

VII. Convene a conference to examine and approve the draft;

VIII. According to the evaluation from the conference, refine the standard again and make it become a draft which will be reported for approval, and then prepare all relevant material so as to be reported to the relevant department for approval.

All the above-mentioned work shall be finished within one year from the just beginning of the work.

Certificate

Promise and Declaration

Date: April 7, 201*
Grss
Holland

Dear Sirs,

We, as the shareholders of the Shanghai Aa Industrial Co., Ltd. which assists Dutch Grss (hereinafter called your esteemed company) to conduct business in China, make promise and declaration to your esteemed company as follows:

1. We are willing to sign the assigning contract for free transferring the share ownership of the Shanghai Aa Industrial Co., Ltd. and all the relevant law documents for changing its legal representative with your designated law entity before the end of July, 201* according to China laws.

2. Within two months after we sign the above-mentioned documents, Shanghai Aa Industrial Co., Ltd. shall, according to China laws, finish the approval and registration procedures of all the above-mentioned documents, failing which we still enjoy the right to exercise power to the company as its legal representative and shareholders based on China laws.

3. Your esteemed company shall admit that all the creditor's right and debt and its responsibilities of Shanghai Aa Industrial Co., Ltd. occurred after it was established will have no any relations with us. If there are debts and responsibilities borne to others arising from the

operation of Shanghai Aa Industrial Co., Ltd. involve us, your esteemed company is willing to exempt us from all the responsibilities or accept these liabilities imposed upon us.

4. Your esteemed company shall open an account in our name in Shanghai with a total amount of CNY500,000 within 7 days preceding we sign the assigning contract for free transferring the share ownership of the Shanghai Aa Industrial Co., Ltd. and all the relevant law documents for changing its legal representative with your designated law entity, allowing us to use the funds in this account provided that the debts and responsibilities borne to others arising from the operation of Shanghai Aa Industrial Co., Ltd. involved us (including but not limited to lawsuits against us, arbitration, disciplinary sanction, claims), and not asking us to refund the funds used by us in this account for these cases. Your esteemed company assures us of our exemption from our debts and responsibilities by taking these measures.

5. Our promises and declaration are complete and indivisible. They will come into force as soon as your esteemed company approves.

Y.R.LIN
(signature)

Contract

Contract for Rent

Rent-collector (hereinafter called Party A): Shanghai Benifit-all Industry Co.
Address: 50* Meiyuan Rd. (W), Putuo District, Shanghai
Legal representative: Li Jisheng, Chairman of the Board
Tel: 6250****   Post Code: 201*33

Tenant (hereinafter called Party B): Shanghai Home-easy Furniture Manufacturing Co., Ltd.
Address: Room 12**, 12th floor, 6** Tongli Rd, Hongkou District, Shanghai
Legal Representative: Wang Liwen, Chairman of the Board
Tel: 6251****   Post Code: 200092

Between Party A and Party B, the following contract is made on the basis of equality and mutual benefit:

Clause 1: Rentable Object

Party A rents the land and factory buildings and the building for office and life attached to Party B, which are located in the Putuo Development Zone at Zhenchen Road. Party A assures Party B of his rentable right.

1. The above-mentioned land (factory area) takes up 10 mu(6666.66 m^2).

2. The total built-up area of the above factory buildings is 3000 m^2; the buildings for office and life totals 500 m^2 respectively.

a. The newly-built factory buildings which take up nearly 1000 m^2 and life buildings with 500 m^2 will be provided by the end of April, 201*.

b. The newly-built standard factory buildings at the 2nd floor, which take up 2000 m², will be provided by the end of June 201*. And office buildings with 500 m² are also provided. Party B should advise Party A in written notice concerning the request to the rentable factory buildings within two weeks after this Contract is signed.

3. The rentable buildings at the factory area should have attached infrastructure. The power supply of the factory building should be 150 kV. IDD, DDD, water supply drainage pipeline, road and green belt should be provided.

4. Party A agrees that Party B can regard the land as its legal address within the rent period after this Contract goes into effect.

5. Party A promises that the surrounding land with 10 mu will be reserved for three years (July 1, 201* - June 30, 201*) for the purpose of Party B's enlarging factory buildings when necessary.

Clause 2: Rent Fee and its Payment

I. Rent Fee

Party A and Party B decide to choose CNY/m²/day as counting unit. It is calculated from the date the area and period are provided according to this Contract.

The rent fee should be:

1. CNY 0.376/m²/day in 201*;
2. CNY 0.376/m²/day in 201*;
3. CNY 0.40/m²/day between 201*-201*;
4, CNY 0.45/m²/day between 201*-201*.

II. Payment

Party A and Party B agree that the principle of payment is "use after payment" and "payment by instalments".

1. Party B should pay CNY 300,000 as earnest money to Party A within 2 weeks after this Contract is signed.

2. The rent fee in 201* will be paid by instalments, twice a year from the date the rentable factory buildings are provided. The earnest money paid by Party B could be used as rent fee and it is deducted accordingly.

3. The rent fee should be paid at the end of January in 201* and June in 201*.

III. Special Stipulations for Rent Fee

1. Between 200* and 201*, Party A and Party B confirm that Party B's beneficial result shall link up with the rent fee, that is, if Party B's output value is over CNY 20,000,000, the rent decreases progressively by 0.5 per cent of the surpassed part; if the output value is less than this standard, the rent increases progressively by 0.5 per cent of the insufficient part.

2. The changed rent resulted from the output value should be paid out in the first payment of the next year.

3. Party A reserves the surrounding land with 10 mu for Party B in return. Party B should

pay CNY 5400/mu/year to Party A as reservation fee, once half a year. If Party B rents the new factory buildings built by Party A on the reserved land, Party A will return all the reservation fee of the land with 10 mu to Party B when Party B pays the rent for the new factory buildings.

4. The rent fee of the newly-built factory buildings on the reservation fluctuates according to Clause 2 (I), with no more than 10 per cent. The rentable period and the infrastructure shall be in compliance with the stipulations of this Contract.

5. As regards the power supply of the provided factory buildings is 100 kV, and Party B needs 150 kV, Party B should pay CNY 100,000 as additional rent to Party A so as to assure power supply of 150 kV when Party B pays the first rent fee. The additional fee will be returned to Party B when this Contract terminates.

6. The initial fee and the use fee of the three IDD and DDD provided by Party A shall be on Party B's account.

Clause 3: Right and Obligations of Party A and Party B

Party A's Rights and Obligations

1. According to the stipulation of this Contract, Party A provides the aimed land and factory buildings on time, and reserve the surrounding land until the valid period ends.

2. Party A assures Party B of the necessary facilities for the rentable factory buildings.

3. Party A is in charge of the coordination with relevant institutions so as to assure Party B of normal production.

4. Party A collect the rent fee according to the stipulations of this Contract.

Party B's Rights and Obligations

1. Pay the earnest money and rent fee according to the stipulations of this Contract.

2. Accept and use the land and buildings according to the stipulations of this Contract.

3. Protect the rented factory buildings and relevant facilities.

4. Be charge of the environmental protection, fire control and public security during the rent period.

Clause 4: Rent Period

The valid rent period of this Contract is 16 years, and it starts from the date all the rentable objects are provided, which are declared in this Contract. If the rent period is extended, Party A and Party B shall sign a contract after negotiation before it expires 6 months. Under the same conditions, priorities are given to Party B to rent the buildings when the contract terminates. Party B should return the rented land and relevant facilities to Party A when this Contract terminates. Except for this, Party B possesses all the property gained during the rent period.

Clause 5: Responsibility for Violation

Party A and Party B should carry this Contract, any Party A cannot terminate ahead of time or fail to carry it, otherwise should bear the liability to pay compensation.

1. Party A will compensate Party B 0.3 per cent of total annual rent fee (CNY) every day if Party A fails to provide the land and factory buildings according to the Contract.

2. Party A should compensate for the loss resulted from Party A's failure to provide relevant facilities.

3. If Party A does not reserve the surrounding area (10 mu) according to the Contract, the rent fee should be reduced 50 per cent.

4. If Party B fails to pay the earnest money and rent fee according to the Contract, Party B should pay the overdue fine at 0.3 per cent of the rent fee (CNY) to Party A.

Clause 6: Others

A supplement agreement should be reached after negotiation if there is something unmentioned in this Contract. And it is of the same legal effect as this Contract after co-signature.

This Contract becomes effective after two partners' legal representatives co-sign.

This Contract is made in octuplicate. Each party keeps four copies respectively.

Party A
Legal Representative (signature)

Party B
Legal Representative (signature)

Relevant Terms

leasing contract 租赁合同	engineering contract 工程合同
joint-venture agreement 合资协议	transfer of technology agreement 技术转让协议
transport contract 运输合同	contract of land use right 土地使用合同

Useful Phrases

to invest in cash/capital goods/technologies 以现金/资本货物/技术的方式投资	to take the lead in 带头，在……中领先
to hold a board meeting 召开董事会会议	to keep sb. further informed 进一步通知某人
seeing that 鉴于	to come into force 生效，开始实施
to take over 接管	to make amendment 做出修订

Summary

International business covers a wider range of business activities than international trade. It includes not only the exchange of commodities, but also international investment, international finance, international economic cooperation, technical exchange, service export and consultation, etc.

Employees are usually required to draft different business documents. It is advisable for employees to find the right sample documents for their reference before drawing up.

Exercises

I. Questions for review

1. How many kinds of documents have you met in your business activities? Please make a list.
2. What shall we pay attention to when we draw up a contract?

II. Choose the best answer

1. We are looking forward_____ your trial order.
   A. for   B. at   C. to   D. with
2. We are now represented _____ ABC Corp. in this area.
   A. for   B. at   C. of   D. by
3. We have specialized _____ chemicals and dyestuffs for more than 15 years.
   A. for   B. of   C. with   D. in
4. We are sure your product will find a ready market here because its taste suits that _____ the local people.
   A. for   B. of   C. with   D. in
5. We enclose you our price list_____ our machines.
   A. for   B. of   C. with   D. in
6. In view of the heavy demand _____ this line, we advise you to send us your first order as soon as possible.
   A. for   B. of   C. with   D. in
7. This product is now _____ great demand.
   A. for   B. of   C. with   D. in
8. It is obvious that such a growing demand will result _____ a price increase.
   A. for   B. in   C. of   D. with
9. The covering L/C should be opened _____ our favor 30 days before the time of shipment.
   A. for   B. in   C. of   D. with
10. There is a good demand here for the captioned goods and we, therefore, write to you _____ the hope of establishing business relations with you.
    A. for   B. in   C. of   D. with
11. For your information, we also hope _____ future orders, you can change the inspection company to SGS (SOCIETE GENERALE DE SURVEILLANCE S.A.) or BV(BUREAU VERITAS).
    A. in   B. for   C. of   D. with
12. We always supply our customers with high-quality goods _____ reasonable prices.

Unit Eighteen Miscellaneous

    A. at   B. in   C. of   D. with

13. As an alternative, please also inform us _____ the air freight to Shanghai via HK.

    A. for   B. of   C. on   D. in

14. We await your repeat order _____ keen interest.

    A. for   B. with   C. on   D. in

15. Please send us a special offer for the purpose of introducing your products _____ our market.

    A. for   B. of   C. on   D. into

16. We can assure you that all the machines are _____ good condition.

    A. for   B. of   C. on   D. in

17. _____ account of a limited supply available at present, we would ask you to act quickly.

    A. For   B. Of   C. On   D. In

18. In the meantime, please keep us informed of the development of the market _____ your end.

    A. for   B. at   C. on   D. in

19. You are welcome to send us enquiries for other products we deal _____.

    A. at   B. with   C. on   D. in

20. We agree to this price and would ask you to accept this order-letter _____ our official order.

    A. for   B. of   C. as   D. in

III. Translate the following sentences into Chinese

1. The Distributor may use all trademarks, brand names and other product marks related to the products of the Principal free of charge during distribution of the products.

2. I'd like to know some information about the current investment environment in your country.

3. Our project must proceed at a reasonably quick tempo. Surely one month is ample time, isn't it?

4. The Distributor bears all costs related to promotion required for sales of the products of the Principal in Australia and New Zealand.

5. The Agreement comes into effect upon signing by the Parties. It may be amended in writing by mutual consent of the Parties.

6. China has proved to be a magnet for foreign investment as companies from around the world have been drawn in by its mix of a skilled workforce, low labor costs and the provisions of investment incentives.

7. The local government welcomes foreign investment in the manufacturing, research and development, and service sectors. New technology is particularly encouraged. Foreign-owned companies are offered more favorable tax rate than the local enterprises.

8. We recognize that our leading science & technology, creativity, innovation and our

ability to add value will be the future for new investment into our country.

Optional Part

9. We are glad to inform you that the 50 cases were profitably disposed of. You will see in the Account Sales that all the goods were cleared at better prices than we expected.

10. We propose to forward you a consignment of 25 cases of Cotton Towels as follows, which please dispose of as advantageously as possible.

11. We note that you are shipping a consignment of wood pulp to us. We are glad to say that the market is in a very strong position, so we are confident that you will be satisfied with the proceeds of sale.

12. The 30 cases canned Pineapples consigned to us by M/V "Big Dragon" arrived safely and we have disposed of them before the landing of other cargoes from your port.

13. We take pleasure in informing you that we have decided to accept your indent for 500 bales of cotton. According to your instruction, shipment will be made in December.

IV. Translate the following sentences into English

1. 对于这份订单，目前我方正面临着与主管当局之间的大麻烦。
2. 政府规定所有的出口商必须把所有的相关文件，随同当地银行的所有的收据缴到当地税务局，并在清关日后至少180天内完成所有的出口会计手续。
3. 税务局将核查退税项目，如果发现该订单尚未付款，我们将不能再获得退税，由此引起的损失将达到订单金额的11%~14%。
4. 我们很高兴通知你方我方将参加于5月15日至17日在巴西举行的201*年圣保罗五金展。
5. 参展后我们想拜访一下贵公司，以便进一步合作。
6. 为了提前申请签证，恳请你方帮我们准备委内瑞拉驻当地大使馆要求的以下材料。
7. 要提供一式二份的邀请函，称呼要单独写上"亲爱的委内瑞拉驻北京大使馆大使"和"亲爱的许知焘朋友"。
8. 随函附上邀请函的样本供你方参考，请用你们公司信笺签发这些文件。
9. 在你们寄送原件之前，请将文件扫描为JPG或PDF格式，供我们检查和参考，以便避免错误或误解。
10. 这一次我们对与你们公司建立一个强有力的商务关系感到很乐观，我们想知道下列产品的定价信息。

V. Case Study Direction

----- Original Message ----- (A)
From: Don Pope
To: lihua88@alibaba.com
Sent: Tuesday, March 12, 201* 8:12 AM
Subject: mode of payment

Dear Snowen:

I am very happy to hear from you again.

I know that the prices have increased drastically, and we are willing to renegotiate. As for the pricing, we can adopt L/C during the first six months, but thereafter, we shall change the mode of payment that we have discussed during our meeting. If that is acceptable, please re-quote the products I originally sent to you and we can start from that point, and go further with the new products.

Best Regards,
Don

-----Original Message-----(B)
From: Snowen
[mailto: donpope@online.net.mx]
Sent: Wednesday, March 13, 201* 8:15 AM
Subject: Re: mode of payment

Dear Friend Don,

Thanks for your e-mail.

After we met each other last month, the prices of the raw materials keep advancing quickly.

However, you said the prices haven't risen while the fact is not--- that may be the reason why we can't go further in spite of the good wills from both sides. Actually, if we produced, we would definitely face a huge loss at that time because the prices of the raw materials increased so much but in the meanwhile you insisted on saying the prices haven't increased.

Furthermore, I'm afraid the mode of payment is not desirable for us. We really hope you can consider again adopting an L/C or 15% T/T for ADVANCE + 75% D/P AT SIGHT, so that we can re-quote you as per the present situation (BRASS increased by 30%, ZINC increased by 50%, STEEL increased by 100%, ALUMINIUM increased by 20%).

We look forward to your respond.

Best wishes,
Snowen

Encl: FAIRS OF THIS YEAR WHICH WE WILL ATTEND:
1) CANTON FAIR (Guang Zhou, China)　April 15th--20th
    Booth No.: ****
2) CHINA SOURCING FAIR (Shanghai, China) April 20th--22th
    Booth No.: 5H08
3) MEXICO FAIR (Guadalajara, Mexico) September 10th-12th
    Booth No.: ****
4) CANTON FAIR (Guang Zhou, China) Oct 15th--20th
    Booth No.: ****

----- Original Message ----- (C)
From: Don Pope
To: lihua88@alibaba.com
Sent: Thursday, March 14, 201* 8:18 AM
Subject: mode of payment

Dear Snowen:

Thank you for your information covering the fairs you will attend. We are prepared to attend some of them.

As to the mode of payment, we are willing to open L/Cs during the first six months. After this period, we need to get on TT with 45 to 60 days from Bill of Lading Date. During the initial six months we hope to build the relationship with you to show our good faith on payments by using L/C. I hope you will understand and agree with our terms. Looking forward to working with you in the near future.

                     Best wishes,
                     Don

VI. Discussion

In your opinion, is it necessary for you and your company to appoint a lawyer to take part in drawing up a contract? why?

Appendix I

Commercial Acronyms and Abbreviations Commonly Used in Business Correspondence

B/E =bill of exchange 汇票

B/L=bill of lading 提单

D/A=documents against acceptance 承兑交单

D/P= documents against payment 付款交单

EUR=Euro 欧元

FCL=full container load 整箱货

LCL=less than container load 拼箱货

M/T, MT= metric ton 公吨

S/C=sales confirmation 售货确认书

ETD=estimated time of departure 预计离港时间

ETA=estimated time of arrival 预计到港时间

C/O=certificate of origin; care of 原产地证书；转交，照管

D/C =documentary credit 跟单信用证

D/N=debit note 索款通知

L/C=letter of credit 信用证

L/G=letter of guarantee 保函

T/T= telegraphic transfer 电汇

FPA =free from particular average 平安险

WPA=with particular average 水渍险

I.C.C.=institute cargo clause 协会货物条款; International Chamber of Commerce 国际商会

KGS, KG=kilogram(s) 公斤

I/L=import license 进口许可证

N/W, NTWT, NWT=net weight 净重

G/W=gross weight 毛重

FOB=Free on Board (…named port of shipment) 装运港船上交货(……指定装运港)

CIF=Cost, Insurance, and Freight (…named port of destination) 成本加保险费、运费(……指定目的港)

CFR=Cost and Freight (…named port of destination) 成本加运费(……指定目的港)

FCA=Free Carrier (…named place) 货交承运人(……指定地)

CPT=Carriage Paid To (…named place of destination) 运费付至(……指定目的地)

CIP=Carriage and Insurance Paid To (…named place of destination) 运费、保险费付至(……指定目的地)

EXW=Ex Works (…named place) 工厂交货(……指定地)

FAS=Free Alongside Ship (…named port of shipment) 船边交货(……指定装运港)

DDP=Delivered Duty Paid (…named place of destination) 完税后交货(……指定目的地)

DAT=Delivered At Terminal (目的地或目的港的集散站交货)

DAP=Delivered At Place 目的地交货

USD=US dollars 美元

L/A= landing agent 起货上岸代理商；letter of authorization 授权书

ASAP=as soon as possible 尽快

ISO=International Standard Organization 国际标准化组织

MAX=MAXIMUM 最大量

MIN=MINIMUM 最小量

RGDS=regards, best regards 问候，致敬

TPND=Theft, Pilferage & Non-Delivery Risks 偷窃、提货不着险

W/W=warehouse to warehouse clause 仓至仓条款

P/INV, P/I=pro forma invoice 形式发票

P&I=Principal and Interest 本金和利息

P/A=Power of Attorney 授权委托书，委任状

C.C. or c.c. = Carbon Copy 副本印送，复写副本，抄送，抄报

Re= Referring 事由

Encl.= Enclosure 附件

O/A= open account 往来账户，赊账

F.A.Q.=fair average quality 良好平均品质，中等品，大路货

G.M.Q.=good merchantable quality 上等可销品质

CBM=Cubic Meter 立方米

Appendix II

Key to Exercises

Unit One Job Requirements and the Forms of Business Letters

Case one

日期：201*年6月18日
收件人：Mr. Henry Ford
发件人：Ms. Vivian Ma
抄送：Mr. Tony Gates
事由：签发中国原产地证书给TONGGUAN(阿根廷)公司

感谢你方在最近文件往来中给予的合作。
TONGGUAN(阿根廷)公司通知我方说在通关方面有一项新的政府规定已被实施。所有工厂对其所有中国制造的产品都要开出中国原产地证书，该规定适合于200*年8月11日当天或之后到达蒙得维的亚和布宜诺斯·艾利斯的货物。详情如下。
文件类型：由中国进出口当局开出的原产地证书，反面必须有阿根廷驻北京领事馆的盖章。
生效日：整箱货——预计6月22日当天或之后驶离香港的船货。
申请：请在预计发船日之前申请原产地证书，并在预定发船日之后20天内将原产地证书寄送WEM。
证书费用：我们正在讨论原产地证书的费用问题，稍后会通知你方。
备注：在原产地证书上注明发票编号和日期是至关重要的(请参考随附的原产地证书样本)。
空运——如果你方要空运，请事先通知我方。
随函附上修改后装运信息及原产地证书样本。如有问题，请即致电6732****与Vivian联络。
感谢贵方的关注。

致
礼！
附件

Case Two

Date: 22July，201*
To: Ms.Jiayin zhu

Fax:
From: Kaili Machinery Trade Co., Ltd.
Fax:
Re: INVITATION

Dear Ms. Zhu,

In order to introduce more information about the foreign advanced machinery and electronic equipment and road construction technology, and promote China's highway construction and its maintenance, we invite Ms. Jiayin Zhu, Mr. Tongwen Ma, Mr. Qi'an Zhao, Mr. Xufu Liu and Mr. Weijun Gao to attend an international exhibition of road construction and maintaining machinery, which will be held in Miami on Sept. 20, 200*. We also want to show you around some famous construction machinery plants.

It is estimated for you to stay in USA for 20 days. We will make arrangements for your round-trip flight tickets, board and lodging and traffic, at your sole expense.

Kindly take it into your consideration. We are looking forward to your early reply.

Yours sincerely,
Henry
General Manager

Case Three

Possible reply

Date: 16 May 201*
To: Johan Dawson
Fax: (613) 9876****
From: Lihua Imp. & Exp. Co., Ltd.
Fax: 86-21-642486**
Re: Freight

Dear Johan,

I am pleased to receive your Fax dated May 16. I am also missing you all very much!

As regards the shipment, I regret to tell you that the forwarding agent misunderstood your instructions, so they shipped the goods on the basis of port to port, not door to door. So, please fetch the goods by yourself at your port and pay the relative fees.

I am sorry that their misunderstanding has caused you inconvenience. But I am still always at your disposal for anything as long as I can.

I am also looking forward to seeing you again very soon.

Best regards,
Henry

Appendix II

I. Choose the best answer

1~5: ACABD
6~10: BCBBA
11~15: BCCDD
16~20: DACBD

Unit Two Establish Business Relations

II. Choose the best answer

1~5: DCDBC
6~10: CDBAD
11~15: CADCB
16~20: CCBCD

IV. Translate the following sentences into English

1. We are an exporter specializing in ceramic products.
2. Our company has various kinds of carpets and other textile floor coverings available for export.
3. We accept orders against customers' samples, specified designs, specifications and packaging requirements.
4. Please immediately quote us your lowest price of your newest type products, CIF Manila.
5. We avail ourselves of this opportunity to inform you that we wish to expand our business into African market.
6. We hope to receive your specific enquiry at an early date.
7. Samples and quotations at favorable prices will be sent to you upon receipt of your specific enquiry.
8. Enclosed please find our price-list and brochure for our new products.
9. We accept orders for goods with customers' own trade marks or brand names.
10. We are looking forward to your favorable reply.

Unit Three Credit Inquiry

II. Choose the best answer

1~5: ABDCC
6~10: DDCCA
11~15: BDCBD

16~20: CBDDC

IV. Translate the following sentences into English

1. Sorry for the delay of our reply due to the 7-day Holiday of National Day from Oct. 1st to 7th.

2. It operates as an importer and exporter of various types of commodities, trading principally with India and Pakistan.

3. We shall appreciate any information with which you may furnish us in this respect.

4. They have always provided complete satisfaction with punctual delivery, moderate prices, and superior quality.

5. They have wide connections both at home and abroad and their financial standing is quite stable.

6. A credit in the sum you mentioned in your letter of Aug. 6 would seem to be safe.

7. The firm's difficulties were due to bad management and in particular to overtrading.

8. We have every confidence in the uprightness of this firm.

9. We should be glad to know if their financial position is considered strong.

10. They have the reputation of keeping their engagements promptly and fully.

Unit Four   Enquiries and Replies

II. Choose the best answer

1~5: DDCBC
6~10: DABDC
11~15: DABCD
16~20: BCDDB

IV. Translate the following sentences into English

1. Please quote us your most competitive prices on FOB Shanghai and send us your quotation to…

2. We are now calculating the lowest price from factory, and tomorrow it will be emailed to you for your consideration.

3. We are now enclosing the pictures and specifications for each item and trust you can manufacture them according to our requirements. Please quote us your best prices.

4. However, we need to obtain more information before making our final decision.

5. If everything is possible, may we have your response by 1 February?

6. To give you more information about our company, we enclose our latest brochure for your reference.

7. We are anxious to establish a solid business relationship between us.

8. Seeing your advertisement in a newspaper, we ask you to send us your latest price-list,

together with an illustrated catalogue.

9. In reply to your email of Oct.12, we are now sending you our brochure by separate airmail.

10. If your quotations are acceptable and the machine proves to be satisfactory, we shall place regular orders with you.

Unit Five   Quotations and Proforma Invoices

II. Choose the best answer

1~5: DBDCA
6~10: BCDDD
11~15: DDDDB
16~20: DCAAC

IV. Translate the following sentences into English

1. We are enclosing our first order for your products and we trust you can allow us 10% discount on your prices.

2. Our prices are extremely low right now.

3. Our incomparable quality enables us to charge higher prices than our competitors.

4. In spite of rising production costs, our prices have remained stable.

5. In spite of the outstanding quality of our products, our prices are lower than those of other suppliers.

6. Our quotation is valid only if the prevailing prices of raw materials do not change.

7. We are able to give you an absolute guarantee on quality.

8. Our products are carefully tested to insure quality before they leave our factory.

9. We guarantee that the articles are in perfect condition when made ready for shipment.

10. We are having great difficulty in satisfying the heavy demand for this article.

Unit Six   Offers, Counter-offers and Re-counter Offers

II. Choose the best answer

1~5: CCDBD
6~10: DCCAC
11~15: CDAAC
16~20: CBCAA

IV. Translate the following sentences into English

1. The rates of export drawback will be reduced by 4% in our country after Jan.1, 200*, and our prices will also be increased accordingly. So, we hope you will accept our re-counter offer as

soon as possible.

2. As the market price is falling, we recommend your immediate acceptance.

3. To be candid with you, we regret that your price seems to be on the high side. So may we suggest you allow a discount on your price, say about 6%.

4. Thank you for your offer dated May 15, but we must point out that other suppliers in your area sent us more attractive quotations in which prices are 10%~15% below yours.

5. We have received a more favorable offer from your competitor, so, please give us a discount, say 10% on your price so as to start our cooperation.

6. Besides, we want to stress again that our usual terms of payment is by D/P at 30 days' sight which is our usual practice dealing with foreign suppliers.

7. If it had not been for our good relationship, we wouldn't have made you a firm offer at this price.

8. Could you please tell us the quantity you need so that we may adjust our price accordingly.

9. If you have taken everything into consideration, you may find our quotation lower than those you can get elsewhere.

10. I think it unwise for both of us to insist on his own price. Let's meet each other halfway.

Unit Seven   Orders and Fulfillment

II. Choose the best answer

1~5: ADDAD
6~10: CDAAD
11~15: CCBCB
16~20: DCCAC

IV. Translate the following sentences into English

1. We'd like to cancel the order for your cultured pearls because of the change in the domestic market.

2. I'm afraid that we are unable to supply as much as you require.

3. The advantages of our products are attractive design, high quality and reasonable prices.

4. Owing to the continual rise in export cost and the excellent quality of our products, it is almost impossible for us to make any further reduction.

5. All these items are urgently required by our clients. Therefore, we hope that you will make delivery at an early date so that they can sell them out before Christmas.

6. We shall arrange for dispatch by the first available liner upon receipt of your sight L/C.

7. As you may not be aware of other products we handle, we will send you a copy of our latest catalogue, by separate airmail, for your consideration.

8. With reference to your order of July 6 for musical instruments, we wish to inform you

that the goods are in production and will be ready for shipment by the end of October.

9. We hope that you will be satisfied with this shipment and we look forward to your regular order in the near future.

10. We are very pleased to receive your repeat order, which, we assure you, shall be executed in due course.

Unit Eight　Sales Confirmations

II. Choose the best answer

1~5: BDDAC
6~10: CDCDC
11~15: DBDAC
16~20: DACDD

IV. Translate the following sentences into English

1. I am ready to sign the agreement.
2. We have no questions about the terms.
3. If one party fails to honor the contract, the other party is entitled to rescind it.
4. Enclosed please find our Sales Confirmation NO. HW-116 in triplicate. Please sign and return one copy to us for our file.
5. A confirmed, irrevocable L/C payable by draft at sight shall be established immediately.
6. The stipulations in the covering L/C shall be in exact accordance with the terms in the S/C so as to avoid subsequent amendments.
7. Emphasis is to be laid on the point that the relevant L/C must be opened in our favor through the Citibank.
8. We have duly signed our S/C and return one copy to you for your file as requested. Meanwhile, we have opened the relevant L/C and it will reach you very soon.
9. If your execution of this Purchase Contract proves to be satisfactory, regular orders will be placed in the future.
10. Please let us have your signed S/C in duplicate for our counter-signing and thank you for your cooperation.

Unit Nine　Terms of Payment

II. Choose the best answer

1~5: CCCAC
6~10: DDCBC
11~15: DDCDA

16~20: BCDCC

IV. Translate the following sentences into English

1. In view of our friendly cooperation, we are prepared to accept payment by D/P at 60 days' sight.

2. We are willing to accept payment by D/P during this sales-pushing stage, but we cannot accept payment by D/A.

3. We regret to inform you that it is our usual practice not to accept payment by D/A.

4. The documentary credit is available against presentation of the following documents.

5. Please see to it that you will establish the covering L/C as soon as possible so as to enable us to effect shipment within the stipulated time limit.

6. The date of shipment is approaching, but we have not received relevant L/C up to date. Please let us have your reply promptly.

7. As the goods against your Order No. 118 have been ready for shipment for a long time, it is advisable for you to open the covering L/C immediately. Otherwise, you will be unable to get the goods before Christmas.

8. We have received your covering L/C, but we find it contains the following discrepancies:

9. Our S/C stipulates that the commission granted for this transaction is 3%, but we find your L/C demands a commission of 5%, so you are requested to instruct your bank to amend the L/C.

10. Please extend the date of shipment and the validity of your L/C No. CHW 118 to July 15 and Aug. 2 respectively and arrange the amendment advice to reach us by June 15.

Unit Ten   Packing

II. Choose the best answer

1~5: CAADD
6~10: ABDDD
11~15: CBBAB
16~20: BDAAB

IV. Translate the following sentences into English

1. We use a polythene wrapper for each pair of gaiters.

2. We intend to switch from carton packing to foil wrapping.

3. We would use cardboard box for this batch of toys.

4. We specialize in the development of plastic packing materials.

5. We hope that you will take measures to reinforce this sort of carton with iron straps.

6. Such packing will make it convenient for us to make distribution to the retailers.

7. Your recommendations on improving packing would be appreciated.

8. When packing, please take into account that the boxes are likely to receive rough handling

at this end and must be able to withstand transport over very bad roads.

9. We pack our shirts in plastic-lined, waterproof cartons, reinforced with metal straps.

10. Such light but strong cases can save shipping space and facilitate the storage and distribution of the goods.

Unit Eleven Insurance

II. Choose the best answer

1~5: ABDAB
6~10: CBDDB
11~15: CABAC
16~20: ABCAC

IV. Translate the following sentences into English

1. Please cover for us the cargo listed on the attached sheet.

2. We have concluded the business on an FOB basis, so the insurance should be effected by you.

3. We shall cover W.P.A for 110% of the invoice value.

4. For goods sold on CIF basis, insurance is to be covered by us for 110% of the invoice value against All Risks.

5. What cover will you take out? We want W.P.A. cover this time.

6. What types of cover does your insurance company usually underwrite?

7. This batch of toys is to be insured against All Risks with the PICC based on warehouse to warehouse clause.

8. We have covered insurance on the 20 metric tons of cotton for 110% of the invoice value against All Risks.

9. We enclose an inspection certificate and the shipping agent's statement and hope that no difficulty will arise in the settlement of our above claim amounting to USD5,000.00.

10. An insurance claim should be submitted to the insurance company or its agent as promptly as possible so as to provide the insurance company or its agent with ample time to pursue recovery from the relative party at fault.

Unit Twelve Shipping Instructions and Shipping Advices

II. Choose the best answer

1~5: DBDDD
6~10: DBABD
11~15: ABCDD

16~20: CDBDC

IV. Translate the following sentences into English

1. The buyer is responsible for chartering a ship or booking the shipping space.

2. For your information, we have already instructed them to contact you to coordinate everything covering this shipment.

3. Finally, we would like to inform you that, due to a new government regulation, this shipment must be shipped out before June 6.

4. We now demand delivery of the said goods in accordance with our Contract No. 3112.

5. The goods will be sent to you by Maersk (China) Shipping Co., Ltd. and should arrive at your port on or about Dec.12 this year.

6. We are withholding delivery for the following reasons: required payment has not been made and you withdrew your Purchase Contract.

7. If you find you can wait for three weeks on this order, please let us know and we will be pleased to ship your goods at the low prices you've come to expect from us.

8. We trust that the goods will reach you in time and give you entire satisfaction.

9. You may recall that we have time and again emphasized the vital importance of punctual shipment because these items are for display at an international exhibition to be held in Kunming on Sept.16.

10. We take pleasure in notifying you that the goods under S/C No.116 have been dispatched by M/V "WASHINGTON MARU" sailing on Aug. 29, 201* for Yokohama.

Unit Thirteen   Trade Disputes and Settlement

II. Choose the best answer

1~5: DACBA
6~10: DBCBD
11~15: BBBAD
16~20: DBABA

IV. Translate the following sentences into English

1. We appreciate you straightforwardness in pointing out that Carton No. 35 did not contain these articles you ordered.

2. To our disappointment, your shipment of our Order No. 268 has been found short weight by 58 kilograms.

3. We have asked our service department to have a thorough investigation of the complaint.

4. We regret to have to complain about late delivery of the goods ordered on Oct.12 because, as you know, punctual shipment is of vital importance to us.

5. Consequently, we think it difficult to file a claim against the manufacturer.

6. We hope that you will be completely satisfied with our future settlement. What do you suggest would be fair?

7. Due to your failure to ship the goods within the time required, we hereby cancel the said order, reserving such further rights we may have.

8. The good were in perfect condition when leaving our warehouse and the damage has evidently occurred in transit.

9. Our goods should be packed in cartons instead of plastic containers.

10. We have made a concession to you to solve this problem. We hope you are satisfied with it.

Unit Fourteen   Sales Promotion

II. Choose the best answer

1~5: CBDDC
6~10: CBDBB
11~15: BAACB
16~20: BCCBB

IV. Translate the following Use Direction into English

Use Direction

1. Connect the wire for special use with this Body Warmer. When it is connected with the mains, the indicator lights on, and it begins to be heated. After ten minutes, heat storing stops and the indicator lights out, meanwhile, the electricity supply is cut off automatically. After the wire is pulled out, it can be used.

2. This product adopts imported special material for storing heat, so its heating can last for five hours after it is once switched on.

3. This product is up to the National Safety Standard for Five Kinds of Insulating Material.

Notice:
1. This product cannot be soaked.
2. This product cannot be used as sports goods and should be avoided beating.
3. This product cannot be heated by a fire.
When it is very cold, this product will make you sense the warmth.

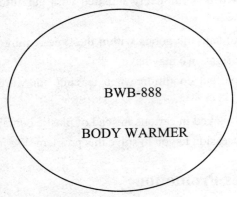

To Give the Aged the Warmth
To Show Solicitude for the Children
To Make the Pupils Study with Undivided Attention
To Bring Your Trip Convenience

Unit Fifteen   Expos

II. Choose the best answer

1~5: DDCCB
6~10: BDDDC
11~15: CADBA
16~20: CDAAB

IV. Translate the following sentences into English

1. We will attend the Canton Fair on Oct. 15th, 200*. We would be very much glad if you could find time to pay your visit.

2. We are pleased to inform you of our Specialized Exhibition for Building & Construction Materials, which is jointly organized with World Expo Group.

3. We organize over 50 successful exhibitions per year in China. Please feel free to contact us for detailed information.

4. We have decided to participate in 10th Dalian International Building & Const. Exhibition in Dalian from 22nd to 25th September.

5. Please tell us your Contact Person, Position, Company, Address, Tel, Fax, E-mail, Website and Products.

6. If you are not interested in our exhibition updates, please email us back with subject "REMOVE" so that we can remove your address from our mailing list.

7. This expo center, located at the heart of the Center Business District in Shanghai, has attracted worldwide attention since its opening in October, 2000. It now hosts more than 50

world-class exhibitions each year.

8. Currently, this expo center has 9 exhibition halls with 125,500 square meters of indoor exhibition space and 90,000 square meters of outdoor exhibition space.

9. Our website aims at offering a more efficient on-line business platform for both international buyers and domestic suppliers.

10. The exhibition halls were separated into four parts as Garments, Home Textiles, Art Deco Gifts and Consumer Goods, covering an area of 105,200 square meters and having 3,652 exhibitors with 5,556 standard booths in the fair.

Unit Sixteen   Flexible Trade (I)

Doc.1 参考译文

独家代理协议

本协议于20**年9月6日在中国上海由有关双方在平等互利基础上达成，按双方同意的下列条件发展业务关系：

1. 协议双方

甲方：   上海****有限公司

地址：

电话：   0086-21-

传真：

乙方：

地址：

电话：

传真：

2. 委任

甲方指定乙方为其独家代理，为第三条所列商品从第四条所列区域的顾客中招揽订单，乙方接受上述委任。

3. 代理商品

4. 代理区域

5. 最低业务量

乙方同意，在本协议有效期内从上述代理区域内的顾客处招揽的上述商品的订单价值不低于一百万美元每年。

6. 价格与支付

每一笔交易的货物价格应由乙方与买主通过谈判确定，并须经甲方最后确认。付款使用保兑的、不可撤销的信用证，由买方开出，以甲方为受益人。信用证须在装运日期前30天到达甲方。

7. 独家代理权

基于本协议授予的独家代理权,甲方不得直接或间接地通过乙方以外的渠道向印度顾客销售或出口第三条所列商品,乙方不得在印度经销、分销或促销与上述商品相竞争或类似的产品,在本协议有效期内,甲方应将其收到的来自印度其他商家的有关代理产品的询价或订单转交给乙方。

8. 商情报告

为使甲方充分了解现行市场情况,乙方应至少每季度一次或在必要时随时向甲方提供市场报告,内容包括与本协议代理商品的进口与销售有关的地方规章的变动、当地市场发展趋势以及买方对甲方按协议供应的货物的品质、包装、价格等方面的意见。乙方还应向甲方提供其他供应商类似商品的报价和广告资料。

9. 广告及费用

乙方负担本协议有效期内在印度销售代理商品做广告宣传的一切费用,并向甲方提交所用于广告的声像资料,供甲方事先核准。

10. 工业产权

在本协议有效期内,为销售有关塑料制品和阀门等产品,甲方可以使用乙方拥有的商标,并承认使用于或包含于塑料制品中的任何专利商标、版权或其他工业产权为乙方独家拥有。一旦发现侵权,甲方应立即通知乙方并协助乙方采取措施保护乙方权益。

11. 协议有效期

本协议经有关双方如期签署后生效,有效期为一年,从×年×月×日至×年×月×日。除非做出相反通知,本协议期满后将延长12个月。

12. 协议的终止

在本协议有效期内,如果一方被发现违背协议条款,另一方有权终止协议。

13. 不可抗力

由于水灾、火灾、地震、干旱、战争或协议一方无法预见、控制、避免和克服的其他事件导致不能或暂时不能全部或部分履行本协议,该方不负责任。但是,受不可抗力事件影响的一方须尽快将发生的事件通知另一方,并在不可抗力事件发生15天内将有关机构出具的不可抗力事件的证明寄交对方。

14. 仲裁

因履行本协议所发生的一切争议应通过友好协商解决。如协商不能解决争议,则应将争议提交中国国际经济贸易仲裁委员会(北京),依据其仲裁规则进行仲裁。仲裁裁决是终局的,对双方都有约束力。

甲方:	乙方:
(签字)	(签字)
20**年9月6日	20**年9月6日

Doc.2　　参考译文

保密协议

本协议(以下称为"协议")自_____年____日起签署并实施,协议双方是_____(以下称为"接受方"),和QQD(以下称为"所有方")。

鉴于 QQD 表示并保证它是与 QQD 产品有关的知识产权的所有人，这包括以口头或书面形式提供给接受方或由于通过对所有方设施的任何参观而了解到的信息(以下称为"知识产权信息")，并且；

鉴于"所有方"愿意将信息告诉"接受方"，并且；

鉴于双方愿意共同保守知识产权信息的秘密。

因此，考虑到这种披露和由此披露而引起的其他保证，约定如下。

1. **目的**

QQD 出于招标目的而将知识产权信息透露给接受方。所有提供给接受方的信息都是所有方的知识产权信息。

2. **接受方义务**

除了由本协议授权或所有方书面授权，接受方同意以下几点：

a. 它将不把知识产权信息提供或部分提供给任何第三方；

b. 它将不出于自身利益的考虑或为其他第三方利益的考虑利用这些知识产权信息或部分信息，不用于除上面所述目的以外的其他用途，也不服务于任何其他个人或实体；

c. 它将负责对所有方提供的知识产权信息或其任何部分严格保守秘密；

d. 它将采取合理措施尽最大努力避免知识产权信息或其任何部分未经授权的泄秘。

e. 它将把知识产权信息或其任何部分在必要的情况下出于执行协议的目的而仅透露给自身雇员或专业顾问，并且使相关人员认识到保密的义务和本协议包含的使用权。

3. **接受方义务的例外**

上文第 2 段的义务不适用于以下几点：

a. 在执行协议过程中已经在公共媒介公开的信息；

b. 在披露给接受方之前已经了解的信息，这一信息并非是从相关保密协议约束下的来源了解到的；

c. 来自有权披露信息的善意第三方的信息；

d. 依照法令、法律、法规或其他政府权威机构要求需要透露的信息。但是，接受方必须：

(i) 立刻通知 QQD 此类要求或需要；

(ii) 至少提前十天，或尽早以书面形式向 QQD 提供有关要求者需求的详情。

e. 接受方自己取得的信息，独立于 QQD 或与知识产权信息无关的信息。

4. **无许可或放弃**

本协议的任何条款并不表示对接受方利用 QQD 知识产权信息的一种完全许可或者对由*国专利、商标、版权法所赋予的权利和赔偿的放弃。

5. **期限**

虽然有上述规定，接受方所有协议上所列的义务从 QQD 执行之日起持续 10 年。

6. 适用法律

有关双方明确同意所有争端、矛盾或可能出现的索赔以及对协议或协议履行情况的解释，都将依据____国____州的法律，排除任何对法律规则或原则的冲突或选择，它们可能导致对本协议的构成和解释要援引另外一个司法主体的实体法。任何诉讼或在衡平法中包括的争端、矛盾，或索赔都将在____州法庭或者如果权限允许的话将在____州联邦法庭进行。接受方同意受上述法庭管辖。

7. 救济

由于知识产权信息的特殊性，接受方需要认识到：一旦接受方不能履行协议下的任何义务，QQD将会遭受不可挽回的损失以及由此带来的难以弥补的经济损失。因此，接受方要同意QQD除了任何其他适用法规或衡平法的补偿外，还应该有权对由于违背协议而造成的后果要求补偿。

8. 标题

各段标题仅为标示方便用，不视为协议的一部分。

9. 信息反馈

一旦QQD要求，接受方应该立即归还，或者在QQD指示下销毁所有的知识产权信息（包括由QQD提供的书面信息和拷贝，以及通知，或其他由接受方准备的有关知识产权信息的编辑文本或其他文件）。

10. 请求

接受方不得在没有QQD资深执行官书面许可的情况下，直接或间接雇用任何一年左右时间后终止与QQD协议的公司雇员；但是，如果前QQD雇员在没有接受方直接或间接指示的情况下自己联系到了并在接受方谋职，QQD是不会阻止接受方雇用他的。

11. 公开声明

在没有另一方事先书面同意的情况下，任何一方不得向任何个人、实体透露有关双方之间正在进行的信息交换、调查、讨论或谈判的事实，除非有必要透露给最接近的顾问，如律师或会计。双方应同意任何公开申明的内容。

12. 赔偿

接受方据此签约并同意，自己负担赔偿QQD总部、子公司、附属工厂以及其他主管、雇员、股东、销售代表、分支机构代理商由于任何相关此协议或接受方不能履行协议引起的损失和任何形式的处罚、花费以及没有限制的损害索赔或人员伤亡损失等。本段和接受方义务的规定将确保协议的顺利执行。

因此，双方已经在前述所写的日期达成本协议。

所有方：**QQD**

负责人：_____

签名：_____

职位：采购与库存主管
接受方：_____
负责人：_____
签名：_____
职位：_____
日期：_____

II. Choose the best answer

1~5: DDCCC
6~10: CDABD
11~15: DACBD
16~20: DABBA

IV. Translate the following sentences into English

1. We thank you for your enquiry regarding the sole agency for the sale of Chinese Qipao in Australia.

2. As regards your proposal to represent us in East Africa for the sale of Chinese hardware, we have decided to appoint your esteemed company as our exclusive agent for a trial period of one year.

3. We think it premature for us to discuss the question of agency during this sales-pushing stage. But, please do not misinterpret our opinion, which in no way implies dissatisfaction.

4. We have to decline your proposal of acting as our sole agency at the present stage. As you see, your annual turnover is still very limited.

5. Unless you increase the annual turnover to the extent with which we are satisfied, we can hardly appoint you as our sole agent.

6. I propose a sole agency agreement for Chinese works of art, collectors' pieces and antiques for a period of 3 years.

7. Party A has the right to revise the selling prices in accordance with the prevailing market conditions and shall notify Party B of the change in time.

8. This Sole Agency Agreement is to remain valid for a period of two years commencing from Sept. 2, 2006 and terminating on Sept. 1, 2008.

9. We have noted your request to act as our sole agent in Mexico City, but before going further into the matter, we should like to know your plan for promoting sales and the annual turnover you may realize in your market.

10. We want to apply for the sole agency of your product in our local market.

Unit Seventeen   Flexible Trade (II)

II. Choose the best answer

1~5: DCDAD

6~10: DBCCD
11~15: BBBDB
16~20: CCCDD

IV. Translate the following sentences into English

1. This is to reply to the Feasibility Study Report and the Articles of Association for Cordial Furniture Fittings (Shanghai) Co., Ltd.

2. Your request to examine and approve the Feasibility Study Report and the Articles of Association for Cordial Furniture Fittings (Shanghai) Co., Ltd. has been received. After studying it, an official reply is given as follows:

3. This corporation produces 6 million sets of various furniture fittings every year, 50 per cent of the products will be sold in the international market.

4. Factory buildings now available there are rented. If the factory buildings are located in planned-land, this corporation will have to move without preconditions.

5. After receiving this reply, please prepare all the relevant documents to apply for the ratification certificate of foreign-funded enterprise, and conduct the registration procedures to the Industrial and Commercial Bureau.

6. The rental conditions may be the same as the above-mentioned two companies. Pollution is not permitted in this development zone. Please make explanation in the feasibility study report.

7. Please take our intent into your consideration immediately so as to catch this good opportunity, because there are a lot of businessmen who come to our company looking for cooperation.

8. To give you a better view of our company, we are sending you our catalogue and video CDs through EMS No: EA56682****CN.

9. In case of any discrepancy, the original Chinese version of this Agreement shall prevail.

10. If every factory follows point by point and prepare all the above-mentioned documents, we will have all the documents required for certification process.

Unit Eighteen Miscellaneous

参考译文：

上海瑞贝咖机械设备有限公司劳动合同

_____(以下简称"甲方")
_____(以下简称"乙方")

根据《中华人民共和国劳动法》以及《上海市劳动合同规定》，双方在平等、自愿、协商一致的基础上签订本劳动合同。

第一条　合同期限

1. 本合同的有效期限为_____年_____月_____日至_____年_____月_____日止。(其中_____年_____月_____日至_____年_____月_____日为试用期)。
2. 合同期满即终止。因工作需要经双方协商一致可续签合同。一般员工期满前7日，干部职员30日之前办理续订手续。

第二条　工作岗位

1. 甲方根据工作需要及乙方的岗位意向，聘用乙方的职位为_____。乙方服从并努力提高工作效率。
2. 甲方因工作需要及乙方的工作能力和表现，可以调整乙方的工作岗位，乙方应服从并相应调整岗位工资福利待遇。

第三条　工作条件和劳动保护

1. 甲方实行每周40小时的工作制度。休息二天。零售部门由于工作需要实行2班交替工作制，其时间安排表由甲方决定，乙方对此表示服从。
2. 甲方因工作需要安排的加班，乙方应该服从，乙方的补休时间安排应事先征得甲方的同意。加班工资按国家劳动法执行。
3. 甲方为乙方提供符合国家规定的安全卫生的工作环境，保证乙方在人身安全及人体不受危害的环境条件下工作。
4. 甲方根据工作需要组织乙方参加必要的业务知识培训。

第四条　工作报酬及福利待遇

1. 根据国家及市政府的有关规定，甲方以人民币形式按月支付乙方工资。试用期月薪人民币_____元。试用期满后月薪人民币_____元。
2. 缴纳个人所得税是乙方的义务，按国家规定在乙方工资内代扣。
3. 甲方按政府规定按期向指定机构为乙方办理养老保险、待业保险等有关保险，其他有关福利费用均按政府规定办。
4. 乙方享有国家规定的法定假日、婚假等假期。乙方在婚假、丧假期间和女员工在妊娠、生产、授乳期间可以享受符合国家有关规定的待遇。
5. 乙方享有公司规定的年假。乙方为甲方服务一年以上后享受带薪休假5天，以后每年增加一天，但不能超过15天(甲方不再提供探亲假)。
6. 乙方患病或工作之外受伤时，参照公司有关规章制度处理，但是与国家有关法规发生冲突时，以国家法规为准。
7. 如果甲方由于经营停止或因破产而宣布解散，甲方将向劳动部门一次性付清必要的劳动保险费用。
8. 乙方因工负伤，甲方负责乙方的治疗、休养。
9. 乙方的退休及失业时的待遇，将依照国家社会劳动和社会保障的法律法规执行。

第五条　工作纪律、奖惩和惩处

1. 乙方应遵守国家的法律、法规。
2. 乙方应遵守甲方规定的各项规章制度和劳动纪律，自觉服从甲方的管理。
3. 甲方按公司的有关规定，按照乙方的工作实绩及贡献大小给予奖励。
4. 乙方如违反甲方的规章制度、劳动纪律，甲方将按照公司的有关规定给予处罚。

第六条　劳动合同的变更、终止和解除

1. 劳动合同依法签订后，合同双方必须全面履行合同规定的义务，任何一方不得擅自变更合同。确需变更时，双方应协商一致，按原签订程序变更合同。双方未达成一致意见的，原合同继续有效。
2. 劳动合同期满或双方约定的合同终止条件出现时，劳动合同即行终止。
3. 乙方有下列情形之一的，甲方可以随时解除劳动合同：
 (1) 在试用期内被证明不符合条件的；
 (2) 严重违反工作纪律或公司规章制度的；
 (3) 严重失职、营私舞弊，对甲方利益受损的；
 (4) 被依法追究刑事责任的。
4. 有下列情况之一的，甲方可以解除劳动合同，但应提前三十日以书面形式通知乙方：
 (1) 乙方患病或非因公负伤医疗期满；
 (2) 乙方不能胜任工作，经培训或调整工作岗位，仍不能胜任工作的；
 (3) 劳动合同订阅时所依据的客观情况发生重大变化，致使原劳动合同无法履行，经甲乙双方协商不能就变更劳动合同达成协议的。
5. 乙方要求解除劳动合同，需提前三十天以书面形式通知甲方。有下列情形之一的，乙方可通知甲方解除劳动合同：
 (1) 在试用期内的；
 (2) 甲方未按照劳动合同支付劳动报酬或提供劳动条件的；
 (3) 用人单位以暴力威胁或者非法限制人身自由的手段来强迫劳动的。
6. 乙方有下列情况之一的，甲方不能解除合同：
 (1) 因病或非因工负伤在规定的医疗期限内的；
 (2) 乙方因工负伤，在治疗、疗养期间的；(经劳动鉴定委员会确认不同程度丧失劳动能力的按《条例》规定执行)
 (3) 女职工在孕期、产期、哺乳期的。

第七条　违反和解除劳动合同的经济补偿

(1) 公司对某些岗位的员工出资培训必须签订培训协议，员工在协议期间必须为公司服务。如有违反，公司保留按培训规定要求赔偿培训费的权利，单位出资培训未签协议的，培训方回到单位服务时间不到五年的，单位可按每年递减百分之二十的比例收取，培训费可酌情收取一定比例的往返交通费和在外期间的生活补偿费用。

(2) 若公司或员工因终止本合同而造成另一方经济损失，该方应按有关的《上海市劳动合同规定》对另一方做出赔偿。

第八条　专利、专有技术及保密义务

1. 乙方在合同期间，使用甲方的资料、设备取得的发明和新技术等的所有权均归甲方，并以甲方的名义进行登记。
2. 即使是未登记的质量管理、操作方法、取得新的有效的创造成果也属于甲方所有。
3. 乙方不得将在合同期间得知的甲方在经营、生产上的专有技术及本条中第 1 项、第 2 项条款所指的一切技术资料向其他公司泄露。假如发生诸如此类的事，乙方则负有刑事上及赔偿甲方遭受经济损失的责任。
4. 乙方无论以何种方式离职，均不得披露、使用或让他人使用其所掌握的甲方的商业秘密。
5. 乙方在离职后二年内不得到同行的企业工作。
6. 乙方如违反保密约定，须承担由此造成甲方的全部损失。

第九条　其他事项

1. 双方认为需要约定的事项：

甲乙双方同意遵守以下的诸规定。

(1)　上海　实业有限公司就业规则；

(2)　上海　实业有限公司工资规定；

(3)　上海　实业有限公司的其他规则。

以上规定如与国家法令规定有所不同，以国家法律法令规定为准。以上规则、规定作为本合同附件，具有同等法律效果。

2. 甲乙双方若发生争议，由争议双方协商解决。协商不能解决时，由争议的一方向单位所在地劳动争议仲裁委员会申请仲裁。任何一方不服从仲裁裁决时，可在收到仲裁决定书之日起十五天内向法院提起诉讼。
3. 本合同条款如与国家法律、法规相抵触，以国家法律、法规为准。
4. 本合同一式两份，甲乙双方各执一份，自签字日起生效，两份合同具有同等法律效力。

甲方：　　　　　　　　　　　　　　　　　　乙方：

法定代表人或委托人：

　　年　　月　　日　　　　　　　　　　　　　　年　　月　　日

承诺与声明

致：荷兰 Grss 股份有限公司

敬启者：

我方，作为一家配合荷兰 Grss 股份有限公司(以下称"贵公司")在华业务运作的上海 Aa 实业有限公司的股东，特向贵公司承诺及声明如下：

1. 我方愿意按照中国法律规定，在 2004 年 7 月底前同贵公司确定的法律主体签署所有有关上海 Aa 实业有限公司免费出让股权的转让合同及变更上海 Aa 实业有限公司法定代表人的所有法律文书。
2. 在我方签署上述法律文件后的两个月内，上海 Aa 实业有限公司应按照中国法律规

定完成所有上述法律文件的批准与登记手续；在对上述法律文件未完成批准与登记的情况下，根据中国法律的规定我方作为上海 Aa 实业有限公司的法人代表和股东仍享有对公司的相应权力。

3. 贵公司应承认上海 Aa 实业有限公司成立以后的所有债权债务及对外承担的责任与我方无关，若有因上海 Aa 实业有限公司运作产生的债务及对外承担的责任涉及我方，贵公司愿尽其所能免除我方的所有责任或承接所有加于我方个人身上的这种债务、责任。

4. 贵公司应在我方签署免费出让股权的转让合同及变更上海 Aa 实业有限公司法定代表人的所有法律文书前的 7 日内在上海以我方名义设立金额为 50 万元人民币的银行账户，准许我方在发生因上海 Aa 实业有限公司运作产生的债务及对外承担的责任涉及我方的情况下(包括但不限于发生针对我方的诉讼、仲裁、行政处罚、被索赔)动用该账户内资金，并且，贵公司对我方因此动用的账户内的所有资金不要求我方退还，贵公司以这些措施作为履行上述免除我方的债务及责任的保证。

5. 我方的承诺与声明是完整不可分的整体，待贵公司全部同意后随即生效。

承诺与声明人：

(签署)

201*年 10 月 11 日

II. Choose the best answer

1~5: CDDBA
6~10: ADBBB
11~15: BABBD
16~20: DCBDC

IV. Translate the following sentences into English

1. As regards this order, we are facing a really big problem with the authorities.

2. The government stipulates that all the exporters MUST deliver all relative documents together with all the local bank receipts into the local tax bureau and finish all the export accounting process within at latest 180 days after the date of custom clearance.

3. The government will check the drawback project. If they find this order has not been paid, we will be unable to obtain the tax refund. The loss arising from it will account for 11% to 14% of the total amount of the order.

4. We are glad to inform you that we will attend the 201* San Paulo Hardware Fair in Brazil, from May. 15th to 17th.

5. We would like to pay a visit to your esteemed company for further cooperation after the fair.

6. In order to apply for the Visa in advance, kindly please help us to prepare the following materials required by the local Venezuela Embassy.

7. The letter of invitation should be offered in duplicate and its salutation should be separately written as "Dear Ambassador of Venezuela Embassy in Beijing" and "Dear Friend Xu Zhi Tao".

8. Attached please find our sample of the letter of invitation for your reference. Please use your company's letterhead-paper to issue the documents.

9. Before your sending the original documents, would you please scan them into JPG or PDF format for our checking and reference in order to avoid mistake or misunderstanding.

10. At this time, we are very optimistic about the prospects of establishing a strong business relationship with your company and would like to request pricing information for the following items.